THE HOLLYWOOD EXILES

THE HOLLYWOOD EXILES

John Baxter

TAPLINGER PUBLISHING COMPANY
NEW YORK

For JUDY GARDNER
A child of the century

First published in the United States in 1976 by
TAPLINGER PUBLISHING CO., INC.
New York, New York

Copyright © 1976 by John Baxter
First published 1976 by
Macdonald and Jane's Publishers Ltd
Paulton House 8 Shepherdess Walk London N1 7LW
All rights reserved.
Printed in Great Britain

Library of Congress Catalog Card Number: 75-34734
ISBN 0-8008-3918-8

CONTENTS

Glad was I when I reached the other bank.
Now for a better country. Vain presage!
Who were the strugglers, what war did they wage
Whose savage trample thus could pad the dark
Soil to a plash? Toads in a poisoned tank,
Or wild cats in a red-hot cage.

Childe Roland to the Dark Tower Came
Robert Browning

ACKNOWLEDGMENTS

I would like to extend my thanks to René Clair, King Vidor, Robert Florey, George Harris, Michael Powell, Emeric Pressburger, Andrew Marton, Douglas Fairbanks Jnr, John Kahan, Sir Bernard Miles, Frank Capra, Marian Nixon, DeWitt Bodeen and the many other film-makers who allowed themselves to be interviewed for this book, and also Kevin Brownlow, Colin Shindler and Barrie Pattison who provided additional material and guidance. Colin Shindler's generosity in making available his own notes and transcripts of his American Film Institute Oral History interviews with Robert Lord was of particular value. Corinna Lassen contributed substantially to the chapter on Scandinavian film-makers with her translations from the Danish and Ray Bowen provided German translations. My thanks also to the Director and staff of the Austrian Film Museum, Vienna; Dr Al Brooks of the Max Reinhardt Archive, State University of New York, Binghampton; the Belgian Film Archive, Brussels, and the Institute of Contemporary History (Wiener Library), London, for substantial help in my research. And to Linda Strawn, who first showed me Hollywood.

BUILDING ON SAND

'I like a fine view,' said Alice B. Toklas, 'but I prefer to sit with my back to it.' Hollywood was no different. One needs only a few hours in Los Angeles to see that, for all the frantic assertion of personality, the city and its film industry have always reposed mainly in the minds of those living there, a group of people who have resolutely refused to see anything that has not fitted their preconceived image. Where the concentration of film activity has faded – down-town, for instance, an area long since abandoned for suburban Hollywood or Beverly Hills – the real Los Angeles surfaces, an industrial city on a temperate shore, not unlike Durban, Piraeus, Melbourne. 'The Coast', that phrase with which Hollywood glamorized itself to Easterners in the 1920s and 1930s, before air travel stripped away the mystery conferred by distance, seems mocking now. Forever looking inward, Hollywood refused to acknowledge its true nature as a colonial port, preferring to interpret isolation in an ambassadorial light. As the farthest outpost of American culture it had a duty to present America to those outside, to offer examples of national perfection, above all to lure into its collective dream the best minds of other nations who would in turn celebrate to their own people the revelation gained there. Ironically, when converts entered the tabernacle they found nothing except that which they had brought with them, but none dared to dispel the mystery, a deception for which they were generously paid.

Few ideas or institutions in Los Angeles belong to California. Even the tall palms shedding fibres into the wide avenues were, like the architectural style in which the houses were built and like the people who lived in them, imported to decorate the dream city. The film industry we know as 'Hollywood' also grew out of foreign ideology. Indigenous American cinema died in the

Hollywood, circa *1925*

1

early 1920s, with its best artists destroyed by their own artistic and business naïveté and the growth of a commercial film industry to which they could not adjust – an industry founded and propagated by Europeans. 'We are building on sand, Rex, just building on sand,' D. W. Griffith confided to Rex Ingram before both turned without much success to Europe. In their place thrived an art that became an industry, a pastime that became a profession and a city that became an expression of both.

In decay, Los Angeles reverts to the geographical self that a few perceptive observers saw and appreciated even in the 'Bagdad' days. Josef von Sternberg and Bertholt Brecht loved the bleak but intensely peopled industrial landscape along the mud-flats of San Pedro, Aldous Huxley the arid alkali gullies of the hills, J. B. Priestley the desert, and all of them the Californian night. 'Neither the things that grow nor the people seemed to have any real roots,' British actor Sir Cedric Hardwicke said. 'Only at night,

Hollywood Boulevard in the mid-1930s, described by this publicity photo as 'the famous boulevard where walk the stars of motion pictures – and those who strive to reach that same goal'

when heavy dews softened the shapes of everything, and lights gleamed delightfully across the hills, did Los Angeles develop a strange kind of deceptive beauty.'[1] Today, the night and the desert are more real than anything that remains of Hollywood's film industry, but on a warm evening, when the scented Sátaña drifts in from the desert, sweeping the streets free of smog, one can sit high above the city, looking down at the pin-sharp lights, and sense how it must have looked to those first émigrés, still convinced that somewhere in this community and its fabulous machine lay a secret that could change the world.

If America's film industry has any true moment of birth, it is that day in 1894 when Mrs Horace Henderson Wilcox, hoping to re-establish in California some vestige of her old Kansas home, gave her husband's Los Angeles ranch the wildly inappropriate but evocative name of 'Hollywood'. Over the next twenty-five years, the natural geographic advantages of the area attracted the more agile of the country's film-makers, most of them wild-cat operators fleeing from the agents of Edison and other patent-owners, determined, vainly, to stamp out the pirated machines with which an increasingly large percentage of the country's films were made. Inevitably, the accidents of Hollywood's early history created a community unlike any other in the United States: hectic, superficial, hedonistic. As late as 1913, Cecil B. DeMille showed only mild surprise at being shot at by patent agents as he rode from his home to the barn which had become his first studio – a trip across what is now the heart of suburban Los Angeles; California's enervating climate and unreal landscape mocked the conventions on which Eastern life rested.

Attracted by this social, industrial and spiritual vacuum, countless film producers joined DeMille and the other pioneers during the green days of the First World War, creating almost by accident a characteristic style of American cinema. Knockabout comedy and action predominated, leavened with ten-minute glosses from classic literature ranging from Dickens to D'Annunzio, as absurdly unreal as the *tableaux vivants* of an end-of-term school show. With the exception of D. W. Griffith and Thomas Ince, film-makers approached their work in the same spirit as the photographers who produced penny postcards, and though both men recognized dimly the potential of the medium in which they worked, some dark fear prevented them from exploiting its potential. In this, the theatrical establishment played an important part. No good actor would think of entering the movies, and those who did treated them as little more than a joke; the star of DeMille's first film, *The Squaw Man*, spurned the stock certificates he was offered in what was later the mammoth Paramount corporation, demanding only his fee in cash and a rail ticket back to New York. Technicians often shared this contempt. Not much could be expected, for instance, of set designers hired from the local vaudeville theatre and expected back there after only a few hours of film work, and Ince was depressed, though probably not surprised, to see on one commissioned back-cloth of a rural scene a helpfully added flight of ducks. (Significantly, the first great milestone in cinema design, Griffith's *Intolerance*, rested in part on the work of foreigners; aiming for a depiction of Babylon far beyond the scope of any Californian engineer, Griffith hired plaster-workers imported to build the 1915 Panama-Pacific International Exposition in San Francisco. Most had worked on the massive sets demanded by Italian opera producers, and a few had perhaps been employed by pioneer Italian film-makers like Guazzoni or Pastrone. It can hardly be a coincidence that the life-sized elephants of Pastrone's *Cabiria* (1913) appear as the rampant supporters of Griffith's monumental walled city a few years later.)

However much one admires the work of the American pioneers, it lacks an essential spark, some flair which the film-makers of other countries were already showing in their work. Like television in the 1960s, the movies of 1918 served an audience so starved of visual stimulation that content mattered hardly at all. The need for a product which would be comprehensible even when shown in a Burmese bark hut or a British slum under projection conditions of appalling primitiveness placed an emphasis on visual sharpness and universal appeal which survived in Hollywood for forty years. Throughout that period, America was to lead the world in all the skills of movie manufacture but to lag well behind Europe in the aesthetics of the medium.

For all its skill, American cinema of the immediate post-war period still had only a precarious hold on the essentials of survival – financial stability and mass appeal. However much the

Intolerance. *Baby-lonian revellers cavort amid the products of Italian plaster-workers originally imported to create pavilions for the San Francisco Panama-Pacific Exposition*

Hollywood studios may have adulated the new productions of Germany and France, it was the American rural audience it most needed to satisfy. The automobile had not yet destroyed the isolation of the country town nor radio eroded its reliance on the cinema and travelling show for entertainment. At the first sign that Hollywood seemed likely to lose touch with this mass audience, the exhibitors, who saw diminishing interest reflected immediately in shrinking returns, brought producers to heel with irate letters to the trade press or the studios themselves. Violently egalitarian, they were particularly incensed by period films, which seemed to them indecently preoccupied with aristocracy; one theatre-owner tersely directed a Hollywood company: 'Don't send me any more of them films where the hero writes his name with a feather.'

The obsession with rural needs went beyond simple considerations of profit and loss. American politics of the post-war period put the seal of approval on small-town life as the purest and truest expression of the national ideal. Rejection of Woodrow Wilson's plans for an entente with Europe underlined the national belief in isolation, and though the election of small-time Ohio politician Warren Harding as President in 1920 ushered in an era of administrative graft and mismanagement, as well as the absurdity of Prohibition, Americans, alarmed by their flirtation with internationalism during the war, glossed over his laxity as country casualness. To them, Harding seemed the archetypal small-town American, simple, unimaginative, even stupid, but essentially good at heart.

Never quick to break new ground, the film industry devoted itself to reflecting the Jeffersonian virtues of thrift, honour, fidelity and honest toil, and the best directors of the time were those to whom such stories came naturally; the well-educated sons of the upper middle class, many of them from the South. Making *Tol'able David* in 1921, from Joseph Hergesheimer's bucolic novel of a young boy's bravery in a small southern village, director Henry King shot on location in Virginia, where he had been born; when his scouts asked for details of the kind of locations they should look for, King told them to find split rail fences. In an area where these were plentiful, everything else would also be right. Richard Barthelmess, a brilliant actor discovered initially by Griffith, distinguished himself in *Tol'able David*, but though Griffith, who had also wanted to film the Hergesheimer novel, did feature Barthelmess in another rural story, *Way Down East*, neither man was ever comfortable with such simple material, preferring the heavy symbolic drama which increasingly alienated American film-makers from the mass audience. Significantly, the only actor to rival Barthelmess in the depiction of rural worth and virtue, Charles Ray, fought bitterly against the attempts of his producer, Thomas Ince, to exploit his skill in such roles. Ray, though superb as the fear-ridden son of a Southern military family in *The Coward* and an unlettered country boy in *The Hired Man*, felt his métier to be 'artistic, uplifting psychological dramas' and lost all his accumulated money and popularity in his own production of *The Courtship of Miles Standish* (1923), a romance of the Pilgrim Fathers which went the unprofitable way of all costume pictures in the early 1920s.

The rural audience loved comedy. Keaton and Chaplin increased wildly in popularity during the post-war period and the early 1920s – but melodrama and sentiment had a wide appeal also. Country audiences particularly liked to see hard work and a winning personality bring deserved success, and books like Harry Leon Wilson's *Merton of the Movies*, which showed how enterprise and friends could make even a country hick into a movie star, were regarded as prime film material. With her customary skill, Mary Pickford exploited rural tastes by combining sentiment, melodrama and enterprise in a series of films, habitually playing orphans coming to terms with farm life, rescuing younger brothers and sisters from danger and finding young love with a sturdy farm lad. Her success in the 1914 *Tess of the Storm Country* as a poor country girl made a fortune for Adolph Zukor – he remade it in 1922 with Pickford again starring in the same role – and she followed it with *Rebecca of Sunnybrook Farm, Pollyanna, Suds* and *Sparrows*, the last a surprisingly sinister picture of rural squalor in which Mary, pursued by the evil farmer, played with skeletal menace by Gustav von Seyffertitz, flees with her fellow orphans through an alligator-infested swamp. Characteristically, for her last film, *Secrets,* made in 1933 when she was thirty-nine and almost forgotten by the public, she returned to the role of rural heroine that had founded her popularity in the great days.

Not all American films of the period were rural pabulum. Epics, sex comedies and even serious dramas did appear, but in most cases their realism and imagination were bounded by the prevailing standards of Broadway, from which the material generally came, and hinged on the contrary prejudices of the country's most famous theatrical impresario, David Belasco. Pompous, pious – he affected a clerical collar as everyday dress though he had no religious qualification – and addicted to spectacle, Belasco's penchant for lavish melodramas found a perfect reflection in the work of Cecil B. DeMille, who shared the latter's gimcrack religiosity and love of costume. Almost forgotten today, DeMille's elder brother William, a director of remarkable skill, struck out on his own, attempting to synthesize rural stories with a modern sensibility to create films which rival anything produced in Europe at the time. His 1921 version of Zona Gale's *Miss Lulu Bett*, with a bravura performance from Lois Wilson as the crushed and despised poor relative victimized by her shallow small-town family, rates scarcely a mention in histories of the film, yet its wry observation of middle-class pretensions and Miss Wilson's calmly accurate playing show DeMille as a considerable talent.

Miss Lulu Bett also offers, in passing, a sharp picture of small-town culture, with the racy brother-in-law hypnotizing the locals with Asiatic curios and tall tales of his travels, trading on an innocence which radio, the automobile and the encroachment of European sophistication via the American cinema would quickly erode. When Pola Negri wanders into a similar town in *Woman of the World* in 1925, much has changed. The upright school-teacher, played so effectively by Milton Sills in *Miss Lulu Bett*, has a more modern incarnation in the crusading district attorney grappling with such city evils as wild dancing and female smoking. Though the town gathers in the parlour of her host to greet the visiting sophisticate as they did in *Miss Lulu Bett*, they now know enough of city manners to sense their own gaucherie and struggle to overcome it, while Negri's highly-sexed, acquisitive and – the ultimate delight – tattooed aristocrat is no mere

William DeMille (left) *with scenarist Jeanie McPherson, authoress Elinor Glyn, and his brother Cecil*

Pola Negri as the refugee countess in Woman of the World

freak, but a woman to be whispered of, gossiped about, lusted after.

In his *Winesburg Ohio* of 1919, Sherwood Anderson summed up the change in sensibility which these films dramatized:

In the last fifty years a vast change has taken place in the lives of our people. A revolution has in fact taken place. The coming of industrialism, attended by all the roar and rattle of affairs, the shrill cries of millions of new voices that have come among us from overseas, the going and coming of trains, the growth of cities, the building of the interurban car lines that weave in and out of towns and past farmhouses, and now in these later days the coming of the automobiles has worked a tremendous change in the lives and in the habits of thought of our people in Mid-America. Books, badly imagined and written though they may be in the hurry of our times, are in every household, magazines circulate by the millions of copies, newspapers are everywhere. In our day a farmer standing by the stove in the store of his village has his mind filled to overflowing with the words of other men. The newspapers and the magazines have pumped him full. Much of the old brutal ignorance is gone forever. The farmer by the stove is brother to the men of the cities, and if you listen you will find him talking as glibly and as senselessly as the best city man of us all.

Hollywood's subjects may have seemed naïve, but at the root of its film-making formula lay a realization that audiences all over the world differed little, and that simple stories had more chance of transferring effectively to other countries than productions created particularly for those markets; a peasant was a peasant no matter where he lived.

At the end of the First World War the Hollywood film industry found its control of the world cinema almost unchallenged, so sweeping and destructive had been the effect of the European war on its traditional competitors, the studios of Germany and France. While the Germans had re-organized their film-making to encourage the war effort and French producers, almost bankrupted by a shortage of material, glumly enlisted in the Army or returned to their former employment, American studios thrived on a booming economy and the new spending power of the urban working class. Even when America joined the war, film-makers, far from having their activities curtailed, were encouraged to produce anti-German features as a contribution to victory.

The shrewder European producers realized that Hollywood's prosperity was no mere accident of politics. American economic expansion into Asia, South America and, to a lesser extent, Europe, provided an infrastructure which the cinema could also exploit. The French in particular watched the process with an envy born of experience; capitalizing on the pioneer work of their travelling photographers, who had penetrated the wilder places of the earth in the 1890s to bring back material for the mushrooming nickelodeons of Europe, the Lumière and Pathé companies already had cinemas in India, Australia, Germany, Scandinavia and the Far East before the war, but one by one the *Cinématographes* died off as local entrepreneurs brought in the later and often bootleg machines of Paul, Edison and Sklandnowsky to rob them of their business. Resignedly the French consolidated their European holdings and even made overtures to the USA by opening offices for both production and distribution in New York, leaving the rest of the world to the masters of the American film business, Zukor, Laemmle and Loew.

By 1914 American films had mass audiences in Japan, Siam, China, India, Australia, Brazil and most other South American countries, not to mention Europe. In many cases the local US

Early French camera-men ranged the world for material to satisfy the European fad for motion pictures begun by the Lumières. Typical of the footage they sent back was this scene of the crowd at the Melbourne Cup horse-race, shot by a Lumière cinémato-graphe in 1896

diplomatic representative protected and occasionally instigated the sale of American films to propagandize the American way of life, though some foreign governments reacted sharply to the mockery of authority, especially the police, and to the sexual innuendo of the Keystone comedies, the country's most popular film export. But no amount of censorship, editing, mutilation or misunderstanding impaired the durable Hollywood film. 'The movie', director Henry King pointed out, 'is the art of the millions of American citizens who are picturesquely called "hicks", the mighty stream of standardized humanity that flows through Main Street': Main Street, USA, the distributors discovered, was not materially different to Main Street, China, or Main Street, France, though all countries had their unusual ways. A 1920 correspondent described a typical evening at the Siamese cinema: 'Sentiment in the film is received in comparative silence by the "chink", but a fight, a motor car or horse chase brings the hall to its feet with yells of delight . . . The orchestra makes no attempt to adapt itself to the action or theme on the screen. It is a thing of fear and wonder as it wanders through pidgin ragtime, Scottish airs, braying with all its force at the wrong moments, relying solely on noise for attention.' The same writer accompanied a travelling film showman into the jungle to witness a scene of Conrad-like grotesquerie: 'In the darkness its semi-naked eager audience squat on their brown haunches on the earth while the hoarse croaking of the night-jars and the shrill singing of insects in the surrounding jungle make a strange orchestra for the old English story of *Comin' Thru' the Rye*.'

In cosmopolitan Japan, Hollywood influence was even more deeply entrenched. By 1920, 1500 cinemas serviced a monthly audience of six million, hampered only slightly by the dictates of censorship – nude statues, kisses, violent struggles were all proscribed – and by the continuing presence of the *benshi*, the traditional narrator who sat to one side of the stage in any dramatic performance and gave a running, often elaborated account of the action. Film exhibitors retained the *benshi* for many years, unconcerned that most of them, unable to distinguish between Occidentals, indiscriminately named all heroines Mary, all heroes Jim and all villains Robert. The *benshi*, like the traditional *Wai-eng* folk dramas of Siam, faded away as Western ideas of showmanship, imposed by America, took hold.

A brief review of 1920s international film events as reported by the *New York Times* encapsulates the spread of Hollywood's influence in the post-war period. In June, Stuart Fuller, US Consul in Tien-sin, China, endorses the value of American films in his work and suggests the distribution of Chinese subtitled prints for the city's six cinemas. 'Films from most of the large American companies are exhibited,' he notes. In the same month a London report mentions that 75 per cent of films shown in Britain are American-produced. In May Famous Players-Lasky, the prototype of Paramount, announces the formation of a $3-million corporation to distribute films in India. By contrast the European cinema languishes. The French announce an embargo on film imports, but the *Times* reassures an alarmed industry that this applies only to film stock, now again being manufactured by a still-shaky group of French factories; completed films are not involved. French producer Léon Gaumont demonstrates a new colour film process to US producers at New York's Astor Hotel. Unimpressed by his flowers, butterflies and landscapes, the Americans ask 'Where are the girls?' and Gaumont immediately cables for cheesecake shots to be sent from Paris.

All these were, however, sideshows. It was Germany to which the Americans looked with caution, speculation and fear. Germany, the conquered enemy, silent, sullen, but showing confused signs of a national resurgence. Cinema-going was said to be booming, new theatres springing up all over the country. Centralized with typical German efficiency during the war, the studios were producing work of surprising sophistication – or so it was said. The German government still forbade the import of American films, an idle regulation since the ricketty Deutsch-mark frightened off major American producers who might have contemplated investment. But they were tantalized by despatches like the one sent by an anonymous German distributor to the *New York Times* on 16 May, 1920: 'The German public demands American motion pictures, and consequently the American product will find a large market in Germany. But in exactly the same manner German films will be demanded in America, be-cause the particular element of interest in German pictures brings the variation that motion picture audiences in America demand.' German pictures in America again? Surely it was too soon. And they probably weren't any good. But even so . . . Discussions, tests of government attitude followed, men sailed discreetly for Europe to acquire copies for 'information'. An important key had turned.

'You know what I call a good invention?' said Thomas Alva Edison. 'Something so practical that even a little Polish Jew would buy it.' Notwithstanding his highly suspect claim to the invention of moving pictures, Edison, anti-Semitic like his friend Henry Ford, would not have appreciated the irony of a booming American film industry controlled by the kind of people he re-garded as fit only to be its audience. For the first twenty years of its existence the American cinema was dominated by a handful of immigrant Europeans, most of them German, Polish or Russian by birth and all of them Jewish. By 1920 the reigning masters of Hollywood were Adolph Zukor and Jesse Lasky of Famous Players, Carl Laemmle of Independent Motion Pictures (IMP), William Fox of the Fox studios; while active as a theatre im-presario but not yet involved in production was Marcus Loew, whose money later brought together Al Lichtman's Metro, the independent Goldwyn and Louis B. Mayer's adventurous little studios as MGM. All had been born in Europe and immigrated to America as penniless refugees. Laemmle came from Laupheim in

William Fox. Because of poor medical work on a broken elbow, his left arm was permanently stiffened

Wurttenburg, Germany, in 1884, as a $22.50 passenger, Zukor and Fox from Hungary in 1888 and 1880 respectively.

The stories of these men's personal success in the movie business have been told and re-told. Less familiar are the assumptions on which that progress moved forward, assumptions bearing directly on the inter-relation between Hollywood and the European cinema for the rest of their existence. The seeds of Hollywood glamour germinated in the gloomy vomit-smelling assisted passage cabins of the immigrant ships, and flowered in the unique atmosphere that would only have existed in a community as unbalanced in its ethnic and cultural make-up as Hollywood after the First World War. Left to itself, the American cinema would have settled for the half-hearted combination of popular entertainment and high-brow dilettantism that ruined the Broadway stage; for all their artistic flair, the best native-born film-makers – Griffith, Sennett, Ince – were undisciplined and devoid of business sense, doomed to be bankrupt by the mid-1920s, ruined not by the immigrants, who on the whole worked to entirely different rules and goals, but by their own inability to judge the public they served. When the new arrivals took control of Hollywood, it was largely by default.

Zukor, Laemmle and Fox believed in the cinema primarily as entertainment. All had come into the business from film exhibition, founding and managing chains of nickelodeons. Film production was primarily a case of guaranteeing material for these outlets. These men bought studios as a clothing retailer buys first a wholesale source – in movies, the 'film exchange' occupied this role – and then a clothing factory in order to eliminate the middle man and maximize profits. Of the American producers, only Thomas Ince grasped and exploited this chain of profit, and his gains were quickly cancelled out by quixotic administration. Ince's efforts, in any event, had not been aimed entirely at profit but, like those of Griffith, at the manipulation and improvement of public consciousness. No European, least of all working-class men like Zukor or Fox, had anything but suspicion for this egalitarian impulse. To them, only the verities of class, race and country were acceptable subjects for entertainment, and to the end Hollywood never deviated from these other than to its peril and loss.

The immigrants believed equally in Europe as the source of

Adolph Zukor is a willing subject for a 3D camera crew (double 3D camera at right) for the shooting of a promotional short

everything good in society, and in immigration as the most effective tool for exploiting its qualities. With a few notable and ill-starred exceptions, the studios never took Hollywood to other countries, preferring to buy the best talents and transport them to America. A network of American-financed studios did spring up in Britain, Germany and France, but in every case circumstances dictated the move – tariff legislation to protect the local industry, as in the case of the UK Cinematograph Act, or the necessity for cheap foreign-language versions of US films which brought about the adaptation of Joinville, in France, as a dubbing factory – and all were closed down when the situation changed. Mere business efficiency was only a rationalizing explanation for this urge to import the best of Europe. Something deeper and more emotional acted on the studio owners as they had themselves photographed amid their accumulated acquisitions: diffident English stage stars, puzzled Polish actresses, European directors, nervous, complacent or eager depending on their importance. The same urge led later to a fascination with royalty, sprinkling Hollywood with spurious grandees and the last scions of decaying royal houses who rated the adulation possible only in a community that retained nineteenth-century Europe's almost fanatical respect for high birth.

Had Hollywood been a conventional business community, one would have expected the first founders to engage in some careful nepotism, to build dynasties and then settle down to enjoy the profits. But on the contrary the Hollywood studios remained under the management of their founders until well into the 1930s, and in some cases later. With the exception of Carl Laemmle, whose son 'Junior' briefly managed Universal under his father before losing his post in the same cataclysm that robbed Laemmle Senior of control, no studio owner built up an organization to hand on to his relatives (though Laemmle's successors did find more than seventy members of his family holding down sinecures in the Universal organization, spawning the quip 'Uncle Carl Laemmle/Has a very large family'). The sons of B. P. Schulberg and Jesse Lasky ended up as writers for the companies their fathers had built. Significantly, the sole Hollywood dynast, Darryl F. Zanuck, who managed to pass some control of Twentieth Century-Fox to his son Richard, was the only studio owner of American birth. To the immigrants, commercial immortality mattered less than success in their own lifetime by the rules of the society they had left.

The indifference, even hostility of established foreign communities in the USA added fuel to this drive for European achievement. Millions of Germans and significant numbers of other nationals settled in America in the nineteenth century, many of them coming over in the same wave as Laemmle, Zukor and Fox. Most founded communities in which their language and culture continued to flourish. But, predominantly Christian, the older immigrants resented the eccentric and essentially Jewish Hollywood society, a dislike the new arrivals returned with interest. Only a handful of people were ever recruited for film work from the earlier immigrants, and even for minor performers, technicians and other staff the studios preferred to recruit outside the United States. On their annual pilgrimages to Europe that continued throughout the 1920s, Zukor, Lasky, Laemmle and other moguls, who seldom allowed employees to execute the task, personally bought up those European artists who took their fancy, a process that must have given them considerable satisfaction. Fugitives from the Europe that had rejected them, they were now kings in their own castles. The blend of truculence and anxiety to please that motivated them is summed up in a cable – probably apocryphal – which independent producer Lewis J. Selznick leaked to the American press on the eve of the Russian Revolution. It was addressed with appealing simplicity to 'Nicholas Romanoff, Petrograd, Russia' and read: 'WHEN I WAS A POOR BOY IN KIEV SOME OF YOUR POLICEMEN WERE NOT KIND TO ME AND MY PEOPLE STOP I CAME TO AMERICA AND PROSPERED STOP NOW HEAR WITH REGRET YOU ARE OUT OF A JOB OVER THERE STOP FEEL NO ILL WILL WHATEVER YOUR POLICEMEN DID STOP IF YOU WILL COME TO NEW YORK CAN GIVE YOU FINE POSITION ACTING IN PICTURES STOP SALARY NO OBJECT STOP REPLY MY EXPENSE STOP REGARDS YOUR FAMILY SELZNICK NEW YORK.

Hollywood missed adding the Czar of all the Russias to its roster of stars, but the assumption toyed with in Selznick's bombastic stunt – that with enough money one could buy the best the old world had to offer – took increasing hold as the post-war slump in movie-making was replaced by a new confidence on the part of the thriving studios. They could afford the best, which to them meant only one thing, the artists of Vienna and Berlin, capitals of the culture that had rejected them and to which they longed to return.

2 BERLIN

European cultural life in the 1920s revolved around Berlin. Paris still excelled in revue, experimental art and the most elevated types of literature, but the war had severely curtailed most of its arts, not least the cinema, whose expansion had been stilled, then reversed by events. An imperial capital without an empire, Vienna, with its neo-Roman avenues and buildings, stood now as a mausoleum to a glory diminishing daily into the past, while London, remote as ever, treasured the theatrical and literary traditions of the nineteenth century, taking little interest in the movements, cultural and political, seething on the Continent – movements that for Berliners were the fabric of daily discussion.

'To go to Berlin,' says the political historian Peter Gay, 'was the aspiration of the composer, the journalist, the actor; with its superb orchestras, its one hundred and twenty newspapers, its forty theatres, Berlin was the place for the ambitious, the energetic, the talented. Wherever they started, it was in Berlin that they became, and Berlin that made them, famous.'[2] Berlin's opportunities were not merely those of a brilliant capital abounding in talented people and an aware audience. Like all its industries, traditionally combined under powerful cartels and controlled by hereditary dynasties like the house of Krupp, German art and publishing had the benefit of expert management and generous patronage from those sections of the community whose attitudes were consistent with the material presented. The Deutsches Theatre, financed by the city government, had naturally offered the directorship to the greatest and most inventive of producers; from 1905 to 1930 it was dominated by the Viennese Max Reinhardt, whose imaginative presentation of the classics with all the new lighting and staging techniques of which he was a master perfectly answered the city's need for a semi-official theatre that combined

19

artistic prestige with neutral politics. Berliners of a political bent could turn to the Volksbuhne, financed by the labour unions, where the socialist Erwin Piscator presented the political parables of Meyerhold and later of Brecht on the bare stage of a theatre devoted to the Constructivist style pioneered in Soviet Russia (and often making extensive use of film). For audiences looking for a middle road, Leopold Jessner at the Staatstheatre, backed by the Prussian state, offered Shakespeare, Hölderlin and Büchner in productions noted for their deceptive simplicity, making ingenious use of the bare tiered stage soon nicknamed *Jessnertreppe* – 'Jessner steps'.

For all its love of argument, Berlin was tolerant, not only of social and sexual idiosyncracies – its brothels, homosexual bars and facilities for all types of sexual deviation were famous, and drug addicts knew it as the cocaine capital of Europe – but of all minority taste, providing that it contributed something to the vitality of their life. The Czech Willy Hoos praised the crackling exchange of opinion, 'the rapid quick-witted reply of the Berlin woman . . . the keen, clear reaction of the Berlin audience in the theatre, in the cabaret, on the street and in the café, that taking-nothing-solemnly yet taking-seriously of things, that lovely dry, cool and yet not cold atmosphere, the indescribable dynamic, the love for work, the enterprise, the readiness to take hard blows – and go on living'.[3] A combination of this tolerance, even hunger for innovation, and the hard reality of state patronage and tough business thinking that underlay the policies of those who catered to it, built the foundation of a German cinema that dominated Europe for the next twenty years.

The war, which had snuffed out the French and British cinemas by cutting off their markets in Europe, far from extinguishing the German film industry actually encouraged it. The Allied blockade provided a forced draught as the audiences of central Europe, deprived of outside product, turned to German films for entertainment. The government supported cinema as a tool of national propaganda, building five hundred cinemas on the Western front and three hundred in the East to show documentary and inspirational film to the troops, and in 1917 General Ludendorff suggested that some of the many small competing companies, mostly left over from successive waves of expansion into Germany by the French and Danes, be amalgamated into a single large concern in which the government, through a generous investment, would have a degree of control. In 1918, through a merger of the studios of Oskar Meester, an early pioneer, Paul Davidson's Union Film and the companies owned by the Danish Nordisk company, the Universum Film A.G. (UFA) came into being, a studio that had a central role in world cinema. The government subscribed DM 8 million of the DM 25 million capital, giving UFA what amounted to a mandate to take over the industry. Though other companies proliferated – in 1911 Germany had eleven film production firms; in 1922, after UFA had been operating for five years, there were 360 – it was UFA, with its big budgets, growing chain of cinemas, laboratories and studios, but most of all its aggregation of great artists, which drew the film-makers and performers of all Europe.

For most film artists, the first step on the road to Hollywood led them to UFA. The war had forced Germany to look to adjacent countries for its stars, and after 1918 the traffic from Austria, Poland, Denmark and Hungary continued. From Denmark a magnetic actress named Asta Nielsen, the precursor of Greta Garbo in her melancholy intensity, led an invasion of Danes, including the

Asta Nielsen, earliest European movie star, in her famous version of Hamlet

actor Olaf Fonss, soon a major star. A Pole, Apollonia Chalupetz, took the name of Pola Negri and lit up every film in which she appeared. Since most stage artists, including Reinhardt, initially refused to work in the cinema – in 1912 the Association of Berlin Theatre Directors even forbade stage actors to appear in films – studios swept up any performer or technician, no matter what his background, who showed promise. Paul Leni, rotund, greedy, a genius of set design; a swarthy Rumanian, vaguely Oriental in looks, calling himself Lupu-Pick; Friedrich Murnau, a tall, stooped Westphalian with the scent of genius; Robert Weine, the Viennese Karl Grune and Fritz Lang, acquired when UFA merged with the Vienna studio of Count Sascha Kolowratz; Henrik Galeen, a Dutchman; Arthur Robison, who was born in Chicago: all joined Richard Oswald, Joe May, Ewald Dupont and other German-born directors to create an industry where only talent and individual ability counted.

There were few common denominators. Many of these people were Jewish, but so were the majority of Europe's talented theatrical artists. It *did* help to have worked for Reinhardt – Weine, Leni, Lupu-Pick, Murnau, Galeen and many other UFA directors, as well as actors like Vladimir Sokoloff, Fritz Kortner, Oscar Homolka, Elizabeth Bergner and Alexander Moissi had all appeared in his productions. It was not merely the Reinhardt charisma that made a person desirable as a film-maker; he had a genius both for seeing talent in a neophyte and nurturing it until it flowered. The twin attractions of Reinhardt and Berlin theatre life drew people from all over Europe. In later years Zoltan Korda, brother of the producer/director Alexander Korda, described in his picturesque broken English how Alex, one of three sons of an estate keeper in Hungary, had set out to find his fortune in 1912:

So comes time when Alex is 18, and I am 16 and Vincent is 14, and mine mother tinks is time for him to go into big world to make some fortune. So she buy him a nice blue suit and – how you say ? – *chapeau melon* ? [bowler hat] And she says to him 'Bless you, my son, into big world must you go. Come back in one year'; and she kiss him and he kiss her, and Vincent he kiss . . . and he is starting to walk. For twenty kilometres we see him walk. Tree hours. Ve can see him no more. And tings grow in the ground and a year passes and is once again a day. From twenty kilometres we see him come. Tree hours he is walking and he comes

zum house and nobody is saying anything. It is breakfast time. So first
he eat my breakfast. And in little time he eat breakfast of Vincent.
Comes mine mother and she says to him 'Alex, not even a little fortune?'
So Alex cries and ve all cry and it is another year. Makes clean the suit
my mother and presses very carefully, and brush the *chapeau melon* and
once again ve kiss and he go forth. Tree hours before he disappear.
And it is another year. And ve are looking twenty kilometres, and
suddenly a very big cloud of dust is rising, and in six, seven minutes it
is here, a very big motor car, a Mercedes. It is open zis motor car, and in
back seat two very fine gentlemen each with big tick cigar. And one of
them is Reinhardt and the other is Alex.[4]

In his first year Korda became a promising cinema director in
Budapest, but the current flowed inexorably toward Germany
and America. A few years later, in 1919, he was one of the leading
film-makers elected to the governing body of the short-lived
Hungarian nationalized film industry set up by order of the
socialist Republic of Councils, only to be crushed four months
later when the Horthy regime destroyed this brief attempt at a
revolutionary state. Alex, Zoltan and Vincent Korda prudently
fled to Vienna. Politics also drove other Hungarians out of the
country, even when their involvement in public affairs was less
than that of the Kordas. Young Emeric Pressburger, later promi-
nent in German and British screen-writing, found, as a result of
the Austro-Hungarian partition after the war, that his nationality
had abruptly become Rumanian: 'Like many others, I had a good
reason to get out of the country. I couldn't speak one word of the
language. I wanted to go to university and I would have liked to
go to a Hungarian university. But understandably they didn't
want these Hungarians to strengthen their feelings towards
Hungary, so they didn't give us passports that were valid for
Hungary. We could go to Germany or Czechoslovakia or, further
away, France, England or America, but these were far away from
our thoughts. It was too far. So a few of us seventeen-year-olds in
1918 decided to go to Germany.'
The plan collapsed when Germany – with the mark already
threatened – refused to admit anyone carrying the much-inflated
Rumanian currency. Pressburger and his friends enrolled instead
in Prague's German-language university; after he had spent six
months learning enough German to pass the entrance examina-
tions, and a further eighteen months of study, the galloping in-

flation of Czech money forced him to try Germany once more. He applied to every university in the country and had an acceptance from only one, in Stuttgart. After two years his studies were again going ahead, but in the time that had been lost his father died, the allowance he had been sending him stopped and Pressburger was forced to strike out in journalism. Within a few years he was at UFA, writing scripts for Anatole Litvak, Robert Siodmak and other major directors. No one seemed to think his apprenticeship an odd one – the cinema has always been an industry that drew the misfits, mavericks and rejects – and Pressburger, being both Hungarian and Jewish, easily found his level in UFA's highly organized supra-national community.

From the stew of talent boiling inside the German film industry a few major names emerged, notably Erich Pommer, a stiff, correct but cunning publicist and businessman who rose in time to control UFA. Hired first by the Gaumont and Éclair companies to manage their German interests, he formed his own subsidiary production company, Decla (For Deutsch Éclair), in 1915, and in

Pola Negri and producer Erich Pommer chat over the samovar during the making of Hotel Imperial *(1926). Shortly afterwards, Pommer returned to Germany and notoriety as the controller of the giant UFA complex*

1919 was responsible for producing *The Cabinet of Dr Caligari*. His involvement in this historic Expressionist work was typical of his career. Realizing that Germany could not compete directly with the American cinema, he conceived the idea of typically national films which guaranteed their individuality and at the same time kept costs to a minimum by exploiting the evocative styles of Expressionist painting and Reinhardt's atmospheric theatre lighting. But after encouraging the collaboration of Hans Janowitz and Carl Mayer on the story of an evil hypnotist and his homicidal 'somnambulist' he angered both writers by demanding a framing story in which the nightmare events were explained as a madman's delusions. 'Without the change, the film would have been a flop,' he explained in later years.[5] As it was, it failed on its first release at the Berlin Marmorhaus in February 1920. After two days during which the audiences, baffled by the Expressionist sets with their painted shadows and the deliberately unrealistic acting of Werner Krauss and Conrad Veidt (both graduates of Reinhardt's *atelier*), demanded their money back, the cinema declined to show the film any further. Undaunted, Pommer embarked on a six-month publicity campaign in which posters and slogans urged the public to see *Caligari*. When it opened again at the same cinema – Pommer had offered DM 30,000 of his own money as a guarantee – the film ran for three months and a new wave of cinema was launched on the world. No artist, Pommer had the skill to choose good people and guide them into profitable associations, as well as the ability to force changes on their work in the name of commercial expediency. The framing story for *Caligari* had a favourable effect on its acceptance overseas, and Pommer later persuaded Carl Mayer to add a happy ending to Murnau's relentless *The Last Laugh*. His commercial drive earned him an unenviable reputation. Emeric Pressburger remembers him as 'a pretty awful sort of chap who waded through human misery and trampled down everything in his way'. Many share his view.

Despite Pommer's hopes of international acclaim, *The Cabinet of Dr Caligari* flopped in America. A puzzled *New York Times* labelled it a 'Cubistic Shocker' and it only succeeded with New York audiences through the addition of an elaborate dramatized 'prologue' that underlined the 'all a dream' explanation. Much more interest had been aroused in New York and Hollywood by

PROLOGUE

¶ Curtains part to disclose a spacious room with the glow from a lighted fireplace at left, while through a large library window at the rear streams soft moonlight. At a table between the window and fireplace the figures of two men are outlined but not fully disclosed. The dialogue begins as soon as the curtain has risen.

CRANFORD.

"I believe you know that I am not given to imagining things—I deal in facts and ignore fancies—and yet I cannot express to you in words the intense distaste that grew on me the nearer I drew to my goal. There was something positively malignant and unnatural in the density of the twisted creepers and shrubbery. That I continued to force my way through the dank, green foliage was due entirely to my pride and not to any liking for my adventure. As I struggled on in the tangled thicket suddenly the green wall in front of me parted easily to my touch and I plunged breathless, confused and shivering with a nameless dread, out of that unhealthy green welter on to a gravelled path which wound away toward the house. Facing me on a marble seat green with mould sat a young man who appeared in no wise surprised at my advent, but more as if he had been expecting me. He was tall and slender, with haunted eyes set in a sad and sensitive face. As I went toward him, he arose and greeted me simply. Being somewhat of a recluse, he said, it was rarely visitors came his way; but they were none the less welcome. He seemed

Written by
KATHERINE
HILLIKER

PRESENTED BY
S. L. ROTHAFEL
AT THE

CAPITOL
THEATRE
NEW YORK
AND AT
THE ALHAMBRA
LEICESTER SQ. LONDON
On FRIDAY
Nov. 2nd, 1923

like a man sleep-walking in a horrid nightmare, and his need to talk was so apparent that despite the warning of danger that prickled my skin I sat down beside him on the ancient seat. 'Did you ever hear of 'The Cabinet of Dr. Caligari?'' he asked me abruptly. As I shook my head and started to reply he laid an admonitory hand on my arm and looked toward the house. Along the pathway came a maiden moving as if in a dream—''

¶ Curtains close, lights out, fade into first scene of picture, showing two characters in garden, with girl in white coming slowly down path.

EPILOGUE.

Same scene as in Prologue. Fire has banked down to glowing embers. On the table the great candles are low

in their sockets. A blue haze of cigar smoke rests lightly on the atmosphere. As the scene is disclosed Cranford rises to his feet, stretches his arms high above his head, then turns quickly to Janes as the latter, who has been comfortably sprawled out in his chair presumably throughout the narrative, struggles up alertly into a sitting posture. Janes' whole attitude expresses intense questioning, but before he can speak Cranford raises an emphatic finger.

CRANFORD.

"And he did! Francis Purnay is to-day a prosperous jeweller in Holstenwall, happily married, with a couple of healthy, normal children. And the strangest thing about his recovery is the lapse of memory that accompanies it. He is like a man suddenly awakened from a bad dream and unable to remember any detail of its horror. The name 'Dr. Caligari,' to-day means no more to him than Smith or Jones. He has completely forgotten his hallucination!"

The 'prologue' to The Cabinet of Dr Caligari specially composed for American audiences

the films of another director who avoided Pommer's net and continued to work in the relatively small studios of Davidson's Union Film. Shrewd, but hiding his shrewdness under a comic exterior; a genius of cinema, but happy to handle any project passed to him; Jewish, German, but broadly international in friendship and ambition, Ernst Lubitsch was a Hollywood character *in petto*, destined for success long before anyone in America knew his name.

Lubitsch's transformation into a Hollywood luminary proceeded far less smoothly than the history books suggest. Cunning and ambition won him his place, as it had everything in his career. The son of a Berlin tailor and an early victim of stage madness, he attached himself to vaudeville and cabaret star Victor Arnold at sixteen, working with Arnold at night and keeping his father's books by day. Arnold, a Reinhardt protégé, introduced him to The Master – probably at the Sound and Fury, a cabaret founded by Reinhardt in 1901 which his minions used as a meeting place and audition spot for new routines. Perhaps because the young

Ernst Lubitsch and Pola Negri on the set of Forbidden Paradise

Lubitsch implied an interest in playing old men – Reinhardt had begun his career as an actor in similar parts – he was offered character roles at the Deutsches Theatre, playing a selection of old veterans in *Faust* and such parts as the second gravedigger in *Hamlet* and the sinister hunchback in Reinhardt's lush Eastern pantomime *Sumurun*, a character he portrayed also in London, where he went too for a successful season of *The Miracle*, Karl Vollmoller's massive religious allegory which the British backer thoughtlessly presented in the huge Olympia exhibition hall, only to see it unceremoniously bundled out to make way for a motor show.

Quick enough to take up a promising actor, Reinhardt promptly forgot most of them, and admission to the inner circle of regular players at the Deutsches Theatre was reserved for the glamorous few: Moissi, Basserman, Pallenberg, Kortner. Seeing no future on the stage, Lubitsch returned to his old trade, vaudeville, by going into movies, quickly establishing himself with Union Film as a comedy actor and eventual director/star of two-reel comedies in which he played a Jewish incompetent named Mayer who bumbled through life, reducing shops, offices and relationships to chaos but somehow surviving every reverse. The Mayer series did well, and though Lubitsch tried unsuccessfully to start his own studio, his continuing association with the wily, monocled Davidson, a German Sam Goldwyn, complete with malapropisms, quickly made him a major director. Working in Union's tiny studio near the Berlin zoo, tantalisingly close to the vast Palast-am-Zoo, UFA's figurehead cinema, he made a series of historical romances whose scope and imagination dazzled European audiences and Hollywood.

Madame Dubarry (1919) put Lubitsch on the map. Lavish, spectacular but subtle in its social and sexual niceties, it followed the rise of Dubarry (Pola Negri) from a flirtatious milliner to the mistress of Louis XV and her resulting fall as a victim of a revolutionary mob – led, in a typical touch of Lubitsch irony, by her first discarded lover. Despite a fiery and calculatingly hoydenish Negri, the role that sticks most in the mind and which accounted for the film's foreign success is Emil Jannings's Louis, a portrait of blowsy vivacity from an actor who became one of Germany's most successful exports to America. Lubitsch had worked with Jannings before, notably in the 1918 *The Eyes of the Mummy Ma*,

Emil Jannings, before his great days as an international star, hams unashamedly in Lubitsch's The Eyes of the Mummy Ma

a fevered mock-Marie Corelli melodrama with Jannings as a religious maniac pursuing Negri around the world. Persuaded by Davidson, Lubitsch used the extravagant Jannings reluctantly as Louis, relying for control on the fact that he had worked a little with Reinhardt. (Among actors who had worked for the great producer there was a freemasonry that helped more than one director. 'On occasion I have used an actor trained by Reinhardt,' Josef von Sternberg later said, 'and, each time, before entering the arena, I would have a little talk with him to let him know that I, too, thought him to be the most valuable human being on earth but that for fear of offending others on my stage I might be forced somehow to cloak this conviction.'[6]) But while Jannings convinced as a fanatic, Lubitsch thought that the role of a king was beyond this bombastic matinee idol and cast instead the subtle and elegant Eduard von Winterstein, with Jannings as Monsieur Dubarry, the aged merchant whom La Dubarry marries to cloak her liaison with the king. Only when Jannings created the part elaborately with costume and make-up for a screen test – 'If I can't play parts I don't look like, then I shouldn't even be on the stage,' he shouted at Lubitsch – did he reluctantly make him the film's star, and, at the cost of overbalancing the drama, gave Jannings his entrée to Hollywood.

With hindsight one can see that Lubitsch may even have made the decision cold-bloodedly, sensing the actor's potential appeal to world audiences, the need for extravagant star figures like Negri and Jannings as pawns in his game. Lubitsch and Davidson were the first German film-makers to sniff the growing American interest in European cinema, but both sides faced a hard task in restarting the interrupted cultural exchange extinguished by a wave of patriotic hysteria during the war, a spirit so virulent that American actors with German names prudently changed them to something undeniably non-Teutonic; Gustav von Seyffertitz, for instance, became 'C. Butler Clonebaugh.' In 1917 and 1918 Attorney-General A. Mitchell Palmer even investigated the Broadway stage in case German playwrights should be slipping propaganda into the classics or having plays presented under pseudonyms. European immorality also concerned the innately conservative American film trade. As late as 1924 a journalist reviewing Josef von Sternberg's *The Salvation Hunters* could launch a vicious attack on Europeans and their films:

It is more in sorrow than in anger that I watch the inept efforts of misguided aliens, whose knowledge of our language is elementary, and that of our mental processes even less than that, trying to make pictures for American consumption . . . To them a clean-minded man is an object of ridicule and a virtuous woman a freak of nature. I know that seduction, adultery and prostitution are prevalent in this country, as well as in others, and I can understand there are those who find pleasure in practising them, but I cannot, for the life of me, see why people should desire to read about them or watch them in pictures . . . Because of some intellectual limitation, I cannot read the putrid stories of Tolstoy, Gorki and all the rest of that tribe. To them it would seem that the meticulous description of a dung hill is art.[7]

The writer would have been sorry to hear that von Sternberg, though born in Vienna, had lived in the United States from the age of three.

With its dissolute king dying in agony as the reward for a life of corruption and his mistress hounded down by a righteous mob, *Madame Dubarry* might have been created solely for its suitability as a Trojan Horse in the German cinema's invasion of America. Even so, Davidson had difficulty in finding a buyer, receiving only one offer, a risible $40,000 – its value was conservatively estimated at $$\frac{1}{2}$$ million – from the First National theatre chain. Reluctantly accepting the deal, Davidson and Lubitsch watched First National remove the film's sexier scenes, change the name to *Passion* and disguise its source by describing Lubitsch as 'Bohemian' or 'Polish' and Negri as 'Italian'. The resulting 'continental masterpiece', as it was called in the advertising, did excellent business in American cities and earned First National more than $$\frac{3}{4}$$ million. Historians like to suggest that this success was due mainly to the total disguise of *Passion's* German origin but, for all First National's caution, newspapers of the day commented openly on its source and speculated, without heat, on the prospects for a revived German film industry. Ideology was noticeably absent from the discussion, which centred mainly on the risks to American films from this new competition, the general unprofitability of costume films in the US, the possible imposition of a tariff on foreign films and warnings from wiser heads that to impose such a tax might lead to similar moves against the showing of American films in Germany. Almost the only political remarks came in a *New York*

Times editorial of 27 March 1921, which commented on the fact that, in the wake of *Passion*, one New York film company had announced it had fifty German films for sale. 'The character of some Germany productions of the recent past,' it said, 'suggests that the wily foe may have a truly German motive in locating all his picture stories in foreign lands,' going on to point out that *Madame Dubarry* exposed the corruption of eighteenth-century France, Lubitsch's 1920 *Anne Boleyn* the evil of Henry VIII's England and a promised *Catharine the Great* would presumably attack low life in Russia's high places – all nations allied against Germany in the war. 'One waits for a pictorial biography of Cesare Borgia,' it continued prophetically; Richard Oswald's *Cesare Borgia*, with Conrad Veidt, came out shortly after.

Like most ideological protests at the state of the cinema from American public and press, the *Times* attack seems thin and un-felt; only money has ever talked with any real authority in the film business, and Hollywood's larger studios had obviously elected to invest heavily in the regenerated German film industry. It is interesting to debate whether Alfred Hugenberg, the crypto-Fascist newspaper magnate who bought a controlling interest in the now-thriving UFA when the German government handed its one-third interest to private banks in 1918, influenced the choice of subjects even in independent companies like Union, but the vogue for historical films had obvious roots in the un-familiarity of French and American audiences with Reinhardt's sweeping use of crowds, a technique plundered by almost every German film director of the time. Acclaim for the new German epics was, however, not universal. Britain's exhibitors volun-tarily suspended screening of all German films for five years in 1918, after the Armistice was signed – a ban not lifted until December 1921, and then only half-heartedly, the Cinematograph Exhibitors' Association merely bowing to a majority vote by washing its hands of the matter; if members wanted to show German films, that was their business. Nor did the American public take to all foreign films equally. In April 1922 the director of the *Motion Picture News*'s Exhibitors Service Bureau mildly explained a few facts of life to the *New York Times*, which had commented doubtfully on an MPN poll placing *Passion, Deception* (the US title of *Anne Boleyn*) and *The Cabinet of Dr Caligari* well down the list of commercial hits. '*Deception*,' the exhibitors'

representative explained,

is a costume bill and it is a tough job to put on this class of production in anything but the big first-run houses. Then, too, the fact that the picture was German-made didn't help matters any. In a number of small cities there was a considerable anti-German demonstration during its run and in some instances the feature was pulled off for this reason . . . [*Caligari*] is in a class by itself. *Caligari* was a flop because very few exhibitors would book it. Those who did were the ones who saw its possibilities as a freak and exploited it accordingly. As entertainment with the fans, *Caligari* just wasn't.

Hollywood knew the truth of these comments even if the newspapers did not, but no studio was prepared to take the next necessary step, that of importing these skilled German film artists to produce in America the kind of films American audiences wanted to see. Except for the immigrant entrepreneurs, American cinema was still relatively free of foreign elements, the only exception being a strong coterie of French producers and technicians who had gravitated to Hollywood from Pathé and Éclair. Maurice Tourneur, Alice-Guy Blaché, George Archainbaud, Louis Gasnier, Albert Capellani and Leonce Perret had all estab-

Erich von Stroheim directs his masterpiece, Greed

lished themselves strongly in American cinema; but, except for mavericks like Erich von Stroheim, Germans and Viennese were rare, and the studios understandably reluctant to bring them in. When the impasse was finally broken, responsibility rested not with Zukor or Fox but with two shadowy entrepreneurs operating in the best tradition of Hollywood's buccaneers.

Little material exists on the background of the Hamilton Theatrical Company, a New York distribution and talent agency founded around the end of the First World War, but in 1918 its owners were the tall, distinguished Ben Blumenthal, who, though American-born, spoke fluent German, and a slippery Berlin theatre-owner named Samuel Rachman. Blumenthal first entered the story at the party given by UFA after the opening of *Madame Dubarry* on 19 September 1919, upstaging such glittering guests as Charlie Chaplin by kissing Pola Negri's hand with some warmth and murmuring, 'Miss Negri, you don't know it yet, but I'm going to be the one who signs you for Hollywood.' Negri, still under contract to UFA for two more films, spent a good deal of time in Blumenthal's company, encouraged by generous gifts of jewellery and assurances of his affection. When First National acquired *Madame Dubarry* and 'Roxy' Rothapfel agreed to open it at New York's famous Capitol, he sent her a diamond and pearl bracelet, and by the end of 1920, when Fox's Winfield Sheehan and First National's J. D. Williams, having seen the reaction to *Passion* in New York, arrived in Berlin to sign her up, a deal with Hamilton, promising her a salary rising from $3000 a week to $5000, was already closed. Blumenthal promptly disposed of the contract at a healthy profit to Famous Players, but Negri remained admiring as she prepared for her trip on the golden road to Hollywood.

The Hamilton duo now showed their true skill in a cunning coup. Rachman, noted for his shady deals, hardly waited for the ink to dry on the Negri/Famous Players contract before hurrying to Berlin's film centre, the Friedrichstrasse, and buying up two old Negri pictures at the bargain price of DM 1000 each. Sailing for New York, he rang Zukor and casually announced, 'I have a couple of Pola Negri pictures if you are interested.' Famous Players took one look and announced that they would pay nothing for such junk, least of all the $¼ million Rachman demanded. 'Such a pity,' he said. 'Perhaps First National or Fox won't be so critical.' Zukor needed only a moment to see that if Rachman sold either of these awful films to a competitor, Negri was finished in America, and rang back to accept the offer. By then, of course, the price had doubled, but Famous Players paid. Having exploited the popularity of Negri, Blumenthal turned to Lubitsch, whom he had clearly identified as the true genius of the star's films, and signed a long-term contract early in 1921 to distribute his films in the USA, his first for them to be the Egyptian epic *The Wife of Pharaoh*.

The Hamilton team underestimated Zukor. Perhaps the first Blumenthal and Rachman knew of his response to their activities was a newspaper report of Zukor's return to New York on 22 May 1921, after a European trip. Famous Players, it was announced, now had a German sister company, the Europaische Film Allianz (EFA). 'Mr Zukor has acquired a large motion picture plant in the West End of Berlin at the Zoological Gardens,' read the report. 'Ernst Lubitsch, Pola Negri and other German stars and directors engaged by Mr Zukor probably will not come to America to make Paramount pictures but will remain in Germany with the EFA.' A few days later an advertisement in the *Berliner Tageblatt* announced EFA's formation and a roster of talent that included Lubitsch, Negri, Jannings, Harry Liedtke, Mia May, Degny Servaes and, most surprising of all, Max Reinhardt, who was supposed to be preparing a film of Milton's *Paradise Lost*, an awesome project even for him. Quite what basis Zukor had for these claims is not clear, but since Lubitsch's *éminence grise* Paul Davidson was named as EFA's General Director, it is probable that Paramount merely bought up Davidson's entire operation – studio, stars and incomplete projects – as a means of gaining a strong foothold in the growing German industry. The theory gains weight from the fact that, immediately after Lubitsch's decision to leave Europe for Hollywood, Davidson's holdings, in which he had long retained a measure of control, were merged with UFA, the growing monolith soon to be owned almost entirely by Paramount.

Zukor's coup crushed the Hamilton Theatrical Co., and on 11 December 1921 the *New York Times* announced diplomatically that 'differences between the Famous Players/Lasky Corporation and the Hamilton Theatrical Company on the distribution and exhibition of certain German motion picture productions have been settled'. Paramount was acknowledged to possess the US rights to all Lubitsch's work, and also that of Pola Negri, Dmitri Buchowetzki, whose *Danton*, renamed *All For a Woman*, was a major hit, Paul Wegener, Emil Jannings, Harry Liedtke and Mia May, while Hamilton was fobbed off with the meagre British Empire rights. With what jaded eyes Blumenthal and Rachman must have viewed the arrival in New York on 24 December 1921 of Davidson and Lubitsch, the latter with a copy of *The Wife of Pharaoh* in his luggage, and the more flamboyant landing a few weeks later of Pola Negri, two harbingers of a flood that fundamentally changed the American film industry.

3 THE LAST GERMANS

The crowd milling about in front of Pasadena railway station seems curiously disoriented. They stare obediently at the camera, a living backdrop to the objects of this gathering, themselves clearly ill at ease. Only the Hollywood host is relaxed. Gleaming teeth clamped on a prop pipe, dressed in jodhpurs and tweed cap like a raffish chauffeur, he radiates a professional confidence; he has seen all this before. Flanking him, the guest of honour and his family, fatigued from a three-day train trip, pose indifferently, the wife and child resigned, resentful, the tall, plump, bearded man, squinting in the sun, already contemptuous of the city that is to be his home for the next three years. The banner behind them, with its extravagant message of welcome to 'the screen's foremost dramatic artist', billows in the warm breeze, the final incongruity; the wind of Hollywood fashion has blown Emil Jannings here – soon it will also blow him, much inflated by publicity and good living, away.

Today Jannings is a legendary figure, best remembered for his roles in Murnau's *The Last Laugh* and Sternberg's *The Blue Angel*, the scandals that surrounded him both in Hollywood and wartime Germany forgotten. Yet, extravagant and unlikeable as he was and repellent as were his social and sexual excesses, Jannings deserves a niche in the history of Hollywood if only for the degree to which his success and failure were controlled by its caprice.

Despite Jannings's success as Louis XV in *Madame Dubarry* and Henry VIII in *Anne Boleyn* Hollywood had been cautious about importing him, mainly because of the continuing box-office resistance to costume romance. Murnau's *The Last Laugh* (1924) did much to alter this view; his portrait of a pompous hotel doorman demoted to lavatory attendant when his strength failed gave Jannings the opportunity to exploit the contradictions of a bizarre character. A natural self-pity and hypochondria gave conviction to the scenes of degradation, and the necessary padding and whiskers encouraged the hysterical identification with the character that had made his Louis XV so effective. He capitalized on the success of *The Last Laugh* with *Variety*, a dazzling

Emil Jannings arrives in Hollywood

novelette about a cuckolded circus acrobat, directed by Ewald Dupont, who may have seen that Jannings, ripe for exploitation by Hollywood, could also carry a clever director with him. Generously assisted by Dupont, Jannings overacted wildly in *Variety*; finding a caricature of his mistress and her lover – the third aerialist in their act – on a marble-topped table in a café, he shatters it and the rest of the café in an orgy of destruction, a contrast with the gentler but sexually explicit sequence where he subserviently undresses his girl and darns her stocking after her performance on the high wire. Dupont's planning paid off. Not only he and Jannings, but also Lya de Putti, who played the girl, scored Hollywood contracts.

Jannings sailed from Cuxhaven on 4 October 1926, into the kind of prepared legend that Hollywood regularly wove around its foreign stars. Even his actual birthplace, Rorschach in Switzerland, was regarded as having too many Germanic connotations, and Paramount announced that Jannings had actually been born in Brooklyn, then taken to Europe at the age of one. (For good measure, his birth-date was also set forward by two years, to

Emil Jannings displays his ability at disguise in The Way of All Flesh, *one of his great American successes*

1884.) Unlike Greta Garbo, whose European background the studios stressed, since her popularity mainly rested with German and French audiences, Jannings was offered primarily as a star for America; outdated in Europe, Jannings's stock character of the humiliated gentleman, his exaggerated use of eyes and eyebrows and his skill with make-up delighted audiences in the US as Paul Muni was to do a decade later. Uninterested in the subtle and naturalistic acting of native performers like Richard Barthelmess and Charles Ray, who had a devoted following among European afficionados, Americans delighted in acting that was readily identifiable as such. Integrity of performance or fidelity to character mattered less than the ability to render one's self unrecognizable by make-up and disguise, and to throw the sort of hysterical fit which had already earned for Jannings the reputation of 'well-poisoning': destroying his colleagues' performances by displays of histrionic fireworks. (The only German star held in greater fear by European actors was Werner Krauss, whose genial alcoholism occasionally led him to invent new dialogue in classic plays and, on one occasion, to wander drunkenly on stage in the middle of a play in which he was not acting to greet some non-plussed friends who were. Despite his acting reputation, no studio dared to offer Krauss a Hollywood contract.)

Delighted to have captured Jannings with a three-year contract, Paramount ignored the unconventional establishment he set up with his wife, ex-singer Gussy Holl, on Hollywood Boulevard in the huge copy of a southern mansion he rented as his home. As he was later to do in the Austrian country house he bought on his return to Europe, Jannings lived the life of a medieval count, eating, entertaining and fornicating massively. In two years his weight swelled to three hundred pounds. Referring always to himself in the third person, he would enthuse over his enormous meals, shouting, 'This is what Emil likes. This is good for Emil.' His house teemed with servants, acolytes and pets. He owned several Chow dogs, including Gilgi, a Hollywood aristocrat whose ownership could be traced back to Rudolph Valentino, who presented him to Hungarian actress Vilma Banky while making *Son of the Sheik*. From Miss Banky he went to another Hungarian, writer Irma Fasekas, thence to actor Andri Mattoni. Finally Mattoni called on Jannings shortly after his arrival and Gilgi refused to leave. Josef von Sternberg remembered Jannings as

Emil Jannings enjoying Hollywood life to the full with Greta Garbo and Norma Shearer (above) *and posing in front of his Hollywood mansion* (below)

extremely partial to dogs and birds. His rooms were full of barking chows, squawking parrots and chirpers from his native forests, among them one whistler known as Pinkus whom he consulted on all financial matters. At the back of his garden was a chicken coop and confined in this annex were Greta Garbo, Pola Negri, Valentino, Jack Gilbert, Conrad Veidt, Lya de Putti and other clucking hens and crowing roosters named after the many visitors who achieved this distinction after bringing a tribute of sausages.[8]

Few people took Jannings seriously, even though his popularity quickly climbed until, in the year he left to return to Germany, only John Gilbert stood above him among the male stars. In Germany he had been the regular butt of practical jokes, notably from the malicious Lubitsch who, while making *Madame Dubarry*, persuaded him that the lavish royal funeral would only carry the necessary conviction if every pall-bearer knew the king was in the coffin. Reluctantly Jannings climbed inside, the lid was screwed down – and Lubitsch ordered the set cleared, leaving Jannings to fume for hours. Victor Fleming repeated the joke in *The Way of All Flesh*, Jannings's most successful American film. Stung by the suggestion that his impression of a man asleep was not sufficiently convincing, he actually nodded off so thoroughly that, when the next shot was set up, he could not be awakened. Fleming moved on to another set-up and Jannings woke eight hours later in the dark, abandoned set. But the public knew him only as the tragic hero of *The Way of All Flesh*, a destitute Russian general in Sternberg's *The Last Command* – two roles which won him the first-ever Academy Award for acting, in 1929 – and the mad Czar Peter of his last film with Lubitsch, *The Patriot*. He might have continued successfully in such roles for years had sound not intervened. A nervous Paramount, frightened by his accent, declined to pick up his option for a fourth year and Jannings, equally nervous about entering sound film with his indifferent English, returned to Germany, rich on the tax-free savings of his years in America ($200,000 of which he had prudently kept in a pillow on his bed in Hollywood), and bought a house near Salzburg where he could entertain such friends as Werner Krauss, and live in the reflected glory of neighbours like Stefan Zweig, Karl Zuckmayer and Max Reinhardt. Zuckmayer never forgot Jannings's hospitality nor a host who was 'larger than life; normal human standards simply did not fit him, in the

Emil Jannings as the Russian general turned film extra in The Last Command

physical sense as well. There on his country property, he was like a Renaissance prince in his *castillo*. Money meant power to him, the power to savour life to the full . . .'[9] Nor had the return to a disciplined Europe altered his character:

He outdid everyone not only in appetite but also in down-to-earth wit and burlesque . . . I never knew anyone who had Jannings's way of pronouncing the most obscene and unprintable words and phrases with such poise and naturalness. Emil's Rabelaisian crudities were completely authentic. Sensitive though he was, sometimes even hypochondriacal, his talent came from his guts.[10]

Jannings gave little in return for his Hollywood fortune, except perhaps some satisfaction to the already wealthy Adolph Zukor. He influenced nobody, founded no style, contributed nothing to the American film; Pola Negri, however, did leave her mark, if only with the extravagant publicity for which she had shown a flair ever since her early days in Budapest when a besotted admirer had financed her first film, a turgid melodrama called *Slave of Sin*, when she was sixteen. Reinhardt chose her for the

Pola Negri communes with nature on a Pacific beach shortly after her arrival in America

Hungarian tour of his *Sumurun* and invited her to join the Berlin cast, where she succeeded instantly. Once in Hollywood, her feuds with rival actresses quickly made the papers, particularly that with Gloria Swanson. In a famous encounter Negri had settled down to a soulful scene in her first American film, for which she had demanded that the studio's customary mood musicians remain discreetly silent, when a brass band struck up outside the set. Though the joke was the director's, Negri accused Swanson, also blaming her for a plague of cats that erupted on her first day at the studios; superstitious about the animals, she refused to work until every one had been rounded up, a task that took all day. First prize in this battle was the Japanese-style bungalow on the Paramount lot vacated by Mary Pickford when she left in 1918 to found her own studio, United Artists. Professing little interest in the building, Negri took possession anyway, to the chagrin of Swanson and other stars who fulminated against the inroads of 'foreign legions'.

She followed the bungalow coup with an even more deadly

insult to Hollywood's actresses: engagement to Charlie Chaplin, wealthiest and reputedly most virile of the city's bachelors. After a meeting at the Berlin première of *Madame Dubarry* – asked on his return about 'the most beautiful thing he had seen there', he replied simply 'Pola Negri' – Chaplin celebrated her arrival in Hollywood with a typically grandiloquent gesture. Woken by her terrified maid with a shriek that 'The Indians are attacking', she found a ten-piece Hawaiian band serenading her, courtesy of Chaplin. Negri and the comedian became a familiar couple in Hollywood society, eventually announcing their engagement even though, Negri claimed, Chaplin's possessiveness and social climbing became wearisome. Paramount's decision to match her in *The Cheat* with handsome French actor Charles de Roche precipitated an argument in which the engagement was broken off; never one to be seen in the wrong, Chaplin instantly issued the story to the press, ensuring that the headline in the papers of 2 March 1923 read 'POLA NEGRI JILTS CHAPLIN'.

No coup so ornamented Negri's Hollywood career as her acquisition of Rudolph Valentino. The harassed Rudy had just emerged from an unhappy marriage to the epicene costume designer Natacha Rambova (a fanciful pseudonym invented by her mentor Alla Nazimova, the Russian star; Miss Rambova was christened Winifred Hudnut) when Negri told the press that she was seriously considering his proposal. Knowing little and caring less about the mercurial Hungarian, Valentino reputedly took the studio's advice that a well-publicized relationship with so heterosexual a lady would do much to rebuild his popularity, eroded by films like *The Young Rajah* in which, at his wife's suggestion, Valentino had appeared dressed in ropes of pearls and other exotica, to the derision of his fans. The romance, from Negri's point of view, could hardly have been timed more precisely. When rumours of impending marriage were at their peak, Valentino died suddenly of an intestinal haemorrhage. Abandoning work on *Hotel Imperial*, an all-star war comedy being supervised by the imported Erich Pommer as Paramount's climactic assault on the European market, Negri set out for the New York funeral, issuing hourly bulletins on her grief, including one description of her visit to the house Valentino had allegedly been building as their home. 'She spent more than an hour at the beautiful shrine of her lost romance,' a press release read, 'a pathetic and heart-broken figure.' Accompanied by a nurse, publicist, secretary and trunks containing $3000 worth of funereal costumes, Negri – after refusing to pose for press pictures with the excuse 'I do not wish to advertise my grief' – boarded the Santa Fe express on the three-day trip to New York.

At Chicago, her private Pullman car, in an unheard-of departure from practice, was transferred across the city and attached to the Twentieth Century Limited so that she would not have to face reporters, who nevertheless besieged the carriage, pounding energetically on the window. By cable she entered into the controversy over where Valentino was to be buried, over-riding suggestions from his family that the body should be returned to his native Italy with the firm insistence that he be interred in Hollywood; after all, hadn't the railway company promised to transport the corpse to California on the unused portion of the return ticket Rudy had in his pocket when he died? In the face of this unassailable logic, her wishes were deferred to.

Alternately screaming, collapsing, fainting and going rigid in nervous seizures, Negri dominated the funeral as unmistakably as her floral tribute – $2000-worth of blood-red roses woven into an eleven-foot long by six-foot wide carpet with 'Pola' picked out in white buds – overwhelmed the wreaths from Chaplin, Fairbanks and other Hollywood notables. Unpleasant suggestions that the Pola/Rudy romance was spurious evaporated with the fortuitous discovery of a letter from the doctor attending Valentino recalling the actor's last words as 'Pola – if she doesn't come in time tell her I think of her'. Thus confirmed in her proprietary rights, Negri carried the funeral and the decision about Valentino's burial. When she returned to Los Angeles the train had two extra carriages: one for Valentino's corpse and the other for floral tributes. Invisible but no less real was the cargo of publicity both for Negri's career and Valentino's last film, *Son of the Sheik*, an additional two hundred prints of which producer Joe Schenck had ordered as soon as Negri set out for New York.

To the end, nobody knew how much of Negri's alleged relationship with Valentino was fake, but novelist Joseph Hergesheimer, who lived opposite Negri and saw her emerge in mourning on the day of the funeral, offered an insight into her grief. As the press cameramen took their shots, one shouted: 'Pola, the light's not good on your face. Will you do it again?' 'And damned

Pola Negri (centre)
leaves Campbell's
Funeral Church after
the funeral of
Rudolph Valentino

if she didn't,' Hergesheimer told Hedda Hopper. 'It's the only time I ever saw a retake on mourning.'

Self-promotion staved off the collapse of Negri's career for a few years only. As sound loomed, Paramount sold the two-year balance of her contract to an English firm for 50 per cent of its value and she disappeared into wealthy obscurity enlivened by desultory guest appearances. Her experience was typical of the first émigrés to Hollywood, hired too quickly in the race between studios anxious not to be outdone. By 1924, when America stabilized the struggling Deutschmark with loans and a readjustment of war reparation payments, control of German film production was almost entirely in American hands, and buyers could afford to be more relaxed in their recruitment. Alfred Hugenberg bought control of UFA and invited Paramount and Metro-Goldwyn-Mayer to acquire further financial interest. In the famous Par-Ufa-Met agreement of 1926, UFA, in return for DM 17 million, agreed to reserve 50 per cent of its cinemas for the showing of Paramount and MGM films, a move which consolidated the shaky industry at the cost of passing a large measure of control in German film production to Zukor and Mayer. Encouraged by the opportunities offered to technicians trained in Hollywood, many artists who had left Germany to work in America returned, led by Erich Pommer, who had spent 1926 and 1927 supervising Paramount's foreign-language productions in Hollywood. Between 1927 and 1933, as head of UFA, he used the new capital to convert its Neu Babelsberg studios into the only European film complex whose facilities compared with those of America.

Despite the flurry of offers to work in Hollywood, Ernst Lubitsch's American career had not gone quite as planned. Having acquired the rights to his German films, Zukor had hesitated over importing the film-maker himself, particularly since anti-German feeling continued to run high. It was left to Lubitsch to break the deadlock by accepting an offer from Mary Pickford to join her at United Artists. Revolted at the image of 'America's Sweetheart' which kept her in pigtails well into her thirties, Pickford periodically rejected the idealized adolescence of her regular work to appear in such relentless dramas as *Stella Maris* – where, as the crippled slum child Unity Blake, she gave a performance of tragic intensity – only to retreat into the old fantasy for fear of angering her fans. (*Stella Maris* satisfied both sides, since Pickford also appeared as the noisomely sweet aristocrat whose happiness Unity guarantees by murdering the drug-addicted wife of her lover.) In 1925 she even asked a puzzled Josef von Sternberg, fresh from his first triumph with the Stroheim-esque *The Salvation Hunters*, to create a new film for her. Sternberg obligingly roughed out a script in which she played yet another slum girl, this time blind, living in the heart of industrial Pittsburgh. Pickford declined with a shudder but the impulse remained, leading her to offer Lubitsch a contract for his first American film.

Lubitsch arrived in 1922 with a distinguished entourage: editor Andrew Marton, assistant director Erich Locke, and Heinrich Blanke, personal assistant, writer and later producer. Anticipating a protest from patriotic groups like the American Legion, Pickford almost seemed piqued when her careful plans to keep his arrival secret proved unnecessary; only the press showed any interest in her decision to smuggle him off the ship in the pilot

Ernst Lubitsch with Mary Pickford (and her mother), Charlie Chaplin and Douglas Fairbanks shortly after his arrival in Hollywood

boat, and they received little information from Lubitsch who, on being met at the Pasadena railroad station, declined with a curt 'Nein' even to answer the question 'Are you going to work in Hollywood?'

According to Pickford, she had chosen as her vehicle with Lubitsch the Elizabethan romance *Dorothy Vernon of Haddon Hall*, a script of which Lubitsch had read and, allegedly, approved in Berlin. On arrival, the director, perhaps not surprisingly, expressed misgivings about the subject and insisted on a new story. After Pickford had rejected a Lubitsch/Edward Knoblock adaptation of *Faust*, the two writers, in conjunction with Lubitsch's regular collaborator Hans Kraly, settled on D'Enrys Dumanoir's *Don Cesar de Bazan*, a romance of nineteenth-century Spain, which became *Rosita*. This, the traditional story of events surrounding Lubitsch's introduction to Hollywood, bristles with unlikelihoods. At Paramount, Pola Negri, in what is surely no coincidence, commenced shooting *The Spanish Dancer*, another adaptation of *Don Cesar de Bazan*, on almost the same day as *Rosita*. Pickford had angered Zukor by leaving Paramount to start production on her own, Negri now occupied Pickford's bungalow, Lubitsch had been Negri's director. Lubitsch arrived in Hollywood in December 1922, yet by September 1923 *Rosita*, a costume spectacular needing elaborate production, had its première. Surely some preliminary work must have been done on the project before Lubitsch arrived, suggesting that Lubitsch was a pawn – or, knowing his talent for intrigue, an active player – in the continuing feud between Pickford and her ex-employer at Paramount. But at this distance one can only suspect and speculate.

In later years Pickford refused to release *Rosita* for general screening, classing it as 'an awful film'. In fact, with Lubitsch's direction, Charles Rosher's glowing razor-sharp photography and, most impressively, the sets of Toledo, designed by the Danish art director Svend Gade, imported into America by Selwyns, the theatrical producers, it is a technical achievement of immense skill. Pickford, however, found Lubitsch entirely incompatible. His broken English, wisecracking humour and inevitable cigar caused friction from the start, a situation not improved by the constant presence on the set of Pickford's watchful mother. She had been scandalized when Lubitsch, explaining his *Faust* script, told her how Marguerite 'stringles' her baby. 'Not *my* daughter!'

Rosita, starring Mary Pickford and directed by Lubitsch. Set design by Svend Gade

she said. 'No sir!' She also attended all screenings of the 'rushes' and, after the first batch, hurried Mary into a corner for an urgent whispered conference. The result was conveyed to Lubitsch, who in turn passed it to one of the writers for imparting to George Walsh, the husky young actor who played Rosita's lover, Don Diego. It had been noted by Mrs Pickford Snr, the astonished Walsh was told, that his snug breeches showed rather more of his manhood than was desirable if Pickford was to remain the centre of attention. For the rest of the film, could he wear not only his usual athletic supporter, but an additional one, and heavy-duty at that? 'In Europe, it would be wonderful,' Lubitsch said wistfully, 'but Mrs Pickford says . . .'

Surviving *Rosita*, Lubitsch moved on to First National and then Paramount, becoming in time its head of production as well as unofficial leader of Hollywood's émigré community. But, for all the affection in which he was held, his career embodies the movie truism, 'If you start with no Hungarians on a unit, it will soon be all Hungarians – if you start with all Germans, you end up with just one.' Lubitsch outlasted friends and enemies alike, and in retrospect his progress looks a copy-book exercise in the acqui-

Lubitsch with Adolph Menjou and Pola Negri on the set of Forbidden Paradise

sition and consolidation of power. One by one, his early colla-borators disappeared. After an argument over Lubitsch's attrac-tive second wife, he and scenarist Hans Kraly had a public fist-fight which ended the latter's Hollywood career. His one film with Negri, *Forbidden Paradise*, flopped and, like Jannings, with whom Lubitsch worked only on the indifferently received *The Patriot*, she returned to Europe and obscurity. During the 1930s after rashly criticizing some of his work and trying to exercise at Paramount the sort of artistic control Lubitsch employed in his Berlin career, Josef von Sternberg found himself out-manoeuvred and finally denied work. He was, he said bitterly, 'liquidated by Lubitsch'.

Even his old editor, Andrew Marton, quickly left the Lubitsch orbit, though to this day he prefers to see only his kindness, and not the handiwork of a diminutive Machiavelli. 'Lubitsch was a marvellous, marvellous man. I remember when I was first en-gaged, my fiancée had to go to Europe because her mother was ill, and she went over on the same boat as Max Schmeling, the boxer. Next thing I know, all my friends send me clippings: 'Who is the mystery woman Max Schmeling is visiting every weekend in Prague?' So I showed this thing to Lubitsch and said 'What should I do?', to which Lubitsch answered, 'I don't know what you should do. I know what *I* would do; hop on the next boat and get her.' I said, 'What about my job?' 'It's yours when you come back.' So I went, and we got married in Vienna. The newspapers had a headline: 'Marton Beats Schmeling In First Round.' Then, on the way back to America, in Berlin, I was staying in an obscure hotel, an unknown person, when the largest electrical firm in Germany, Tobis Klang Film, rang and said, 'Mr Marton, we know you cut *Alibi* and other sound films. Would you consider staying here and working for us?' They wanted me to train thirty-eight student editors in sound cutting technique, after which I would have the opportunity to direct my own films.' Marton took the job, not discovering until forty years later that Lubitsch had wired Tobis saying, 'Andrew Marton is passing through Berlin. You couldn't do better than sign him up.'

So Marton went the way of other collaborators, and Lubitsch, the last German, remained.

4 'TAKE YOUR BALLS IN YOUR HAND AND CHUCKLE'

When Sergei Eisenstein came to the US in 1930, one of his first interviews was with Sam Goldwyn, an ardent admirer, he claimed, of the Russian director's work. *Battleship Potemkin*, Goldwyn said, had been a rich emotional experience for him. Would Eisenstein prepare something similar – but with a smaller budget, of course – as a vehicle for Ronald Colman? Eisenstein's reaction is not recorded, but his astonishment was shared by many of the distinguished directors lured to Hollywood in the mid-1920s by the short-term contracts handed out promiscuously by the Berlin offices of the big Hollywood companies. Many came to Hollywood – it is hard to find a single major European director of the period who did not make at least a token visit to Los Angeles – but only a fraction, seldom the cream, stayed there. Recognition did not come easily even to Lubitsch, and was in many cases withheld entirely. Unlike the refugees of 1933 and 1940, fleeing from persecution and thus entitled to a certain sympathy from the film community, European film-makers of the 1920s often encountered Hollywood's worst face, wearing the familiar triple mask of xenophobia, apathy and ignorance.

By the time *Passion, Deception*, Buchowetzki's *Danton* and the remaining post-war epics had been released in the US, Hollywood's ardour for the German film was considerably diminished. Having bought up every new production of any reputation in order to keep it from competitors, the studios viewed their accumulated holdings with alarm. Relentless Expressionist works like Lupu-Pick's *Shattered* and Paul Leni's *Backstairs* showed little commercial potential, and though both had minority releases in the US, public interest fell even below that shown in *Caligari*. Even more alarming were such productions as Joe May's 1919 *Mistress of the World*, a sprawling multi-feature designed, like

*Joe May was one of
the many German
directors whose work
Hollywood found too
humourless and prolix*

Fritz Lang's *Mabuse* and Nibelungen films, to be run on two or
three consecutive nights. With the benefit of their eighteen
months' experience, the studios felt they understood the German
art of film, and their reaction was relieved contempt. Famous
Players set up a department exclusively to re-edit and re-title
foreign films, and Robert Kane, general production head of
Famous Players and a leading figure in the Famous Players/Para-
mount foreign version business for many years, summed up the
prevailing attitude in a 1922 interview. Films, Kane confided,
'were produced in Germany in a shape that the most amateurish
of American picture fans would laugh at'. Comedy came in for
particular criticism. 'The German sense of humour is perverse
where it is not just cheap slapstick. . . . When we laugh at their
'comic' actors in our projection rooms it is not at their comedy but
their attempts at it.' The German moral sense and insistence on
realism also caused Kane some sleepless nights. 'In some pictures
the Germans, like the French and the Italians, go the limit. I have
seen films built on some of the stories of Sudermann and Haupt-
man . . . that could not pass a blind censor in any Anglo-Saxon
country. In most of the films we are producing' (from German

originals) 'dozens of shots must be eliminated. They are the last things in the risqué.'

Shortly before the interview, Kane and his staff had been wrestling with *Mistress of the World*, the length of which gave them particular trouble. 'In these German films,' he explained,

it is the Teutonic mind we have to struggle with. The German mind cannot condense. It is prolix . . . Editing seems to be a totally unknown art in the film studios of Germany. It is as though a newspaper should print every word in all the Associated Press stuff that comes over the wire at night – just slap it in . . . Our task is to boil these stories down to from five to nine reels without losing the guts of the story and keeping the beautiful shots intact. It is often a herculean task.

May's film, he explained, 'as it came to us originally was in fifty-four reels, with 94,000 feet of stuff we could not use. It took four months of work to cut it to twenty reels, put titles on it which match up with the action and strike the American tempo.' Americans finally saw *Mistress of the World* as three separate features, *The Dragon's Claw*, *The Race for Life* and *The City of Gold*, comprising altogether about a third of May's original film.

What Famous Players cut from these films of 1921 and 1922 is less interesting than what they left in. The basis for selection conveys exactly what Hollywood admired about the cinema of Europe. 'These German films excel in pictorial effect,' Kane said,

because artistic Europe has eyes. Europe is all colour, scenery, variety, a clash of cultures. She is theatrical – she is always looking for 'effects'. . . . We need more of the bizarre, the grotesque, the exotic in our productions – but always retaining those things . . . that we excel in – story-telling, mechanical technique and picture tempo.[11]

It was the extravagant which Hollywood admired in European cinema, the sense of period and of place conveyed by the epics of Lubitsch, Oswald, Buchowetzki and May, and it is not surprising that German and Austrian set designers, cameramen and costumiers were wooed as energetically as directors. In 1923 Hans Dreier, a pupil of the great designer Jean Perrier, left UFA/EFA to join Paramount and become head of its design department, a major influence for good taste in Hollywood for the next thirty years. (He had been preceded at the Famous Players studio

by Paul Iribe, the French couturier and jewellery designer whom
Lasky had imported to trump Cosmopolitan's employment of
Ziegfeld Follies designer Joseph Urban in 1920. Despite his
Viennese background and experience with Reinhardt, Urban did
not adapt to Hollywood as Lubitsch had done and as Dreier and
Warner Brothers' Anton Grot were to do so effectively during the
1920s and 1930s.) For his 1927 MGM adaptation of *The Student
Prince*, Lubitsch imported his costumier on *Madame Dubarry*, Ali
Hubert, soon to become a Hollywood fixture as did Hans Kraly,
cameraman Theodore Sparkhul and assistant Henry Blanke, all of
whom left Lubitsch's team to establish pockets of European
technical skill at other studios.

By contrast with the technicians, most of whom came to stay,
the earliest imported directors had Hollywood careers as brief as
they were variable. Brought out for the most part on the basis of
a single European success, their talents and temperament seldom
fitted the Hollywood mould. Here at least Kane's remarks about
the opacity of 'the Teutonic mind' were borne out. Despite a
narrowing gap between Hollywood's product and that of UFA,
practice in the two studios remained vastly different. Germany
brought to its film-making a polished and unemotional professionalism typical of all its enterprises, a calm expertise that mini-
mized glamour in favour of efficiency. British director Michael
Powell visited UFA in the 1920s and still remembers 'the efficiency – those dust-free oiled floors. All UFA was like that.' But
this polished plant merely reflected a rigid internal discipline.
Arriving in Berlin in 1929 to make his first German film, *The Blue
Angel*, Josef von Sternberg was astonished to be told by Erich
Pommer that 'not only would he have to know precisely what
scenes I contemplated photographing, the angle of the camera and
its exact range, but that he would have to be so informed every
morning'.[12] Sternberg successfully appealed against this strict
regime, but few German directors would have thought the restrictions odd or even unwarranted. They found Hollywood's casual
system and lack of respect for the director profoundly disturbing.

In addition to the problems of control, artistic freedom and
technique, those of language could be almost insurmountable.
Lubitsch's broken English made communication difficult, as did
that of other émigré directors like Paul Stein. Screen-writer
Lenore Coffee recalled strolling past Stein's set one day with her

William Dieterle, seen here with his photographer, perfectly epitomized the UFA-style director, complete with autocratic manner and white gloves

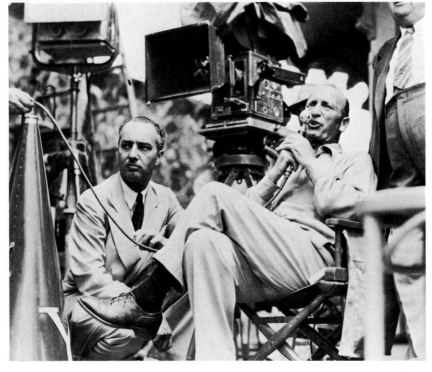

Michael Curtiz directs

husband Will Cowan when they heard the director's heavily
accented voice instructing an actor, 'I vant you should take your
balls in your hand and chuckle.' Wondering if he had mis-heard,
Cowan walked onto the stage, conferred briefly with Stein in
German and told the puzzled actor, 'All Mr Stein wants is you to
take those balls over there and juggle with them.' Neither Joe
May nor Michael Curtiz ever totally mastered English, and Curtiz
in particular communicated in a pidgin Hungarian/German/Eng-
lish only totally understood by a British grip nicknamed 'Limey'
who could always be found on Curtiz's films. The director's
multi-lingual background also made him the source of some
famous malapropisms, including the famous 'Bring on the empty
horses' and, describing a horror film, 'This will make your blood
curl.'

Language problems were overshadowed by those of temperament. Some directors proved themselves so incapable of handling
the Hollywood machine that they spent years in California making
a single film. Young Rumanian Marcel de Sano was signed by
Goldwyn in 1926 to direct four films, including *The Ordeal* with
Garbo and Lon Chaney, but this project folded after de Sano
announced to the press that the idea of Garbo falling in love with
the grotesque Chaney was too ludicrous for him to contemplate.
Shortly after, at Warner Brothers, screen-writer and, later, producer Robert Lord was assigned to work with him. 'He was a very
sad young man,' Lord recalled, though his sympathy declined as
de Sano turned up late for conferences or not at all, disappeared
for weeks and finally told Jack Warner that Lord's constant
changes to the script made it impossible to start the film. After
Warner had talked to Lord and rejected this story, an abject de
Sano confessed to Lord that he was terrified to go on the set with
such a big film and merely wanted to put off the evil day in every
way possible. Shortly after, he left for France and committed
suicide there in 1939; all that remains of his Hollywood career are a
lost melodrama called *Peacock Alley* and a few photographs of the
parties he attended with the urge to mingle and to please that
seized all émigrés. Slim, swarthy, handsome, he gazes out sadly
from the beaming groups on the beach, expressionless in a sea of
grins.

Other directors started well in Hollywood but lacked staying
power. After the smash success of *Variety*, which influenced

NORMA TALMADGE HOME MAY 1925
SANTA MONICA, CALIF.

TOP ROW - L TO R
1. FATTY ARBUCKLE 2. MAE MURRAY 3. WARD CRANE 4. VIRG VALLEE 5. RONALD COLEMAN
BESSIE LOVE 7. JACK PICKFORD 8. RUDOLPH VALENTINO 9. POLA NEGRI

SECOND ROW - L TO R
1. RAYMOND GRIFFITH 2. CHRIS GOULDING 3. LOUELLA PARSONS 4. LILLA LEE 5. CARMEL MYERS
6. ALLAN FORREST 7. BERT LYTELL 8. CLAIRE WINDSOR 9. DICK BARTHELMESS 10. CONSTANCE
    TALMADGE 11. BEATRICE LILLIE 12. AL HALL 13. MRS. JACK MULHALL 14. MR. JOHN ROBERTSON
15. JULIANNE JOHNSON 16. AGNES AYERS 17. JOHN ROBERTSON 18. MRS. TALMADGE
19. HENRI DE FLAIS 20. MICKEY NEILAN 21. HOWARD HUGHES

THIRD ROW - L TO R
1. "TONY " MORENO 2. PRINCE DAVID MDIVONI 3. CHAS. LANG 4. EDMUND GOULDING
5. MARCEL DESANO 6. MANUEL D'ARCE 7. HARRY D'AROST 8. DORIS DEAN ARBUCKLE
9. MRS. ANTONIO MORENO 10. EDDIE KONE 11. NATALIE TALMADGE 12. MRS. SEDGWICH
13. CHRISTINE FRANCIS 14. ALLIE MAC INTOSH 15. KITTY SCOLA 16. BLANCHE SWEET

Paramount to import Jannings, director Ewald Andreas Dupont also received an offer from Universal to direct in America. Movie tradition has it that his debut, a Viennese-style melodrama called *Love Me and the World Is Mine*, flopped so spectacularly that he immediately fled back home, but one is forced to be sceptical. England's leading trade paper, *The Bioscope*, wrote: 'It would be difficult to speak too highly of this production, containing as it does so many points of appeal.' The true author of Dupont's decline was, his contemporaries claim, an autocratic temperament; short, choleric, a perfectionist, he exasperated everyone with whom he worked by his insistence on 'realism,' a common problem with intense and serious-minded German artists. Leaving Hollywood, Dupont arrived in London in 1927 with a script on the Paris music hall which he insisted must be filmed inside

A typical Hollywood party at the home of actress Norma Talmadge at Santa Monica in May 1925

*E. A. Dupont (in hat)
directs* Love Me and
the World Is Mine, *
his first Hollywood
film*

the real Moulin Rouge; when the owners declined, Dupont reluctantly compromised with the Casino de Paris. *Piccadilly*, which
followed *Moulin Rouge*, was equally accurate in its London setting, and Dupont completed his extraordinary trilogy with
Atlantic, a mammoth recreation of the *Titanic* disaster in which a
full-size replica of a section of the liner was lowered realistically
into the studio tank. Actors in *Atlantic* complained of the heavy
'significance' Dupont put into their dialogue with his Expression-
ist-influenced direction, but, never one to take too much interest
in his casts, Dupont returned to Hollywood where he expected
his temperament to gain some respect. After a few programme
pictures he was working on Warner Brothers' *Hell's Kitchen* in
1939 when one of the Dead End Kids pushed too hard and the
director slapped him. Though smoothed over at the time, the
incident became such a subject for gossip that Lewis Seiler replaced Dupont, who did not work in Hollywood for another
eleven years. Unable to return to Europe, he resourcefully set up
as a talent agent, at which he was a considerable success, and also
edited a gossipy weekly newspaper, *The Hollywood Tribune*.
Paradoxically, Dupont did better in America than the remaining

Variety team. Jannings died in Germany, rich but discredited, and Lya de Putti, after a brief career complicated by her heavy drinking, returned to obscurity and an early death. Only cameraman Karl Freund, also brought out by Universal, had a true Hollywood success.

If temperament caused Dupont's downfall, luck played a far greater role in the Hollywood careers of two other émigrés, Benjamin Christensen and Paul Leni, both masters of the horror film in their respective countries and imported in the pursuit of the grotesque and bizarre foreshadowed by Robert Kane. In his native Denmark, Benjamin Christensen's audacity with unusual material had established him as a master of fantasy. *The Mysterious X* (1913), *Night of Revenge* (1915) and notably *Haxan* (1920), a quasi-documentary of witchcraft through the ages with hideously beautiful recreations of satanic rites, shook even the most phlegmatic of Hollywood talent scouts. Attending a screening of *Haxan* with another of his Scandinavian imports, Victor Sjöstrom, Louis B. Mayer asked: 'Is this man a madman or a genius?' After some thought Mayer, who chose his European employees almost entirely from Scandinavia with a view to personifying the concept of the tall, blonde American which MGM films exemplified in story, photography and design, offered Christensen a contract.

From his arrival in February 1925, bad luck dogged Christensen. 'The beginning was brilliant,' he reminisced, 'insofar as the first day the firm sold one of my stories, *The Light Eternal*, for £1500. It was not so marvellous afterwards; about twenty American writers were let loose on my script and altered the whole tone and message.' Mayer put Christensen onto a circus story, *The Devil's Circus*, a curious melodrama in the style made popular by Lon Chaney, whom Christensen was also to direct in *Mockery*. For *The Devil's Circus* Christensen used Karl Dane (Dehn), another of Mayer's Danish imports, and Norma Shearer, then a relatively new star who had, however, worked with Sjöstrom. These Nordic associations, exacerbated by extensive and confusing rewriting of the script, made *The Devil's Circus* look like a parody of the Hollywood 'Scandinavian' film, some critics even speculating that it might in fact be a Danish film with American actors cut in to the close-ups.

Hollywood might have overlooked the adverse press for Christensen's debut, but their superstitions were aroused when

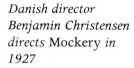

*Danish director
Benjamin Christensen
directs* Mockery *in
1927*

two of his assistant directors on the film committed suicide within
a week of its completion. 'It did not look too good,' said Christensen. 'For some time I was put in ''cold storage'' and Lionel Barrymore put some light on the matter for me. ''You can surely understand that no one wants to work for anyone whose assistants take
their lives.'' I also added to my unpopularity by having my shoes
soled and heeled. No one else did this; one *always* bought new
ones when the old were worn out. In the end I got one of Hollywood's most well-known fortune-tellers at my throat. He told
everyone they should keep away from me, because I brought bad
luck. Later I got to know the reason why he disliked me – I had
bought an antique Chinese figure he had wanted himself.'
Christensen had the frustrating experience of seeing his friend
Sjöstrom (his name anglicized as Seastrom) widening his already
considerable reputation with films like *The Wind* while the
former's ideas were turned down as uncommercial. 'The producers just said, ''We are here to make films that make money.''
When I came up with some original ideas, they asked me what I

thought the American "farmer" would say to that and advised me to forget it.' What the American farmer thought of *The Wind*, with its nihilistic, almost Strindbergian depiction of rural life in the Mojave Desert one can only imagine.

The real truth of Christensen's case was that, having been brought to America on the strength of his fantasy and horror films, it was in this field he was expected to stay, just as Sjöstrom, a skilled realist, had to pursue the rural drama form. In the curious way Hollywood had of tailoring its legends to the pattern of its films, Christensen's bad luck and the sinister events that dogged him provided support for his role as a master of horror. Pressed to do a Lon Chaney vehicle, he rejected the fantasy form entirely and insisted that MGM base it on one of his own stories set in the Russian Revolution. With Chaney miscast in the sympathetic role of a serf who poses as a count to help a noblewoman escape from the Bolsheviks, *The Mockery* flopped. MGM moved Christensen indefatigably to another fantasy subject, Jules Verne's *Mysterious Island*, but the director made such extravagant technical demands, including £15,000 adaptations to the studio tank for underwater shots, that Maurice Tourneur and finally Lucien Hubbard completed the film.

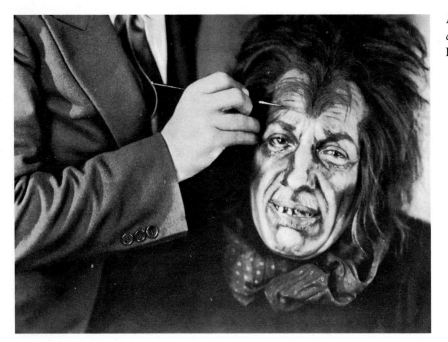

Making up an actor for Seven Footprints to Satan

Released by MGM, Christensen slipped into a job with the less prestigious First National, for whom he resignedly made his most popular American films, a series of horror comedies including the delightful *Seven Footprints to Satan* (1929), a spoof on the superstitions of which he had been a victim. The silly-ass hero, complaining of the boredom of his life, finds himself a prisoner in a house inhabited entirely by monsters, wild animals and screaming victims – all, he discovers at the climax, played by his friends, who have collaborated on a huge hoax to show him that reality can be as bizarre as any fantasy. *Seven Footprints* and the three films that followed became Christensen's premature farewell to America. In 1929 he returned to Denmark, hoping to reassure the film industry there that he was still interested. The directorship of a new theatre was offered to him, but paradoxically his American citizenship prevented him from accepting it. A return to Hollywood by the contrite Christensen and attempts to set up his own production company with the help of his friend Wid Gunning, the eccentric film journalist and editor of the respected if at times incomprehensible trade paper *Wid's Daily*, failed when New Deal legislation made his plan illegal overnight. Back in Denmark, this time for good, he contented himself with programme films – 'sweet things with music' – and a long career as the industry's elder statesman, his reward for which was the managership of a cinema in Copenhagen. 'Large sums of money, many years of work,' said one critic, synopsizing this frustrating career. 'Hollywood had taught Benjamin Christensen one thing and that was to bend his head and say "Yes, Yes".'[13]

Not all those who returned to Europe did so in disgrace. Paul Leni, brought out in 1927, adapted well to Laemmle's Universal, for which he produced a handful of superb horror films. In Germany Leni had proved his genius with fantasy, first as set designer for Lubitsch, then as a director in his own right. Jovial, portly, addicted to huge meals and practical jokes, Leni seems an unlikely candidate for a king of horror, but Laemmle obviously saw in his earlier work, particularly *Dornröschen*, a luscious version of the 'Sleeping Beauty,' and in the sinister *Backstairs*, an Expressionist drama of urban squalor co-directed by theatre producer Leopold Jessner, that delight in the grotesque and absurd which Robert Kane rightly isolated as Hollywood's greatest gift from German art. Leni munched the rituals of horror

Conrad Veidt in The Man Who Laughs

film as a glutton eats a peach, with an almost lascivious relish. In *The Cat and the Canary*, a classic exercise in the 'old dark house' tradition, curtains billow in ghostly perspective down a hall-way, taloned hands grope for the heroine, shadows twist and flee across the lamp-lit walls, though Leni scored his greatest Hollywood triumph in *The Man Who Laughs*, the grotesque fable of an orphan rendered a circus freak when his mouth is mutilated into a hideous and permanent grin. The fastidious and correct Conrad Veidt, who had left Germany after his success in *The Student of Prague* (1926) to try Hollywood, played the freak, giving the role some of the sly malevolence that had distinguished his playing of the somnambulist in *The Cabinet of Dr Caligari*. The film's sardonic mockery of royalty was Leni's personal contribution; he viewed all his films, like his trip to Hollywood, with amiable contempt, an attitude borne out by his working methods. Dissatisfied with the reactions of his cast in *The Chinese Parrot*, Leni arrived on the set with a huge gong, which he kept by his chair and struck with nerve-racking effect whenever he wanted

An all-British cast in a horror classic: Colin Clive, Elsa Lanchester, Boris Karloff and Ernest Thesiger in The Bride of Frankenstein

them to register shock. Technicians expected some eccentricity from foreign directors; Dmitri Buchowetzki insisted on having a piglet presented to him on the first day of any new film, and many émigrés, including Stroheim, Sternberg and Dieterle, affected the white gloves and autocratic methods of UFA. But Leni's gong proved too much. After one morning the cameraman issued an ultimatum – either the gong went or the technicians did. Leni's comic flair for the horror film and his genius with design promised much, but in 1928 he returned to Berlin, and died the following year of a blood disease. Universal's admiration of his work is reflected in the fact that Laemmle hired young English set-designer/director James Whale in 1930 and put him to work on a series of horror fantasies – *Frankenstein, The Bride of Frankenstein, The Old Dark House* and *The Invisible Man* – which closely resemble Leni's black-humoured and elegant creations.

'He lived alone with his servants in a castle perched on the highest hill in Hollywood,' a friend said of F. W. Murnau in later years.

I felt flattered to be the only guest at the long table, which gave an eagle's eye view of the lights of Hollywood and Los Angeles far below. His face glowed as he told me he had just purchased a yacht. She was a beauty – there were the pictures of her – *Pasqualito*. But he was changing her name to *Bali*, for to that far-distant paradise he would sail her. Hollywood was taking too much out of him. He would break out of his prison. . . . Lord, how I envied him.[14]

F. W. Murnau, William Fox's 'German genius' and the classic case of an artist destroyed by the Hollywood machine

This lugubrious dinner presaged the end of perhaps the brightest talent ever to be ruined by Hollywood. With his *Faust*, *Nosferatu*, and particularly *The Last Laugh* Murnau, the gangling ex-art historian, had created something new in film, an alternative to the intense Expressionism of his avant-garde contemporaries and the slick professionalism of the mainstream. In Murnau's world the camera glided sinuously through landscapes made unreal by mist or shimmering light, confronted individuals whose lives existed only in part on the physical level, analysed emotions and motivations so obscure that one still finds astonishing the vividness with which they leap into the mind. With *The Last Laugh* Murnau triumphed; the trivial story of a pompous hotel doorman's demotion to lavatory assistant, then elevation to wealth by the most fortuitous of accidents became in his hands the grimmest human tragedy redeemed by a delicious jest. But when Murnau took the film to Hollywood in 1924 with hopes of an American sale, few companies showed any interest. On the basis of his Lubitsch films, Jannings, the star of *The Last Laugh*, had already been snapped up by Paramount, and Murnau's remaining work seemed too uncompromising for Hollywood. Guided by his producer, Erich Pommer, who knew that *The Last Laugh* would eventually have its effect, Murnau returned to Berlin and took the opportunity of a German tour by Mary Pickford and Douglas Fairbanks to hire Pickford's cameraman Charles Rosher for a year as consultant on *Faust*. Murnau, Rosher recalled, asked constantly; 'How would they do this in Hollywood?' Consequently, when *The Last Laugh's* critical success persuaded William Fox to offer Murnau a four-year contract, the director had a grasp of American film-making technique few other émigrés could boast.

Delighted with his 'German genius,' as he called him, Fox promised Murnau $125,000 for the first year of his contract, rising to $200,000 for the fourth, all for a leisurely one film a

year; any additional films would net another $125,000 each. His requirements as to collaborators were scrupulously observed. Carl Mayer was paid $50,000 for his adaptation of Sudermann's *A Journey to Tilsit*, and Murnau's regular designer Rochus Gliese was imported to plan his first film, a version of the Sudermann story now named *Sunrise*, which his old adviser Rosher was to shoot. The most beautiful and subtle of all late silent films to come out of America, *Sunrise* earned Murnau a critical and professional acclaim achieved by few émigrés. Hollywood directors, including John Ford, adapted and absorbed his style, and American film gained a new depth to its vision, soon sadly to be blinded by the eruption of sound.

Throughout the production of *Sunrise*, Fox uncomplainingly agreed to the wildest flights of Murnau's fancy, over-riding even his own lieutenant Sol Wurtzel, who pointed out that, by omitting a brief dust storm from a longer storm sequence, thousands of dollars could be saved. Murnau resisted, even when the rain machine accidentally flooded the set before the dust flurries could be filmed. Rather than bow to events and shoot the rain sequence, Murnau sent a thousand extras home until the streets dried out, then brought them back for the dust and rain in proper order. Later, to get a particular tree he admired, Murnau had it shipped from Lake Arrowhead by road and its withered leaves replaced by new foliage glued on by three hundred Mexican labourers. On re-erection the tree looked unconvincing, so all the leaves were removed, again by hand, and replaced with others. While the job went on, contented extras hung about on full pay. *Sunrise* could not hope to make a profit, but for William Fox, anxious to hold up his head in a film community briefly obsessed by foreign genius, critical acclaim was reward enough.

Having made the gesture, however, Fox felt enough money had been expended on art and stressed to Murnau the necessity of turning a profit on his next film. Preliminary correspondence on the project chosen, a circus drama called *The Four Devils*, shows Fox gently but firmly demanding that work be completed 'at a reasonable cost,' to which Murnau acquiesced by shooting entirely in the studio with a little-known cast; like Christensen, he had 'learned to bow his head and say "Yes, Yes" '. A 'happy ending' was also added against Murnau's will, as had been the case with *The Last Laugh*, and he responded by retreating, as

many others had done, into the distant haughtiness of the
offended artist. Although his homosexuality would have gained
him entry to the highest Hollywood circles, Murnau remained
aloof, surrounding himself with a coterie of Latin servants and
intimates. He had, one senses, begun to lose the iron control that
had taken him from Berlin to Hollywood's high places, fatally
ignoring the fact that the film community required one to conform socially in return for artistic freedom. In 1928 he announced
that his third film would return to the lavish exterior style of
Sunrise with a 'woodcut' of country life showing, as he put it in a
letter to Fox, 'the sacred nature of bread and the alienation of the
modern city dweller and his ignorance of the basic sources of
nature.' In the circumstances he could hardly have expected it to
succeed.

Enmeshed in the financial negotiations that were soon to destroy
him as a power in the film world, Fox approved the project with
little thought, and Murnau moved his unit to a farm near Pendle-
ton, Oregon, specially purchased for the production. Mounting his
camera on a sledge, he deliriously ploughed down acres of ripe
wheat while the Fox people, having gratefully declined another
intricate Mayer script on the grounds that he had not met the
deadline, shook their heads over an equally 'un-American' story
by Berthold Viertel, imported by Murnau for the task. From the
start everything was stacked against *Our Daily Bread*. Murnau
was intransigent, Fox distracted and impatient with his
German genius, the temper of the country hostile to rural subjects
and the whole idea of silent film, and the money men obviously
aware that, should Murnau remain on the payroll very much
longer, he would become eligible for a rise to $200,000 a year. In
February 1929 *Our Daily Bread*, then close to completion, was
shelved, and the Murnau/Fox contract terminated by mutual con-
sent. (In 1930 a much-altered version of the film, with additional
material by Murnau's assistant A. F. 'Buddy' Erickson, was released as *City Girl*.)

An embittered Murnau headed, symbolically, for the South
Seas. With extraordinary flair he had teamed up with another
Hollywood renegade, the documentarist Robert Flaherty, and
persuaded a tiny company, Colorart, to back a co-directed film on
Polynesia, Flaherty's second attempt at such a subject; *White
Shadows in the South Seas*, set up as a co-directed production with

MGM in 1927, had collapsed when Flaherty and his associate director, W. S. 'One Shot Woody' Van Dyke, had failed to collaborate. The second attempt, *Tabu*, worked out no better. Arriving in Tahiti after a leisurely voyage in the *Bali*, Murnau found Flaherty broke, Colorart having gone bankrupt, and the production stalled. Determined to finish the film, Murnau offered finance from his own Hollywood earnings, and paid off all but a few essential technicians. A painful eighteen months followed in which *Tabu* slowly went ahead in the face of illness, bad weather, accidents, diminishing funds and deteriorating relations between Flaherty and Murnau. By the middle of 1930 all Murnau's money had gone and he was contemplating selling the *Bali*. Even his pleasure in the simple hedonism of the islands where he felt so much at home, comfortable in his bungalow, surrounded by his library − sent from Berlin − and the friends and lovers he had found among the Tahitians, was beginning to fade. At the last minute Flaherty made a deal with Paramount to finance the completion and distribution of *Tabu*, and the studio, then riding high on the success of its European sex comedies made by Lubitsch and the growing coterie of Germans on its payroll, offered Murnau a ten-year contract. Murnau returned to Hollywood in triumph, the artist who had defied the establishment and fled into the wilderness to return with a masterpiece. With the question of his Hollywood future still to be settled, he decided to attend the première of *Tabu* on 18 March 1931, and return to visit his mother in Germany. The fortune-teller he habitually consulted before any major decision told him puzzlingly that he would arrive at his mother's home on 5 April, but not in the way he thought. On 11 March Murnau was thrown from a speeding car on the coast road outside Los Angeles and killed. His coffin arrived back in Germany on 4 April and was claimed by his mother on the 5th.

5 COCKNEYS AT KEYSTONE

'We were basking in the brilliant Indian summer of a popular art,' J. B. Priestley wrote of the music hall in his novel *Bright Day*,

a unique folk art that sprang out of the gusto and irony, the sense of pathos and the illimitable humour of the English industrial people, braving it out in their mills and foundries and dingy crowded towns; an art that flourished, withered and decayed well within a man's lifetime, but that, before it lost all its vitality, scattered its seeds, its precious seeds of rich warm humanity, all over the darkening world, and sent an obscure droll called Chaplin as far as California so that his flickering image could go out and conquer the earth.[15]

Most writers emphasize Chaplin's importance in transferring English music-hall comedy to other countries, but despite his success, immeasurably greater than most other comedians who moved to Hollywood in the 1910s and 1920s, it is debatable just how typical he was of the breed. For all the reduced circumstances of his childhood, Chaplin was never at heart one of 'the English industrial people' but rather a representative of the middle class. The emphasis in his autobiography on faded gentility, a ruthless pursuit of profit in his American career that has none of the characteristic British working-class contentment with a living wage and an established home, perhaps most convincingly the films he made as an independent director, elaborate comedies of manners in which, as Robert Florey noted, 'the players had to mimic, to imitate each gesture, each expression, each movement of Chaplin even if the scene had to be shot fifty times or more,' betray his true personality. Acquisitive, snobbish, ruled above all by the profit motive both in intellect and business, he was a Hollywood man long before he even knew the place existed.

In Chaplin's light, lesser talents have paled: Stanley Jefferson, a colleague in Fred Karno's Mumming Birds troupe, who later achieved success as Stan Laurel; Jack Richardson, a Sennett graduate who died alone and alcoholic in London after the introduction of sound; even Karno himself, whose brutal tutelage of many great artists ended with a spell in Hollywood as destructive as it was absurd; and George Harris, a diminutive Liverpool comic who turned his five-foot height, Jewishness and hustling manner into a successful lifetime career that began 'on the halls' and ended in top management.

Comedian Jack Richardson hangs high over suburban Los Angeles in Sennett's Wall Street Blues

Harris's introduction to movies reads like a two-reel comedy in itself. In 1924, a successful specialist in cheeky bell-boys and similar roles, Harris was appearing at the Holborn Empire in London following a successful Australian tour. 'I had seen something in the paper about a representative of Mack Sennett being in London looking for talent. The last thing in the world I figured was that I would be considered. I'd come off after doing my act when the door-keeper told me there was a man waiting to see me. He handed me his card, and it read 'Jack Root, Mack Sennett Studios, Glendale Boulevard, Hollywood, California'. The penny still didn't drop, but I went down to see this huge man – he'd been a boxing champion – and he laughed. 'Gee, you're smaller than I thought you were. How would you like to go to Hollywood?' I was taken aback, but of course I said I'd love to. He said: 'Well, you come tomorrow morning to the Savoy Hotel and we'll talk about it.'

'I didn't sleep that night, and the next morning I walked into his suite at the Savoy and it was loaded with photographers. Root pointed to me and said: "Well, folks, there it is – the funniest face in Britain." ' (Root later explained that, harassed by the London press for a story, he had announced alcoholically that his mission in Britain was to find and purchase for Sennett the country's Funniest Face. Realizing belatedly that no candidates were available, he noticed the reviews of Harris's performance at the Empire, caught his act and sensed that the tiny comedian might fit into Sennett's team. The rest was publicity.) Taken aback by the demand from photographers that he pull a funny face, Harris said: 'I'm not going to pull a funny face because that would be mugging. If I'm going to be taken to Hollywood I want to be taken for what I am.' Root quickly stepped in and explained: 'Don't worry, we'll make that face funny when we get there.' Before he had fully grasped the situation, Harris was on his way to a contract with Mack Sennett.

With hindsight, one can see that Root and Sennett knew they had miscalculated in signing Harris to a contract, but hoped for some profit from a bad deal. Sennett, who had no faith in the star system, put few of his performers under contract, preferring to employ them on a weekly basis. A contract comedian who did not readily fit into the wildcat Sennett style was a liability. Harris remembers Sennett vividly. 'He had a cap on and a mouthful of chewing tobacco; a leather coat. He looked at me, gave a guffaw and said: "You're a little one, ain't ya? We'll have to get them to put you on a wire and throw you round the joint," which terrified me at the time. I was told to get on the set and watch.

'After watching for a while I'd got friendly with most of the people there. They were all very kind to me. Then Sennett said: "While you're waiting round till we find something for you, how about going up into the Tower? [The three-storey building where Sennett's writers worked was known as The Tower.] You've been on the halls in England and in pantomime. You might be able to give them some ideas." Sennett always had a high regard for English pantomime. He'd had Chaplin, Billy Bevan and other knockabout comedians from the halls who had been masters of pantomime and slapstick. He said: "Go and sit with the gagmen and if you'd like to suggest something, don't hesitate." '

'Sometimes Sennett had an idea of his own. He would come into the comedy department some mornings and, without any notes, start relating a routine he'd thought up. I remember him coming in one morning and starting to laugh before he'd even opened his mouth. "Heh heh heh . . . Jesus . . . I had an idea last night. How about getting Turpin . . . heh heh . . . getting him into a women's Turkish Bath? Y'see, this guy's sent out by his wife to get some shopping and he finds himself in this Turkish bath . . . a *women's* Turkish bath! Imagine . . . imagine that son of a bitch. . . ." He couldn't stop laughing at the idea. That was enough for men like Frank Capra and Jack Jevney, two of the top gagmen of the time. If you've got any comedy mind at all you don't have to be given more than the basic idea. The writers would kick it around, thinking of all the comic possibilities that could logically develop from this idea. Once we got an outline – just one sheet of paper – the director and the gagmen would get on the set and one gag would beget another. If one situation appeared to be extraordinarily funny we would continue with that for a while – "go along with the gag", as they say. When you had men who really knew what it was all about – comedy writers like Capra and Adler, directors like Lloyd Bacon, Al Santell, Del Lord, Eddie Cline, and also a man who could write good comic titles like the best in the world, Ralph Spence – well, you couldn't go far wrong.

'After I'd been with the writers for a while, Sennett decided to put me into some films. One morning I was told to get made up and go down on location. I didn't know the name of the film; it probably didn't have one at the time, just a number. A couple of the boys and I were picked up and taken down to a little side street off Glendale Boulevard on which there was a coffee stall. It was a prop, of course, but the traffic was going by unconcernedly, taking no notice. People were used to it by then. I knew Del

Lord, the director, and behind the stall was a very pretty girl, whom I recognized as Madeline Hurlock. Del came up and said: "George, here's what I want you to do. You go up to the stall and order a cup of coffee. Taste it, register a dislike for it, take another taste, then push it away and say to Madeline 'I just don't like it'. Then we'll cut." That wasn't too bad. "Do you want me to rehearse it?" "No, it'll be fine." So I walked up to the stall – the camera turned – I said "I'll take a coffee," tasted it . . . nasty . . . another taste. I put it down and said "I don't like it". Madeline said "Don't like it, eh? Then I've got something that you will like." Her hand went down and I got a custard pie right in my face. When I got the shaving soap and flour paste out of my eyes I said "I didn't know *that* was coming." Del said: "That was the idea. It's your first introduction to the pie. If I'd told you, you'd have registered anticipation. That's a perfect take. Even the fact that you wiped it off was so natural."

'Even in Hollywood, life could get boring. By then, I wasn't too smitten with what I was doing, drifting from a bit here to a bit there. I couldn't see myself getting into anything really worthwhile. And this wasn't the kind of comedy I was used to at all. At least in pantomime you knew what you were going to play; here it was entirely different. You were at the mercy of gagmen and people in the studio who picked on you for anything they wanted you to do without knowing whether you thought you could do it. It was a great experience but it wasn't quite my cup of tea. I'd been with Sennett for seven months and done about eight or nine films, along with bits here and there. Mr Sennett always said that he was waiting for some way to feature me, but nothing came along. But, as they say, there's a divinity that shapes our ends'.

'I was then beginning to know several people in Hollywood, and Raymond McKee, who was a good friend, said "I'd like you to join the 233 Club." It used to meet at the Masonic Hall on Hollywood Boulevard, and though it wasn't a Freemasons' Club there were similarities to the Masons. Harold Lloyd belonged to it, and so did Tom Mix. I said I'd love to. When they accepted me, I had to appear for a sort of cod initiation ceremony, and at that meeting was a cameraman from Fox named Glenn McWilliams. The following morning, I'm told, there was a meeting at the Fox studios in the office of Jim Ryan, the casting director. Victor Schertzinger, the director, was there, and McWilliams. They were talking about the casting and location work for a film called *The Wheel*, based on a John Golden play that had run on Broadway. Came the moment when they began to discuss who could play the part of a little Jewish fellow, a messenger boy who had been a jockey. It wasn't easy to find an actor with these qualifications, but Glenn suddenly said: "Wait a minute. I saw a little guy last night who could be ideal." Ryan rang the Sennett casting director, who agreed to let me go over and talk about it. And when I walked into Ryan's office and he and Victor Schertzinger saw me, I thought they were going to put their arms around me. Victor gave me one smile and that was all. Next thing I knew, Mr Sennett sent for me and asked me if I wanted to do the part. I said I'd love to, so he agreed to release me. And I hadn't been on the Fox lot for twenty-four hours before I knew this was my metier.'

Harris became a regular featured player in such Fox films as John Ford's *Three Bad Men* and *The Shamrock Handicap* as well as his own series of two-reel comedies, *East Side West Side*, variations on the popular formula of Jewish/Irish romance established by *Abie's Irish Rose* and *The Cohens and the Kellys*. Poised to reach what would have been the apex of this form, a parody of *Brown at Harvard* called *Ginsberg at Yale*, he was thwarted when Fox's increasing involvement in the money market took control of the studios out of his hands. Undaunted, Harris moved into radio, experimental television, British films and finally public relations, an irrepressible and highly clubable little man whose spirit Hollywood could never crush.

Though Harris succeeded, many talents of greater stature in the music hall failed, destroyed by their inability to conform to Hollywood's rules or, in a few cases, by the weight of their own past careers, the sins of which came home ironically to roost. No name is more famous in vaudeville than that of Fred Karno, legendary mentor of Chaplin, Laurel and a school of knockabout comedy that gave Sennett the foundation of the Keystone style. 'The Guv'nor', as he liked to be called, coloured an entire generation of music hall, though one looks in vain for the 'rich, warm humanity' of Priestley's description in Karno's ruthless rise and speedy fall, the latter an object lesson in the dangers of making enemies on the way up. In most other respects, Karno fits Priestley's vision of a music-hall artist; uneducated, brutally treated at home, the young Frederick Westcott was on the road early as an itinerant glazier, circus hand and eventually an acrobat, a trade in which he earned the name Karno when he and two friends, loitering among the shivering unemployed on Poverty Corner, the spot near London's Waterloo Station where 'resting' music-hall artists gathered in the hope of casual work from the theatrical agents of nearby York Street, grabbed a job substituting for The Three Carnoes, a gymnast act suddenly unable to fill an engagement. Liking the name's theatrical ring, Westcott became Karno, later changing his name officially by deed poll. Gymnastics gave way to pantomime and that in turn to comic sketches, for which Karno had a genius. 'Fred Karno's Speechless Comedians' were soon touring the music halls of England in such successes as *Jail Birds*, a series of routines unarguably the basis of Sennett's Keystone Cops – Karno even transported his team in an ex-police 'Black Maria' identical with the Kop Wagon later driven for Keystone by Del Lord – *Early Birds* and finally the famous *Mumming Birds*, a forty-five-minute parody of vaudeville itself which was to run, in one country or another, continually for the next forty years.

Like all Karno's successes, *Mumming Birds* was a self-contained vaudeville bill with singers, dancers and a good deal of low comedy. As the curtain swung back, audiences saw a mirror image of the theatre, with boxes set up on stage to view a variety performance. One by one the 'audience' took their seats in the boxes: a toff in evening dress, much the worse for drink; an odious boy, well armed with fruit, pies and other refreshment; his affectionate uncle and other patrons. The master of ceremonies then proceeded to introduce a series of acts notable only for their appallingly low quality: poorly synchronized can-can girls, abysmal song-and-dance men, a lady vocalist who lurched through the sentimental *Come Birdie Come and Live With Me*, a thunderous recitation of the poem *The Trail of the Yukon*. Each act was greeted by furious abuse from the audience, fusilades of fruit from the boy and occasional alcoholic incursions from the toff. Finally, the star turn, Marconi Ali, the wrestler, offered to fight anyone in the house, the toff confidently flattened him, took his prize and demanded beerily 'Bring on the girls'. With *Mumming Birds* companies touring Europe and eventually America, Karno could attract the best young music-hall comics despite the low

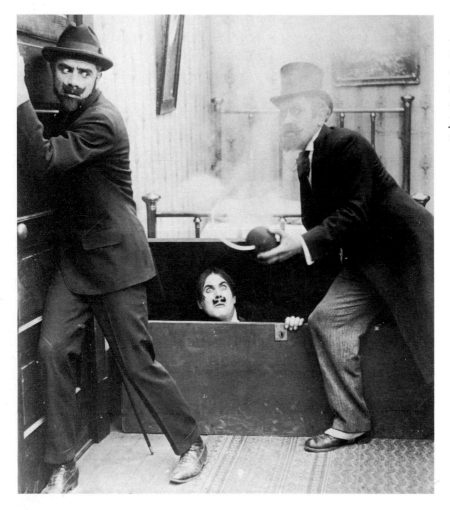

Widely regarded by Fred Karno as funnier than his younger brother, Sid Chaplin (in trunk) never achieved even a fraction of his fame in the movies

salaries he offered. Among those who regularly played the toff in *Mumming Birds* were Charlie Chaplin and his brother Sid, Stan Jefferson – later Laurel – and Billy Reeves.

Karno's parsimony was the least of his odious accomplishments. His wife Edith bore permanently on her cheek the mark of his small steel-tipped shoe where he had stamped on her as a punishment for failing to scrub the stage after a performance. Sexually voracious, he carried on numerous affairs, including one which coincided with the birth of his last child. Three weeks after the delivery, Karno's wife received a large parcel from her husband containing pornographic photographs of him and his showgirl mistress copulating in a field, his hint that the marriage was at an

Early advertisement for the vaudeville show which carried Charlie Chaplin to America and fame

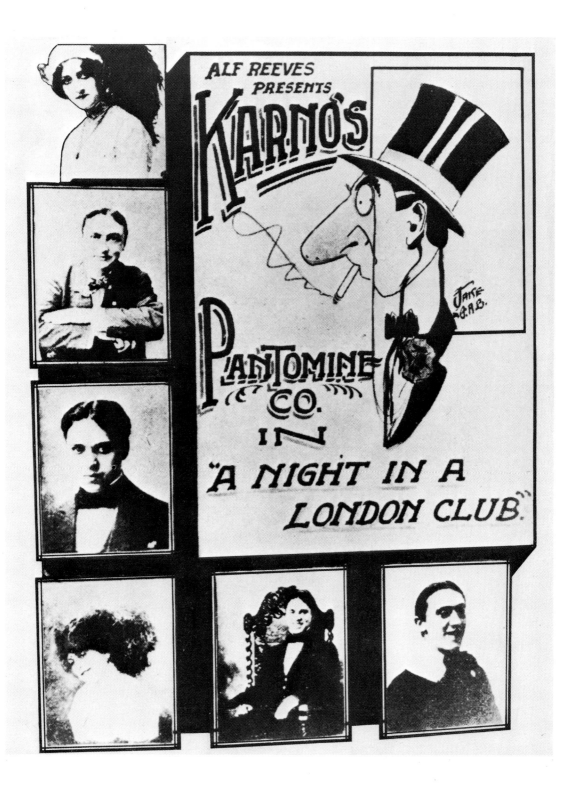

end. His business judgment may have become cluttered by such problems. In 1911 he sent *Mumming Birds* on tour in America as *A Night In An English Music Hall* with a cast that included Laurel, Chaplin and Reeves. Regarding Charlie as inferior to Sid, Karno kept the latter in his English company, a move he was later to regret. As word went round of the tour's success, film companies put in offers to all three stars that dwarfed the £15 a week Karno paid. Chaplin deserted the tour to join Keystone, Laurel went to Hal Roach, and Reeves too accepted a better deal. Indifferent to the fact that his performers could barely survive in New York on his meagre salaries, Karno suspended the show on half-pay while shipping out replacements, a move which panicked the American agents into slashing the contract to $200 a week as a protest against 'lesser performers'. The US company of *Mumming Birds* closed its tour in 1913, by which time most of its talents had found niches in American show business and the movies.

When the company folded, Karno had already embarked on the course that was to destroy him. Tagg's Island, a quiet haven on a secluded reach of the Thames, contained a casino which Karno leased in 1911 for £7000, turning it at vast expense into the Karsino, a combination hotel, restaurant, music hall and casino around which he hoped to establish a Riviera atmosphere. He himself lived with his current mistress in a luxury houseboat moored on the island, furnished with every conceivable appointment, including marble bath-tubs. The Karsino proved a total flop, soaking up every penny of Karno's fortune. Flashy attractions – Pavlova is supposed to have danced there and Karno even offered Chaplin £1000 a week to appear – did not help. In 1926 Karno went bankrupt.

Now forced to live off his second wife, Karno reconsidered the offers from America made to him in his days as a major name, notably a suggestion from a New York agent that he conceive some routines for the Marx Brothers. Sailing to New York with high hopes in 1929, Karno was jolted by the indifference of East Coast theatrical people, all of whom knew about his bankruptcy and bad reputation. The agent who had invited him was evasive, and even Jesse Lasky, once a theatrical agent with whom Karno had done much business but now head of Paramount/Famous Players, refused to see him. A determined Karno followed Lasky to California but found Hollywood even more alien and uninterested. Only Chaplin, now in business on his own, extended any welcome, though Stan Laurel, then successfully teamed with Oliver Hardy at the Hal Roach studio, offered to help also. In what sounds like a subtle revenge on 'The Guv'nor', Chaplin treated the low-brow Karno to a two-hour organ recital as a way of demonstrating his new-found sophistication, then took him to dinner at the home of Marion Davies, where the gold door-knobs and unlimited bootleg liquor administered the *coup de grâce*. Thereafter Chaplin was kind, using his publicity machine to boost the arrival in Hollywood of 'Britain's comedy king', finding him an apartment and even giving him £500 to set himself up. But, no longer interested in music-hall comedy, Chaplin could offer no work, nor did the interviews and articles following Chaplin's publicity campaign lead to any offers.

The only concrete proposal came from Stan Laurel. Introducing him to the expansive Hal Roach, Laurel suggested that Karno might be allowed to hang around the studio. 'Sure,' Roach agreed. 'You can see how we do things out here, Fred.' The quick-tempered Karno bridled at the suggestion that he could learn from anyone, but Laurel's hint that Roach might also put him on salary as a 'consultant' persuaded him to accept. He was promptly offered $1000 a week, a luxury office, full access to all story conferences and an attentive audience for any ideas he might have to contribute. A shrewder man would have seen this offer for what it was, a charitable sinecure, and used the respite to make contacts in the movie colony, but Karno had little diplomatic sense. Making clear his contempt for the Roach brand of slapstick, much of it based on routines he had developed in the 1890s and long since discarded, he quickly alienated everyone in the studio. The crisis came when, at a story conference, Karno interrupted the discussion with his usual brusqueness to suggest an improvement to the routine being discussed.

In the script, a rich man, his silk hat on the table beside him, is waiting impatiently in a hotel lobby while a tiny black dog mopes on a leash. Animals obsessed Karno, and in various shows he used a pack of hounds, a stolen pair of deer and, on one occasion, a tiny Scottish terrier under whose tail a red light glowed derisively at the audience. All these ideas ended in disaster: the hounds relieved themselves against the scenery, the deer's antlers became entangled in curtains – and this occasion was to be no exception.

Why not, he suggested, have a waiter come by and knock the silk hat to the floor in passing, then pick it up, note the tiny dog and use it to brush off the hat? Everyone laughed, the routine was accepted, not without reservations from the unit manager, who knew the unreliability of animals in films, and Karno went off to choose the right kind of dog. Next morning, as the kennelman arrived at the studio with Karno's choice, it jumped out, ran across the road and was killed by a car. Someone gave the impatiently waiting Karno the news; screaming 'It's a plot!' he stormed off the stage, burst into Roach's office and resigned at some length. A relieved Roach paid him off for the few weeks he had worked and on 27 April 1930 Karno left Los Angeles for the last time, already full of the tales he was to tell in later years of how Hollywood had 'ganged up' on him. His remaining years were taken up in a fitfully successful attempt to make movies in Britain, cut short when he died in 1941.

One is tempted to see some justice in the relative fates of George Harris and Fred Karno, and also in the career of Charles Chaplin, an apt illustration of Hollywood's ability to draw out and illuminate the flaws of an imperfect character. Rejected as 'too shy to get on' by Karno, Chaplin had been regarded as second-rate even in childhood, a fact which made him gauche and naïve, pathetically anxious to see good in people and to rise in their estimation. Even so, Karno had paid a member of the *Mumming Birds* company sixpence extra a week to make sure that Chaplin bathed at least once a week while on tour and when he went to America it was very much as a means of keeping his brother Sid in Britain, where the audiences were more critical and the routine more demanding. But Chaplin's contradictory personality harboured an extraordinary vision which did not emerge until America stimulated his vanity and skill. Stan Laurel swears that as the S.S. *Cairnrona* neared New York, Chaplin went to the rail, stretched out his arms and cried: 'America, I am going to conquer you. Every man, woman and child shall have my name on their lips – the name Charles Spencer Chaplin!'

From his first weeks in America Chaplin adhered to this vision of his destiny, leaving *Mumming Birds* for a job with Mack Sennett's Keystone, only to swap it for better contracts with Essanay and Mutual until in 1917 he signed a $1 million-a-year deal with First National to become the richest and most independ-

Chaplin clowns on the ship which brought him to America

Chaplin (in life preserver) and Stan Laurel (far left) on their way to America

ent star in Hollywood. By 1919, when he formed United Artists with Griffith, Fairbanks and Pickford, his career was safe from anything Hollywood could do to him. As one of the few actors to control his own work, his financial position was inviolable, but his personality demanded that he continue on his set course of self-improvement. He became a skilled musician, playing the violin, piano and organ, and composing tunes for his own films. His literary pretensions seeped into his productions, and press and public fidgeted nervously as he made subtle Europeanized films like *A Woman of Paris* and financed von Sternberg in his *A Woman of the Sea*, destined never to be seen because Chaplin, dissatisfied with the realism of Sternberg's style, shelved the whole production. Sexually attractive (and athletic), a brilliant mimic and generous host, Chaplin became part of a Hollywood set whose pretensions to cultural sophistication matched his own, though outsiders often found his posturing absurd. Pola Negri, briefly his fiancée, quickly penetrated the façade when she arrived in America. 'One evening,' she wrote,

when he came to pick me up for a party, I entered the living room to find him engrossed in a dictionary. I asked him what he was looking up and he replied: 'Nothing in particular. I make it a practice to learn a few new words every day.' After dinner, I was startled to observe him turning the conversation to a topic that permitted him to use the words I had heard him committing to memory. Everyone was humbled by his brilliance. I decided to have a little fun by jumping in with some of the words before he could get to them . . . On the way home he was absolutely furious with me for having stolen the scene. He shouted: 'How dare you use terms you don't understand!' I laughed and responded: 'How dare you be such a fraud!'[16]

Even at Pickfair, the home of Mary Pickford and Douglas Fairbanks, leaders of Hollywood society, Chaplin was regarded ambiguously, as much a butt as a guest. (For his part, he privately described his hosts as 'Babbitts'.) Hotelier Frank Case attended many Pickfair dinners and observed Chaplin's social climbing at close range:

I stayed four months . . . During this time I don't think Chaplin ever missed a weekend. He would arrive Friday or Saturday for dinner and stay until Monday, and these were the occasions I loved. We would be

Chaplin (above) *with the great French comedian Max Linder, and* (below) *directing* The Gold Rush

five or six at table . . . After the coffee Douglas would make a stodgy speech introducing every one at the table but never by his own name or in his own person. You might be introduced as the Mayor of Los Angeles, the chief executive of one of the big companies, some notorious criminal currently in the headlines, or Hearst, Zukor, Garbo, any-one. . . . And you were supposed to respond in character. This was not nearly so difficult as it sounds, for if any one hesitated for half a minute, Charlie would jump up, and accept the assignment, sometimes speaking for everybody. One night I introduced Douglas as Mr Chaplin and he responded with a burst of egotism, conceit, and braggadocio that had Chaplin in spasms. When Charlie got up to reply, we all walked out on him.[17]

Not all the jokes were quite so subtle. At one Pickfair party Chaplin remarked that his greatest ambitions were to play Hamlet and Napoleon, an idea that set the table rocking with laughter in which Chaplin immediately joined, passing the remark off as a joke. When a reporter asked him in 1931 if he had any ambition to play a tragic hero, like Napoleon, he said: 'I do not intend to appear in any tragic role. Life is tragic enough. My ambition is to be as funny as possible for the good of the world.' Even his ambi-tion could not survive the prospect of mockery.

The more Chaplin tried to transcend his beginnings, the more they forced themselves on him, though when he met old pro-fessional colleagues he preferred to give, as he did to Karno, a dramatic demonstration of how high he had climbed. British gagman George Carney avoided the two-hour organ recital given to Karno, but when Chaplin brought him to Hollywood in order to recreate an old routine they had done together on the halls, he lay chatting about the old days beside Chaplin's pool for six weeks on full salary, occasionally pausing to rough out some remembered lines from the sketch on which they were supposed to be working. Although such routines often appeared, polished beyond recognition, in his films, Chaplin's previous life proved less easy to burnish. As soon as his position in Hollywood was assured, Chaplin tried to have his mentally ill mother admitted to the United States, a request consistently refused by the Immigra-tion Department despite two years' discussion and many personal visits to Washington. In March 1921 she and his secretary Thomas Harrington arrived incognito on the *Celtic* but immigration offi-cers discovered Mrs Chaplin's identity and confined her to Ellis

(Above left) *A search into Chaplin's ancestry produced this coat of arms.* (Above right) *Chaplin calls on Winston Churchill and* (below) *George Bernard Shaw*

Island pending deportation. Chaplin, who announced he 'would spend any amount of money within his power to have his mother cured of her illness' – which he attributed to shell-shock from zeppelin raids on London during the war – found his money of little use, though he did gain temporary admission by posting a bond for her care and safety. She later died in California.

All Chaplin's latent nostalgia for England came out on his 1931 visit to promote *City Lights*. 'I want to visit the places known to me in childhood,' he announced. 'I want particularly to visit the north of England. I want to smell the baked bread, to see them using bluestone, to hear the clatter of clogs in the morning. . . . I want to capture something I used to experience as a boy of sixteen or seventeen.' The reality proved elusive. At the request of the press Chaplin made a ritual return visit to his old haunts in London's slums, where he was mobbed by gawping and resentful residents. The only sign of the old days came when the ex-Karno comic who had been hired to make sure he bathed recalled to a horrified Chaplin how he and his wife had had to scrub his back. For Chaplin, England existed only in the fanciful form of a Dickens novel, which he had recommended to von Sternberg as an acceptable model for his *A Woman of the Sea*. Actual poverty and squalor merely horrified him, and he quickly fled back to the artificial haven of Hollywood.

Although he transformed his own life, those of other people proved as impossible of improvement as did his public, who rejected his elaborate tracts on social evils and yearned consistently for the tramp in the funny hat that had made him famous. Against all logic, Chaplin tried to prolong the career of Edna Purviance, the actress who played opposite him in his early films but who had become by 1926 a heavy drinker. *A Woman of the Sea* was intended as a vehicle to re-launch her career, but for an actress so confused that the director had to use the rhythm of a kettle-drum to set the tempo of her scenes there could be no hope of a professional future. Drink, the spectre of his childhood, haunted Chaplin, but his response was always to try and bribe or buy his intimates out of its control. He even offered his mistress and eventual wife Paulette Goddard a thousand shares of General Motors stock if she would stop drinking for three months, but his attempts to stem her intake were as disastrous as those of making her – or Edna Purviance – into a great actress. If anything, the

Husband and wife, or just good friends? Paulette Goddard lost the plum role of Scarlett O'Hara in Gone With the Wind *when she could not produce a certificate of marriage to her constant companion Charlie Chaplin, whom she claimed to have married at sea*

effort merely hampered them. Pola Negri's career suffered in the aftermath of her engagement to Chaplin when the actor, sensitive to his reputation, broke the news publicly that she had jilted him, and Paulette Goddard was dropped as a potential source of scandal from the short list to star in *Gone With the Wind* when he could not substantiate his claim that they had been married at sea. For all his dreams, Chaplin could not create the ideal world that Hollywood promised him, and when he added his weight to the utopian ideals of the 1930s Communist revival the public turned on him so vehemently that he retreated with his millions to Switzerland, no less an exile there than he had been in California. His image had conquered the earth, as Priestley said, but the man could not even conquer himself.

6 THE LAST OF ENGLAND

Whatever extravagant claims the studios made as to their desire for a cross-fertilization between the American cinema and that of Europe, a true synthesis was the furthest thing from their minds. The moguls' belief in importation rested on their own experience as poor and ignorant immigrants who had thrived in America by adopting local customs, responding to local needs, taking local names and wives. Artists who merely wished to repeat in Hollywood the themes and techniques of Europe held little interest for them, as Murnau, Christensen and Karno soon found. Significantly, the Europeans whom Hollywood wooed most earnestly in the late 1920s and who established themselves most strongly in the film community were British actors and authors, a group which soon rivalled the growing German community in numbers and influence. One need not look too far to find reasons for their success. For a century the British stage provided most of America's plays and players, the bulk of its reading, scholarship and education in the arts, and by the 1920s Shaftesbury Avenue was established as the richest source of material for Broadway.

The first Hollywood buyers of London talent, predictably, were Adolph Zukor's Famous Players, which, having scored handsomely with adaptations of European stage successes under the banner 'Famous Players in Famous Plays,' now urgently needed both. Jesse L. Lasky, an ex-vaudeville impresario with connections in the British theatre, crossed the Atlantic on buying forays, returning from each with a glittering array of acquired heads. In July 1920 he announced on the New York dockside that he had 'arranged for contributions to Paramount Pictures by James Barrie, Henry Arthur Jones, Arnold Bennett, H. G. Wells, R. C. Carton, E. Temple Thurston, Max Pemberton, Compton Mackenzie, Edward Knoblock and Robert Hichens'. Few of these writers seem to have done more than sell the movie rights of a novel or West End success to Lasky, with little interest in its eventual fate as a film, but since Hollywood had already established precedents for its cavalier attitude to Continental ideas of artistic integrity, Lasky could afford to be optimistic almost to the point of absurdity about the significance of his acquisitions. 'These men realize that through the films they can reach an audience immeasurably larger than that available through stage plays and novels,' he said expansively, 'and they are devoting themselves to a study of the technique of the screen, so that they can write their stories and plays directly for pictures. In this respect American authors face a very great danger, for unless they learn how to write directly for the screen they may find French and British authors dominating the rich field of the motion picture art. . . .' With the blend of distortion, patriotism and proprietorial pride that now distinguished Hollywood's pronouncements on the movies, Lasky warned Americans not to let the cinema become, 'like aviation,' a technical triumph 'invented and perfected by Americans [but] left to the Europeans to develop its possibilities'.

Lasky's hoped-for flood of stories written directly for pictures failed to materialize (though Barrie and Knoblock did provide departure points for films like *Peter Pan* and *Kismet*, both directed by one of Hollywood's more ambitious artists, Herbert Brenon), and active recruits to the movie community from English literary circles were rare. Henry Arthur Jones, then aged 70, did visit Hollywood in 1920 and Paramount finally snared Sir Gilbert Parker, a Canadian who had lived in Australia before settling down in Britain as a Conservative MP and moderately successful novelist. Failing to gain re-election in 1918, he was ripe for an offer from Jesse Lasky to live in Hollywood, where he became an occasional scenarist and tame apologist for the excesses of the movies; his measured pronouncements against murmurs of anti-British sentiment, sexual licence and dollar diplomacy among the companies vying for European talent appeared regularly in British papers for the next ten years. Lasky had to be content with such burnt-out cases as Parker, or the odd lecturing literateur who could be lured into a contract. Hugh Walpole had his first offer in 1919, while on a lecture tour, but it was not until 1934 that he took the plunge. The greatest effort was expended, with

Cecil B. DeMille poses with Elinor Glyn and Sir Gilbert Parker (left), *two of Hollywood's captured literary lions*

no success, on trying to persuade George Bernard Shaw that his work should be filmed, a campaign as doomed as it was hilarious. Shaw's celebrated reply to Sam Goldwyn's flattering offers to create great films from his work – 'You are interested in art whereas I am interested in money' – was invented by publicist Jack Dietz, but S. N. Behrman did recall:

To one of the Hollywood bigwigs who sent Shaw an interminable, exquisitely composed telegram describing his qualifications to put Shaw on the screen, the successor of Voltaire replied by cable: 'Your telegram is too literary. It is obvious that your aspirations would conflict with mine. I am the literary man. Besides, the costly and unnecessary length of your cable convinces me that you are a poor businessman and I want a good businessman'.[18]

Film exhibitors greeted Shaw's loss with equanimity, since the whole hunt for literary lions seemed to them a dangerous aberration in a field where only money talked. In 1921 Burton Rascoe of London's *Bookman* magazine attacked Hollywood films as intellectually bankrupt, charging that, according to the National Research Council, the average mental level of the American film-

Sam Goldwyn and Ronald Colman entertain yet another distinguished European visitor, Alastair MacDonald (centre), son of British prime minister Ramsay MacDonald

going audience was that of a 14-year-old boy. Even Gilbert Parker found it hard to resist Rascoe's logic. Only 75 per cent of American films were *really* bad, he said, and a number – *Broken Blossoms, The Three Musketeers* and *The Kid* were cited – had 'significant ideas'. But he acknowledged that the American cinema 'was and is the mirror of the aspirations of a peculiarly unimaginative, repressed and mentally starved people, a people who in the overwhelming main have been taught to value only a devitalizing and despiritualizing material success, arrived at by a curious duality of ethical teaching and practice'. Such harsh words, even had they understood them, would have left the cinema owners unmoved. Wid Gunning, in the trade paper *Wid's Daily* for 14 November 1921, reassured his exhibitor readers that they had nothing to be ashamed of. Why had some recent beautifully-written films failed at the box office?

Because they were out of focus. They couldn't please a 14-year-old child with them. No. So why try on his elders? When th' intelligence is th' same. An' conversely, as they say in Columbia: why not give 'em what they can understand? The producers who do are getting money. Th' distributors too. An' most important of all – th' exhibitors.

Gunning went on to point out that theatre producers Al Woods and Charles E. Blaney were selling off their turn-of-the-century melodramas to the movies. Offers for *Parted on Her Bridal Tour, Child Slaves of New York, Nellie the Beautiful Cloak Model* and *More to Be Pitied Than Scorned* were apparently flooding in. 'If this isn't somethin'. To make y'u get th' ol' bean workin' – to get th' ol' think tank oilin' up. Then I'd like to know what it is.'

Gunning accurately reflected the film industry's true attitude to literary subjects and 'Famous Players'; for all their eagerness to buy up writers and their works, Lasky and the rest had little idea of what to do with the material or the men, even when they knew what they had bought. Plays totally inappropriate to film were often purchased on the basis of outlines or reviews, and little-known writers ripe for a career in the movies left to struggle in minor jobs. When the London financier and investment banker Edward Beddington-Behrens visited Hollywood in 1925, he spent his first evening with an old friend, Robert Nichols. One of the lesser 'war poets', an intimate of Aldous Huxley and his circle, Nichols had become fascinated with the movies and in the early 1920s moved to Hollywood, a decision Huxley at least found unaccountable. 'Is [film] a good medium to work in?' he wrote to Nichols in 1926. 'I say no, because you can't do it your-self. You depend on Jews with money, or 'art directors' or little bitches with curly hair and teeth, or young men who recommend skin food in the advertisements, or photographers. . . .'[19] How much more scathing Huxley would have been had he known that the best job Nichols had been able to land was as a gagman for Douglas Fairbanks. 'Nichols had arrived in Hollywood,' Bedding-ton-Behrens said,

and written to various film people explaining who he was, that he wished to write scenarios, and giving his qualifications. They naturally took no notice, as they were not interested in finding talent. Unused to the American cinema mentality, his arriving unannounced was quite the wrong tactic . . . Had he been written up beforehand as a distinguished foreign visitor, with introductions from Bernard Shaw and Barrie, all would have been well. The big producers would have rushed to get a contract out of him to prevent his being taken up by somebody else.[20]

Beddington-Behrens had, of course, come with all the right intro-ductions, including letters from producer Walter Wanger and the

New York investment banker and theatre 'angel' Otto Kahn. A word to Fairbanks that his unknown young gagman was actually a famous poet and contributor to the London *Times* galvanized the star. Nichols, Beddington-Behrens said, 'was immediately brought into Doug's intimate circle, and his pay and status on the set was raised.'[21]

In his visits to the studios Beddington-Behrens had a rare chance to measure Hollywood's investment in the craze for Europe and literature, and his findings appalled him. Famous Players alone had $8 million tied up in story rights. 'Famous Players produced seventy full-length pictures a year and were always short of stories,' he wrote incredulously, 'yet every executive who went to Europe bought plays and stories, but no proper record was kept of these.' He left California with a healthy scepticism for Hollywood's much-vaunted financial skill, which may have contributed to his success in the 1930s as a film financier and eventual owner of United Artists. His contempt was far from unusual; between the urbane, well-educated British literary establishment, obsessed with gossip and the nuances of society, and the unlettered and aggressive movie men, most of them products of middle Europe, yawned a gulf as profound as that between species. 'The minds of Hollywood producers seem to have the characteristics of the minds of chimpanzees,' Aldous Huxley wrote, 'agitated and infinitely distractable', and Joseph Conrad in the 1920s confided to Hugh Walpole 'that in selling his book in America he felt exactly like a merchant selling glass beads to African natives'.

Between European writers and those of Hollywood the differences also seemed irreconcilable. Most working scenarists had come up from title or gag writing, and possessed little but native wit and a flair for the medium. In the 1920s they were joined by magazine writers and newsmen, hard-bitten, wise-cracking, a type unknown in Europe. S. J. Perelman has given some acid parodies of them in his pieces on Hollywood – one who took him home to smoke marijuana and be entertained by his girl-friend, a Mexican from a nearby cannery; the hypochondriac whose tics 'pursued each other across his features like snipe'; another who could only work with a vibrating massage appliance strapped to his head and whose dialogue, Perelman acknowledged, left him 'deeply shaken' – but for the habitués of Shaftesbury Avenue the

Count Ilya Tolstoy reads from the works of his father to Dolores Del Rio, in preparation for a film of one of Tolstoy's short stories

impact was less funny than numbing. Invited to America in 1929 to script a film on Sherlock Holmes, a character for the film rights to which Paramount had paid $5000, Basil Dean, one of London's most respected producers, found himself confecting a new Holmes story in collaboration with Bartlett Cormack, author of the underworld classic *The Racket*. 'He seemed unable to begin work until externals were arranged to his satisfaction,' Dean recalled. 'Jacket off and hung over the back of the chair, tie and collar loosened; sleeves rolled up, eye-shade adjusted, and never less than three packets of Camel cigarettes and attendant books of paper matches stacked in front of him, the Chicago news editor to the life!'[22] Depressed by the New York heat, Cormack insisted they move somewhere cooler; as a result, *The Return of Sherlock Holmes* was written mainly in the Ritz Hotel, Atlantic City.

British actors found the movies' eccentricities easier to handle. Since the turn of the century they had travelled in large numbers to appear on Broadway, beneficiaries of a tradition that only a Londoner wore evening dress with the elegance demanded by the drawing-room dramas so popular before the First World War. Americans also appeared in London plays, a practice established

during the wartime embargo on German performers and bitterly
resented by both players and audiences when it persisted into the
1920s. In 1920 a demonstration broke out on the first night of
J. Hartley Manners' *A Night in Rome* after imported Broadway
star Laurette Taylor told a US paper she would be glad to leave
'that dreadful England'. Critics asserting that there were English
actresses easily as good as Miss Taylor who might have played in
the part were surprised to find Broadway impresario Morris Gest,
who was in the audience, agreed with them. 'There are English
girls quite as clever,' he said wolfishly. 'That is one reason why
I am in London – to engage some of them for America.'

Gest's remark underlined the extent of American influence in
the theatre and particularly the cinema of Britain at this time. (In
1918, 44 million feet of film were imported into Britain. By 1919
the figure had shot to 81 million feet. By 1920, 75 per cent of the
films shown in Britain were from Hollywood.) Many ailing live
theatres were converted to movies, a fact welcomed by the public
but deprecated by the better critics. The *London Daily Post* saw
the dangers: 'We have been assured that the cloud has a silver
lining in the dollars pouched by English actors who, unable to
obtain employment here, have migrated to the States. . . . There
is but cold comfort in the reflection that, although our theatre has
closed her doors to the English playwright, she is at the same time
throwing the English actor out of her windows.' By March 1921
it was estimated that two thousand chorus girls and small bit
players were out of work, and a spokesman for the trade commented: 'We heard not long ago about Americans who were
coming here with millions and millions of pounds to do big
business in the cinema line, but nothing has come of it.'

Had they known the debilitating effect American money was to
have on the British cinema when investment did begin, London
would have complained less bitterly, but like the fortunate stars
being signed up for Broadway by enterprising producers they
saw only the dream of international success, not the inevitable
cost to integrity and reputation, aspects of the deal their employers were at pains to disguise – if, in fact, they were aware of
them at all. One by one, the actors who had scored such successes
in the plays of Rudolf Besier, Frederick Lonsdale and Somerset
Maugham drifted to Broadway; Clive Brook, Percy Marmont and
A. E. Matthews were just the sort of willowy young men with

patent leather hair and ramrod backs who inhabited the fantasy Britain built by Broadway and Hollywood, a stereotype that was to outlast the original by decades and guarantee most of these men movie employment well into the 1940s.

The chief architect of this invasion was the American impresario Gilbert Miller, a freelance producer who specialized in buying up drawing-room dramas in Britain along with their casts and selling them to the larger managements of Broadway. His blend of shrewd commercial sense and a flair for theatre distinguished him from his first effort, a 1919 production of *Daddy Long Legs*. Later he produced on Broadway such milestones as Lonsdale's *The Last of Mrs Cheyney*, Laurence Houseman's *Victoria Regina* and Sherwood's *The Petrified Forest*; Leslie Howard, Cedric Hardwicke and Herbert Marshall all came to America under his personal management, which operated with the backing of his father-in-law, the Wall Street banker Jules Bache, just as Morris Gest, who, except in his preference for German stars and companies, exploited the same vogue for European performers as Miller, financed his activities with the money of Otto Kahn and of his own father-in-law, the producer David Belasco. Dubbed 'the culture-kick banker' by Lillian Hellman, Otto Kahn occupies a curious and important position in American cultural history of the 1920s. Distinguished, white-haired, sporting an imperial moustache, this investment banker and patron of the arts was frequently approached by impresarios for the financial advice and help which, as head of Kuhn, Leob and Co. (and a millionaire) he was uniquely fitted to give. He backed the Theatre Guild in its early years, chaired the Board of the Metropolitan Opera Company, and advised Zukor on the critical Paramount stock issue which gave Wall Street its first control over Hollywood film production. Genuinely disinterested, he offered equal help to the leftist dramas of Dos Passos and John Howard Lawson and to Morris Gest's grandiose productions of Reinhardt's *The Miracle*. Many artists praised his personal intervention on their behalf, ranging from investing the capital of *The Miracle*'s star Diana Manners to funding tuition for promising young sopranos. Josef von Sternberg credits him with persuading Paramount to release *The Last Command* when it was thought anti-Hollywood and William Wellman with vital intervention in the case of *Wings*.

Kahn exemplified the Broadway spirit of cultural dilettantism which consistently evaded the film industry. Both Gilbert Miller and Morris Gest owed their success to this odd blend of showmanship and savoir faire. Not for them the vulgar head-hunting raids of the movie moguls, the disinterested deals for properties whose merits were hardly understood. When an actor signed with them, it was with the conviction that a great favour was being conferred on Broadway. Negotiations having been completed at Claridge's or the Ritz, he found himself booked into the plushest stateroom of the *Europa* or the *Berengaria*, his comfort obsessively catered to by a producer perfectly accustomed to liner life. In 1920 Basil Dean, making his first trip to the US as Miller's guest on the *Olympic*, noted that his host 'was one of a group of passengers . . . who appeared to be immediately at home with the ship's daily round'. From the ritual of morning gymnastics to the marathon meals, always ordered in advance from the French restaurant, where the fastidious could eat ostentatiously at their own expense while regular passengers dined free elsewhere, Miller pursued a hectic life-style he kept up tirelessly until his death, unconcerned by changing fashion or world events. When Cedric Hardwicke crossed to Broadway in 1934 as Miller's latest prize, he had to travel without him. Although the *Europa*, of the North German Lloyd line, had the best food and service, Miller, out of consideration for his Jewish father-in-law, felt he could not patronize a German line himself. Each day, however, Hardwicke sat down to a meal ordered by radio, complete with wine, from the ship in which Miller was also crossing the Atlantic a few hours behind the *Europa*. Among Hardwicke's companions on that trip were Leslie Howard, en route to star in *The Petrified Forest*, Charles Boyer, making another try at a Hollywood career after a disastrous 1929 visit, Erik Charrell, director of *Congress Dances*, also bound for a brief and inauspicious Hollywood visit, and scenarist Monckton Hoffe, a commuter who rivalled even Miller in total trips. Such a glittering list was far from unusual. A 1925 voyage of the *Majestic*, which replaced the *Olympic* in the early 1920s, included Basil Dean, Noel Coward, his mother and acolytes Gladys Calthrop and Lilian Braithwaite, Eugene Goosens, Michael Arlen, Leslie Howard and Ruth Chatterton. Dean noted how the other passengers 'stared askance at "these noisy theatre people" ', implying the slightly suspect status they enjoyed in a society for whom the transatlantic liner was the last bastion of gentlemanly travel. In *Brideshead Revisited*, a novel, paradoxically, which MGM wanted very much to film, even bringing Waugh to Hollywood in a vain attempt to obtain the rights, Evelyn Waugh lashed out waspishly at the ostentation of the theatrical sailors, on whose glamour the ship-owners seized as a publicity device. Waugh stigmatizes a private suite as 'a cinema-actor's dream' and a character remarks: 'It's crazy to go to the restaurant and pay extra for exactly the same dinner. Only film people go there anyway.'

Miller, Gest and their actors cared little. They knew that Broadway and Hollywood regarded with reverence, even awe, the products of Europe's sophisticated theatre companies, even if the general public was indifferent. Lacking its own repertory system, American theatre was dazzled by the technical skill and adaptability of German companies like the Volksbuhne and Deutsches Theatre, the Yiddish Habimah Players, the Comédie Française, the Moscow Art Theatre or the polished performers turned out by the almost continuous employment offered by London's West End. Playwright Elmer Rice in his novel *The Show Must Go On* contrasted the European system with that of Broadway. An agent lectures a young writer on the idiocies of the American stage:

In Europe, a director like Leroy Thompson would be the regisseur of an established state of municipal theatre. He would have at his command a permanent company of trained actors and a permanent staff of technicians . . . Your play would have been read and discussed for many weeks . . . and the actors would come to the first rehearsal thoroughly familiar with every line of the text . . . The theatre would be equipped with a complete and flexible machinery for staging and lighting the play . . . and it would have a storehouse filled with scenery, properties and costumes . . . But what happens here? On the stage, at the first rehearsal, sits a group of actors who have never seen each other before and who have not even read the play in which they arc to perform. And in exactly four weeks . . . they must be prepared to give a finished performance before a critical audience . . . And so with the production. Everything is started from the beginning – scenery, costumes, lighting equipment – and when the play closes everything finishes with it. The actors are disbanded, the scenery is burned, the costumes are sold to the ragman . . . Nothing is learned, nothing is saved, there is no permanence, no continuity, no pattern, no objective, no ideal. It is all waste, waste, waste . . .[23]

Not surprisingly, actors trained in this ramshackle school regarded Europe's sophisticated technicians as demi-gods. In 1922 John Barrymore gave one of the worst performances of his career when Konstantin Stanislavsky and some actors from the Moscow Art Theatre – one of Morris Gest's highly successful importations – attended his legendary *Hamlet*. Brooks Atkinson recalled that night's performance as 'embarrassingly overwrought . . . [the cast] were shocked and puzzled. Even when his sister and others told him during the intermission what he was doing, he was unable to regain control.'[24] This extraordinary respect for foreign expertise had a direct bearing on the establishing in 1926 of the Theatre Guild, which attempted, finally with only limited success, to encourage a quasi-European production system with a permanent company. But, as so often happened in the cinema, the adaptation of European methods led to a Europeanizing of the product. The Theatre Guild presented so many Hungarian plays, notably those of Ferenc Molnar, that it was nicknamed The Budapest House, and one of its producers, Lawrence Langer, told a reporter that it was 'not an essentially American institution. Half the actors are English and up to now English plays have dominated in the productions.'

If Broadway was deferential to European companies, Hollywood prostrated itself. Stanislavsky made a ritual Hollywood pilgrimage, and when Gest brought the Habimah company to Broadway, MGM asked them to Hollywood and, though they were cordially contemptuous of movies, offered them a 'courtesy film test' with which they were to be presented as a souvenir. Ironically the director chosen to supervise the shooting was Josef von Sternberg who, though Viennese-born, hated the Expressionist style of acting perfected by the Habimah. But he had his orders:

I was asked not to guide them in any manner, merely to allow them to express themselves, as they were loaded with talent to which no one could make a contribution. I was only to see to it that their demonstration of acting finesse would not be lost by the camera. This proved to be not quite so easy as had been anticipated. The cameraman threw me a glance of desperation and I took over the control of the mobile tripod mount to keep the performers from eluding the lens. Theirs was the agility of rabbits. I managed to swing the turret in time to follow one giant leap as an actress about to hurtle through the air was nailed to the floor by a nimble fellow actor, who seized her by the throat and bellowed 'Prostitute!' before the others attacked to pry him loose in a witches' sabbath of acrobatic histrionics.[25]

No prize more consistently evaded Hollywood in the 1920s than Max Reinhardt, the genius of German and Austrian theatre whose pioneering work at the Josefstadt in Vienna, the Berlin Deutsches Theatre and later in Salzburg at the festival he was to make a personal showcase, dazzled even the moguls of Hollywood. Paramount had promised a Reinhardt film at the time of its EFA deal and hardly a year went by without the announcement of some film project which would rival the scope of his stage work. Even when Gest brought Reinhardt to the US in 1924 with his production of Karl Völlmoller's epic morality play *The Miracle* and the producer and author visited Hollywood, the Viennese genius remained elusive. Producers who made the pilgrimage to Berlin or Salzburg so appalled the sophisticated artistic society – and were sometimes so appalled by it – that deals became impossible. Invited to one of Reinhardt's famous after-theatre suppers at Salzburg, held at midnight in his private castle where antique candelabra illuminated the cream of European culture and aristocracy, Louis B. Mayer took in the candles at a glance and remarked sympathetically to his host 'A short circuit, Mr Reinhardt?' That evening's performance had been of Hoffmansthal's adaptation of *Everyman*, presented, like many of Reinhardt's productions, in the open air to exploit the architecture of Salzburg's churches and squares. Subtitled 'A Play About a Rich Man's Death', *Everyman* left Mayer, in Reinhardt's words, 'utterly dashed, his brow beaded with sweat'. 'You can't put that on in America!' he insisted. 'There are too many rich people there.' Cultural innocents like Mayer were easy meat for the Salzburg guests, who parodied their actions with icy malice. Noting a visiting Hollywood producer goggling at Reinhardt's exquisitely dressed and jewelled guests, Ferenc Molnar confided straight-faced that most of them were extras hired for the night to impress him; the disenchanted visitor grunted in unsurprised irritation and left. Many years passed before Reinhardt came to Hollywood and then, as another immigrant looking cap-in-hand for a job, his treatment was as heartless as one would have expected from a community which never forgave a slight.

Sir Charles Aubrey Smith at his most urbane in The White Cliffs of Dover

To nobody's surprise, the people Hollywood seized and held from the stage in the 1920s were those who, by accidents of talent, inclination or career, might have been born to the trade. Ronald Colman and Leslie Howard had only the most fitful of stage careers; their talents perfectly suited the cinema of which they became such tasteful furniture. Skilled stage actors like Herbert Marshall, Ernest Torrence, Sir C. Aubrey Smith and Sir Cedric Hardwicke went to Hollywood at the peak of their powers, found movies a comfortable refuge in the evening of distinguished careers, and settled down without rancour to steady work in supporting roles. No European author or dramatist of proved worth, no great actor or actress from the European stage ever stayed in Hollywood for longer than he or she could help. But in its recruitment as in its product, it was Hollywood's particular genius to make the dross sublime.

Hollywood's recruitment policy was not quite as mindless as it sometimes seemed. Its failure lay in the fact that decisions were made according to rules, not of talent or appropriateness, but of

prejudice, superstition and assumption not unlike those governing the movies themselves. The films succeeded because they
created a fantasy remote from the experience of mankind and
therefore an ideal refuge for the world. Its producers and directors
were influenced in all artistic choices not by literal truth but by
the reigning illusions of this fantasy world. It was a world which
reflected the mind of a shallow, ignorant, stateless community, to
which any foreign country was an amalgam of stereotypes
remembered from a book, landmarks seen from a hotel window or
glimpsed from a speeding train, characters imperfectly recalled
from history or fiction. Zukor and Fox did not need to be told
about London. They knew it as a city of fogs where horse-drawn
cabs clattered over cobbles and ancient mansions loomed over the
thatched cottages of the poor. Paris was the Eiffel Tower, apaches
in striped jerseys and berets, net-stockinged whores with hearts
of gold. And even when they knew better, as in the films set in
Vienna or Berlin, they realized that the mass audience who
flocked to these films shared similar illusions – illusions that
could not be disturbed for risk of commercial failure.

When actors or writers were hired from overseas, it was
necessary that they fit the archetype created for them. Men like
Colman and Howard became so immersed in their Hollywood
roles that real life seldom intruded, while the publicity machine
ensured that the self-parody soon became too well established to
avoid. One can see the pointers to success in the careers of those
actors who accepted the need to be national symbols rather than
people – Garbo, the stark, brooding Swede; spurious sons of
Empire like Colman and Howard; the archetypal Junker Stroheim,
who fought unsuccessfully to be taken seriously as a director but
never lacked work as an actor – and the seeds of failure in other
individuals who could not or would not see what the studios
wanted of them. The Germans in particular succumbed to the
illusion that talent would eventually triumph – a fantasy soon
shattered, though seldom soon enough. Europeans often commented later on the almost cruel kindness of Americans when
forced to reject a potential employee. One visitor of the 1930s –
not to the movie colony – remarked:

Germans frequently mistake a friendly reception of themselves or their
projects for genuine interest and hence meet with cruel disappoint-

ments. A German looking for a position or help of some kind may be met with 'I'll see what I can do for you' or 'I'll consider you for the position' which, if nothing more definite is added, such as 'Call me again in a few days' or 'I'll let you know by next Monday' is likely to be merely an evidence of friendliness or sympathy . . .[26]

Many imports to Hollywood in the 1920s and 1930s, particularly actresses already famous in their own countries, took movie hospitality for an adulation similar to that which they enjoyed at home and confidently awaited the fame and easy money that never materialized.

One of the most tragic cases was that of the legendary Mrs Patrick Campbell, creator of many roles in the plays of Shaw, with whom she carried on a long and famous correspondence. Aged, plump and eccentric, 'Stella' Campbell came to Hollywood in 1930, at the height of its feverish pursuit of stage names with clear diction. In February 1930, acting in New York, she gave a lecture on *Beautiful Speech and the Art of Acting*, demonstrating her splendid delivery by parodying a scene from *The Matriach*, a role she had created but for whose New York lead she had been passed over in favour of Constance Collier. MGM seems not to have been put off either by the propagandist point of her talk or by the actress's waning appeal which led her at the lunch that followed to greet critic John Mason Brown with a stern: 'Dear Mr Mason Brown, please stand over here and let me turn my back to the light. I do not wish to have you look too closely upon my ruined face'; they immediately signed her to a contract. The honeymoon which followed was glittering but brief. Cedric Hardwicke recalled the cast and crew of her first film being told to treat her with the respect due to a monumental talent. She was not even screen-tested, a barbed compliment, since neither her face nor her acting style suited the cinema. Her unconventional behaviour baffled the MGM executives, and though Hardwicke put this down to less than perfect recall – 'Manner grew more regal as memory faltered' – a residue of genuine eccentricity remained. Her first appearance at MGM fanned rumours of her unusual manner. Arriving a few minutes early with her inseparable pet, a white Pekinese named Moonbeam, under her arm, she was greeted by the camera operator with, in her words, 'a kindly smile and a "Hullo, babe, what's the little dog's name?"'

Not wishing to be outdone in cheerfulness and humour . . . I answered with dignity "Tittiebottles". From that moment I was dubbed a nut. . . .'[27] A series of classic gaffes marked her progress through Hollywood society. 'She made enemies right and left with her caustic tongue,' her biographer recalled. 'She had developed a new line in *fausse naïveté* or pretended ignorance. . . .'[28] Meeting famous stars at a party, she would suggest 'You pretty little thing. Why don't you have a screen test?' Noting a particularly striking young man, she accosted him with a booming 'You are a very beautiful young man. Why don't you make a film?' 'But my dear Mrs Campbell,' he replied, 'my name is Joseph Schildkraut!' She winced and said: 'But you could change it.'

MGM soon realized its mistake, but it was not done to break the news quietly and pay her off. Small roles in English stage adaptations like *Riptide*, most of which was cut, and odd cameos like the pawnbroker in Josef von Sternberg's *Crime and Punishment* gradually reduced her importance in the studio hierarchy. Sternberg, himself totally unconventional, saw Stella Campbell's

Mrs Patrick Campbell as the pawnbroker in Crime and Punishment

tragedy with a clear if unsympathetic eye. She was, to him, 'a woman who was once a celebrated beauty, lovely enough "to turn the heads of countless cavaliers" as George Jean Nathan put it, but now only her little dog named Moonbeam turns its head when she passes. . . . She has read neither the book nor the script. . . .'[29] After criticizing Sternberg as 'a nasty man' for asking Marian Marsh to shed a few tears by way of a test, she asks him: 'What does this manuscript of yours require me to shed?' 'Only your impudence, Stella.' 'I am not impudent. I only want to know what I am to portray.' 'Your part calls for a pawnbroker.' 'I cannot possibly become a *tradesperson*. . . .'[30] In *Dinner At Eight*, Marie Dressler parodied her as the blowsy old actress Carlotta Vance, complete with a Pekinese named Tarzan. Despite such assaults, Hollywood maintained the fiction that she had a future in movies. Edmund Goulding, her director on *Riptide,* cabled with evident sincerity: 'I honestly urge you to dismiss from your mind the possibility of your name and appearance being ineffective photographically. You are Mrs Patrick Campbell and you are being put on the screen with all the charm and technique that made you that lady. Relax, trust, don't worry, sleep well, feel well and give me your confidence.' She was even invited to dine with Irving Thalberg and his wife Norma Shearer for the discussion of a possible part, a meeting that, as one would expect, ended in disaster. Borrowing $400 from her friend, the playwright Lillian Hellman, Stella blew every penny on a dress. Far from resenting the extravagance, Miss Hellman thought it 'a splendid gesture for a proud old lady' and when they met later asked if MGM had offered her the role. 'No duckie, and I don't think I'll get it. So I'll give you a few of Bernard Shaw's letters as repayment.' Declining the gift, Miss Hellman pressed her on the reasons for this failure. 'You see, dearie duckie,' Mrs Campbell giggled. 'I was doing rather splendidly at first. And then, well, it's true, isn't it, and *that's* the important thing, I said to Mr Thalberg "Your wife has the most beautiful little eyes I've ever seen".'[31] Since Norma Shearer's unfortunate squint was a sore point with both the star and her husband, it is not surprising that she didn't get the role.

By 1934 Mrs Campbell could see the truth. In one of her last letters to Shaw she confided bitterly: 'The studios say I am too celebrated for small parts and too English to star – that Kalamazoo and Butte, Montana, and Seattle would not understand my English style and speech. Whenever I ring up my agents they answer "MGM is thinking of you but nothing suitable has come along. . . .".'[32] In the hope that publicity might help, she replied with bitter frankness to *Los Angeles Times* drama critic Edwin Schallert when he interviewed her on radio in May 1935: 'I don't mind going home and saying "I wasn't wanted in Hollywood". But I do mind going home and saying "They didn't realize the quality of my work, and gave me no real opportunity of showing it".' But the interview produced little reaction, and in her last sixteen months in Hollywood she worked, she confided to Shaw, only thirteen weeks. Finally she took a cabin in the mountains one hundred miles from Los Angeles and spent seven months writing some scrappy and rambling memoirs with only Moonbeam for company, returning shortly after to Europe, where she died, poor, querulous and forgotten, at Pau, France, in 1940.

Hollywood has no monopoly on stories such as Stella Campbell's, though few artistic communities would have reacted to her sarcasm and failing powers with the same calculated withdrawal of professional help and friendship, nor would the effect have been so destructive. In the case of other émigrés, a certain macabre irony intervenes, as if Hollywood, in ordering its activities in the creation of art, allowed fiction to impregnate fact. Few cases illustrate this more effectively or show so plainly the gulf between British theatre and American fantasy than those of Ivor Novello and Edgar Wallace.

Britain had few more famous names in the 1920s than these two. The willowy, classically beautiful Novello dazzled the country with his prodigality, writing such hits as 'Keep the Home Fires Burning', scripting, scoring and acting in his own plays as well as those of others. Edgar Wallace, though vastly different in background – he had been variously an unsuccessful war correspondent, playwright, editor (mainly of racing papers) and journalist before finding his metier in the racy crime romances that he cranked out in a steady stream for the last twenty-seven years of his life – was equally in the public eye.

Spotted by D. W. Griffith in 1922 while dining at the Savoy, Novello was taken to America to co-star with Carol Dempster in *The White Rose*, his appearance heralded by a flood of publicity announcing him variously as 'The British Adonis', 'The Valentino of England' and 'The Welsh Genius'; the *New York Evening Tele-gram* quoted him as pleading with a reporter 'Please don't write me up as the handsomest man in England'; despite the build-up he flopped in films, and only agreed to return in 1931 when MGM offered him a contract both to act and to write, mainly on the strength of his play *The Truth Game*, in which he appeared on Broadway. His first job was to adapt *The Truth Game* for films, a project that took nine months and eight scripts, at the end of which little but the title and character names remained. Relaxing in the beach house of Edmund Goulding, Novello hardly noticed the inexorable recession of Hollywood interest in him, until the lead in *The Truth Game* – by then retitled *But the Flesh Is Weak* – went to Robert Montgomery and MGM exercised its control over his writing activities by having him collaborate on the script of a weepie called *Lovers Courageous* and then, ultimate insult, assist Cyril Hume with *Tarzan the Ape Man*. The dialogue of this film has some unforgettable lines. 'You're laughing at me,' a stilted Ian Hamilton accuses Jane (Maureen O'Sullivan). 'A little bit, per-haps,' she agrees, 'but very tenderly', while outside the jungle mutters. In 1931 he persuaded Thalberg to release him from his contract and packed for his return to England.

Among the British émigrés he invited to his going-away party was Edgar Wallace, who had fled from the combined difficulties of income tax investigation, ill health and an unsuccessful attempt at gaining the parliamentary seat for Blackpool (under the slogan 'A Showman For a Showman's Town') to the peace of Hollywood, where RKO had offered him two months' work at £600 a month with options for double that period. Wallace spent more time at Agua Caliente and other race-tracks than was strictly necessary for the purposes of research, but in between meetings he managed to write a number of original stories, including *The Beast*, which became in time *King Kong*. He seemed well on the way to becom-ing a movie stalwart; his clubable character, interest in horse-racing, a favourite hobby of the Hollywood rich, and slickly com-mercial methods gave him the mark of success, and writer Guy Bolton, himself an adoptive Californian, remarked, on the occa-sion of RKO picking up Wallace's option, that 'he was the biggest success among the writers that have come out here'. Under-standably, Novello was slightly disappointed when Wallace announced that a chest cold made it impossible to attend his farewell party, but the actor, busy with his packing, gave it little thought. Two days later, as the carriages of the Chief (the Santa Fé Super Chief express) were being joined to those of the Twentieth Century at Chicago, Novello dropped by the baggage car to see that his dog Jim was being well looked after. He found the guard sitting on a large wooden crate. 'What an enormous case,' Novello commented as he fed Jim his lunch. 'I hope that no one's inside.' 'Sure there is,' the guard said. 'A film writer who died in Hollywood.' Novello looked at the label. He was sitting on the corpse of Edgar Wallace, who had died in a diabetic coma the day Novello left Los Angeles.

7 THE SILKEN LADDER

Screenwriter DeWitt Bodeen has vivid memories of Hollywood society in the golden days of the 1930s and particularly of the soirées in private homes like that of playwright Ernest Wajda. 'Wajda's famous Sunday nights – they were really something. All the Hungarians would be there, and the Germans; they stuck pretty much together. Very dressy affairs too. Up to then I had been labouring under the delusion that one never wore evening dress on Sunday nights, but you did at the Wajda's.'

The cosmopolitan Bodeen can be forgiven for imagining that in Hollywood society all would be as it was in New York, where manners generally reflected the trends of Europe. But as one moved farther from the east coast social habits blurred into one another, until by the time they reached California many had taken on the peculiar individuality of the movie colony. Social conventions seldom disappeared altogether – the flow of Broadway and European émigrés ensured a continuing standard – but many were adapted to serve as weapons in the battle for status that dominated movie society. To dress for one's Sunday nights conferred a special character on both host and guests; not to know the ground rules marked one as a parvenu. Knowledge of the latest 'in' person or place could fundamentally affect one's social standing. British director/writer John Paddy Carstairs analysed the phenomenon as it struck him in the early 1930s:

Hollywood is funny 'that way'; you've got to know the spots. If you go to the wrestling match on Monday, you won't find many stars, but if you go to the boxing match on Friday you are sure to see Mae West, Lupe Velez, Johnny Weissmuller, Bruce Cabot, Wheeler and Woolsey, Ruby Keeler, Al Jolson, Pat O'Brien, Jack Oakie and a good dozen more. It is the same with the night-spots . . . I've been in the Trocadero when,

inside, there was enough talent to make a dozen films . . . And yet, if you pick another night, you may not see a soul. I've known people to spend a small fortune at the places they've been told to visit, only to learn when it's too late that the place is no longer popular (and gosh! how quickly Hollywood can tire of you and yours!)[33]

Mr and Mrs Ernst Lubitsch at home to the German community. Guests include E. A. Dupont, Peter Lorre and Otto Preminger

The foreign visitor's crash course in Hollywood status-seeking began as he landed in New York, to be greeted by a barrage of flashing light-bulbs and inquisitive reporters – if he was lucky. Whether one was met on board ship or on the dock, the speed with which one's baggage was whisked through customs, the nature and degree of the official studio welcome – which could range from, as in the case of Marlene Dietrich, a celebrity banquet attended by Jesse Lasky to the brusque delivery of a train ticket by messenger usually allocated to writers and other minor figures – were all barometers of one's importance in Hollywood's eyes.

On the journey to California distinctions became even more marked. Until commercial air travel became established in the early 1930s, the rail trip by the Twentieth Century Limited from New York to Chicago and then, after a four-hour delay during which one had to cross the city to the Dearborn Station, the three-day trip on the Santa Fe Line's Super Chief, offered the only feasible route to California. Crossing New Mexico and Arizona the Super Chief gave travellers a breathtaking panorama of the American landscape, but its popularity had less to do with the route's superiority over that of the Union Pacific, which took a more northerly line via Salt Lake City, than the Santa Fe's greater luxury and shrewd emphasis on the number of film personalities it carried. After killing time in Chicago according to individual tastes – DeWitt Bodeen found the four-hour delay ideal for a quick visit to the Chicago art galleries; Frank Capra, on being asked how he spent the time, replied 'How else? We got drunk' – the Chief's passengers wandered into the Dearborn Station to find an ambience which reproduced many characteristics of Hollywood. Any film people of note would be shown the day's passenger list as a matter of course; they would be interviewed for a radio programme about 'Who's On The Chief' and asked if they wished to have name cards on their doors. To decline this particular courtesy indicated an unwillingness to entertain guests during the trip, and few cared to travel incognito, though occasionally some eccentric would elect to spend the trip working. Making his first visit to America, Edgar Wallace spent his four hours in Chicago boning up on the current situation in the gang wars over lunch with a newspaperman. During the trip to California he wrote the whole of his play *On The Spot*, based on the stories he had been told, which ran for a year in London and boosted the careers of its stars Charles Laughton and Anna May Wong.

But Wallace was exceptional. For most of the Chief's passengers socializing began even before the train left, with old associates reviving their acquaintance and fellow professionals mixing in the sort of exploratory social intercourse only possible in the relative freedom of travel. During the 1940s a radio-telephone link was installed in the Chief but until then its passengers were luxuriously free of the pressures of Hollywood front office or Wall Street boardroom. Michael Powell remembers the train trip he made to Hollywood with his colleague Emeric Pressburger as a delightful experience. 'Fritz Lang was on the train. We had never met him but he came along and introduced himself. We had a drawing room so we spent most of the three days telling stories and making jokes with Lang, who was a lovely person. We were going through marvellous places like Albuquerque and Santa Fe. Exhausting? No, my dear fellow – it's the only way to travel.'

Arrival had the same subtle significance as travel. The truly famous avoided Los Angeles altogether, being taken off at the tiny Pasadena station rather than having to endure the tedious Los Angeles suburbs and the irritation of fans and the press. Garbo and Dietrich received this accolade but other actors were generally given a tepid reception at the down-town terminal, with the dubious garnish of a press conference. Having been met by fellow émigré Nigel Bruce, who took him out for a quiet dinner, Cedric Hardwicke was astonished to read the next day in the press that a chauffeur had picked up the 'English nobleman' and driven him in style to his hotel. Some hopefuls exploited the perfunctory nature of the press reception with stories designed to get them known in Hollywood. A destitute young English actor fantasized freely to the press about a recently-collapsed indoor-horse-racing plan in which he had been involved and earned the headline 'British Sportsman Arrives. Plans to Buy Over 100 Head Of Polo Ponies', though it was some time before David Niven achieved fame as either sportsman or actor. The honeymoon period during which one's remarks were taken down and printed with the lack of concern for status due only to the unestablished lasted a few days. Within twenty-four hours, on his first visit to the studio, a newcomer was asked to fill in an elaborate questionnaire detailing everything from famous ancestors and pet aversions to the name, tonnage and accommodations of his yacht, information on which the publicity department based its categorization of his image and career.

To most visitors, the city and society they encountered as they stepped off the train were as alien as those of Afghanistan, but made doubly confusing by the jumble of familiar elements from which they had been confected. Aldous Huxley's wife Maria said Hollywood reminded her of 'a permanent International Exhibition.

(Above) *Classic Hollywood architecture: the Brown Derby restaurant.*
(Right) *Hollywood's Cream Can snack-bar*

The buildings are ravishing, fantastic and flimsy. They are all surrounded by green lawns and huge palm trees and flaming hibiscus and to finish it off the population wear fancy dress costume. . . .'[34] The opening of Huxley's *After Many a Summer* reflects an almost identical reaction to the miscellany of Los Angeles architecture. If private homes were fanciful copies of French chateaux, Austrian schlosses or English manors, places of entertainment needed to be even more bizarre. The city boasted restaurants in the shape of a crouching dog ('The Pup'), a bowler hat ('The Hat') and a sphinx, not to mention a gas station surmounted by a twin-engined aircraft with revolving propellors, while Grauman's Chinese Theatre, an eccentric copy of Shanghai's Opera House erected more as a background for premières than as a cinema, and the Coconut Grove night-club with its decor of branching palms so superbly evoked in George Cukor's *A Star Is Born*, both characterize an attitude to architecture found nowhere else in the world.

A classic boom town, Hollywood had soared in population from 5000 in 1911 to 35,000 in 1919 and 130,000 in 1925, initially outstripping the available real estate, though a post-war building

The oppressive decor of the Coconut Grove night-club, gathering place of many Hollywood stars

boom vastly over-supplied the town with private residences at the expense of the apartment blocks then so urgently required. By the mid-1920s Hollywood had become both congenial and cheap. Arriving from New York, producer Robert Lord found a five-room flat for $60 a month – half what he would have had to pay in New York, and with salaries high and the cost of living low, most low-income film people could live well. Among the stars, a glut of elegant mansions gave a wide choice of residences and services. 'In those days,' Gloria Swanson said, 'the public wanted us to live like kings and queens. So we did – and why not? We were in love with life. We were making more money than we ever dreamed existed and there was no reason to believe that it would ever stop.'[35] At the time Miss Swanson was occupying a twenty-four room mansion in Beverly Hills originally built for the razor magnate King Gillette, but many newly-successful actors preferred their own ideas. 'Almost the first thing a player does upon attaining fame and a sufficiency of fortune is to buy a house,' one British report of 1926 said. 'Quite often the house is designed by the owner himself, and the result is a polyglot of styles, some of definite architectural tendencies, others with no particular style but plenty of originality.'[36]

Miss Swanson's comparison of the stars with royalty held true in other respects. Money in the quantities available to the top stars in those days when income tax was less than 1 per cent on the first $20,000 rendered any whim or fantasy a reality overnight. Fortune tellers, astrologers and graphologists thrived as fruitfully as art dealers and merchants of rare books. Émigrés unsuccessful in the movies often opened restaurants or, like director Harry Lachman, became antique dealers. Some Hollywood homes boasted furnishings as priceless as any in a European museum. Dame Edith Sitwell called George Cukor's house

one of the most beautiful in Hollywood, full of gaiety, charm and originality. It is quite unlike any other house I know, and reflects in every way its owner's extraordinary subtlety and distinction of mind. Among other treasures he has some exceedingly beautiful 18th-century chairs whose backs are made of gigantic mother-of-pearl shells. They have gilded legs. Among his pictures is a particularly lovely Renoir.[37]

Hugh Walpole lamented the ease with which dealers identified him as an easy mark and would seek him out day or night, seductively telling him 'You don't have to buy anything' as they unwrapped the latest over-priced old master. In six months he managed to accumulate three Cézannes, three Renoirs, two Picassos, a Gauguin, a Braque, a Derain, plus drawings by Beardsley, Toulouse-Lautrec, Laurencin and countless rare books and manuscripts.

Walpole's genuine love for and knowledge of the treasures he bought contrasted with the attitude of most film people, to whom the status acquired by possession mattered far more, a philosophy which reached its apotheosis in William Randolph Hearst's San Simeon. Walpole was shocked and horrified by his first visit to the newspaper magnate's Californian castle with its aimless accumulation of art:

What a place! A huge imitation stucco building like a German health resort, planted on a hill between the mountains and the sea. Magnificent tapestries and everywhere marble statues, sham Italian gilt and a deserted library where the books absolutely weep for neglect. In the grounds there is a zoo with some superb lions and tigers, but the cages are too small. Water buffalo and zebra look in at your bedroom window.[38]

The art motif and Hearst's Spanish-American taste in architecture also extended to the palatial bungalow occupied by his mistress Marion Davies, a collapsible building towed from studio to studio as Hearst's Cosmopolitan Pictures, formed to showcase her talent, wore out its welcome with one company after another. The bungalow, with its figure of the Virgin over its door, inspired Dorothy Parker to one of her most acid rhymes:

> *Upon my honour*
> *I saw a madonna*
> *Sitting alone in a niche*
> *Above the door*
> *Of the glamorous whore*
> *Of a prominent son of a bitch.*

Far from engaging the interest and affection of its guests, the Hearst ménage at San Simeon earned only pity and contempt, though ambitious newcomers hung around in the hope of making useful contacts; while planning the Davies vehicle *Page Miss Glory* Robert Lord spent many days there in company with a young English actor named Archie Leach – later Cary Grant – who 'was laying Marion Davies, or trying to'. As Leach and Lord played tennis on the excellent composition courts, 'Popsy' Hearst, clearly baffled by the identity of the many guests and their reasons for being there, wandered about while his guards tried in vain to keep Miss Davies sober and away from the men, a job rendered irrelevant by her bribes. By persuading guests to leave their cocktails on a window ledge from which she could conveniently steal them or, if this failed, resorting to a special stock of liquor kept in a lavatory attached to the play-room, Miss Davies became progressively drunker as the evening went on while the guards pointedly looked elsewhere. Confronted by Orson Welles and Herman Mankiewicz with the idea for *Citizen Kane*, producer John Houseman reflected: 'Not only Mankiewicz but every male and female columnist in Hollywood, not to mention actors, directors and film executives by the dozen had been entertained at San Simeon and had witnessed the embarrassing boredom of their ageing, unmarried hosts. To expose this in a movie seemed unethical, ungrateful and dangerous.'[39] Houseman may also have recognized San Simeon as a potent symbol of the Hollywood ideal, the decaying apotheosis of that pursuit of status and possession which dominated the movie colony all its life.

For the Europeans, San Simeon was no more absurd than the rest of Hollywood society. 'Placed' by salary and status, condemned to a round of the same old faces and conversations, the better film-makers found refuge in work. Michael Powell summed up the disillusion and alienation Europeans felt at life in Los Angeles. 'California is a hell of a place to live. Miles from anywhere. In those days it was much further than it is now. We were Europeans. We liked to be near theatres and opera and ballet and galleries and people. There weren't any of these things in California. The reason why these highly intelligent people who went to Hollywood immersed themselves in work and just made film after film after film was, I think, because . . . well, what could they do in California? No theatre, no opera – until radio and television came in it must have been the end of the earth. And people too . . . Europeans love people. It's talk as much as anything that keeps things going in Europe, particularly central Europe, where most of these people came from. Where was the café life in California?'

The little talk to be heard in Hollywood centred, naturally, on movies, and nowhere was it more concentrated than at Pickfair. Pola Negri, newly arrived in 1922, found the Pickford/Fairbanks soirées grotesquely funny:

They always took the same form. Mary would sit at one end of the table, with Doug beside her, so they could hold hands as they told us the grosses of their respective films . . . After dinner, we would see a new film and discuss 'the industry'. It might be production plans, it might be the pictures being made by those present, it might be the casting of some important role, but it was always the movies. [40]

Like the Wajdas' Sunday Nights, Pickfair evenings also had their own ground-rules. Invited on the basis of his knighthood and stage reputation, Sir Cedric Hardwicke arrived punctually at 7.30 p.m. to a Pickfair dinner party, to be admitted by a startled butler and shown to the empty bar. It was nine o'clock before other guests began to arrive and Miss Pickford made her grand entrance at the top of the staircase on the stroke of ten. Like most visitors who stayed, Hardwicke came to see this carelessness of form less as rudeness than an immersion in movies which excluded all else, even a personal reaction to individuals or works of art, both of which existed for them only in relation to 'the industry'. More impressionable travellers, however, often responded only to the superficial barbarism of Hollywood's indifference. Lady Diana Manners confided to her diary that she found the Los Angeles first night of Reinhardt's *The Miracle*, in which she starred,

cruelly alarming and altogether rude and miserable. The house was packed with screen celebrities. In my unblinking gaze I saw Pickford, Fairbanks, Norma Shearer, Marion Davies, William Randolph Hearst, Emil Jannings, Elinor Glyn. To my surprise no one did anything in honour of Reinhardt or any of us – no party, no flowers, no telegrams, no visits to congratulate. Hollywood is unlike any other American city . . . I hate this town, hate it, hate it! I believe they despise us for being 'legitimate' stage. [41]

A waste of time to explain that artists not yet processed by the studio machine, disturbing in their foreign eminence and skill, dangerously at liberty to supplant those already precariously in command, could hope for little more than guarded interest from these nervous and unsure exiles.

Lady Diana Manners (right) *and Rosamond Pinchot in Reinhardt's production of* The Miracle

Predictably, styles of living in Hollywood followed rules as strict as anything in a film script. The decision to purchase or rent a house – rental was more popular, implying a disdain for the film business and a readiness to pull out if things should not suit you – and how to staff it bore importantly on one's standing. Houses reflected not only one's salary but a chosen image. The British community announced its desire to remain aloof by electing to live in the mock-Elizabethan or French houses dotting the hills above Sunset Boulevard. A 1926 British fan magazine article referred approvingly to the 'picturesque half-timbered' house owned by British character actor Ernest Torrence, and remarked sniffily 'there is a decided preference for stucco and red tile, of which the majority of Californian houses are made – Ernest Torrence's house is one of the exceptions. . . .'[42] Servants too had their significance, and though the large Mexican/American 'Chicano' community in Los Angeles provided a pool of cheap labour (on which studios relied for their heavy work and the 'swing gangs' who manhandled scenery and equipment) it was accepted that Filipinos, Chinese or, on occasion, an English butler indicated true success. Gloria Swanson complained of the sellers' market in high-class help: 'You'd have someone for a year and then he would quit. Then you'd go to Rudolph Valentino's house and your former butler would open the door and say "Good Evening, Miss Swanson".'[43] Sensible émigrés soon learned the rules on servants. Offered a job adapting Alan Crosland's 1929 Barrymore hit *Don Juan* as a vehicle for Errol Flynn, puzzled German playwright Karl Zuckmayer asked his friend Fritz Lang for advice. Lang told him to grab the job. Historical films, notoriously long in gestation, offered the prospect of indefinite employment and, more important, the acquisition of status. 'I ought to rent a nice house and hire a Filipino couple as domestics, buy a car on instalments, bring my family here and be "happy",' Zuckmayer recalled. 'Besides I would have a three-month holiday every year during which I could do my own writing.'[44] To Lang's astonishment and that of the émigré community, Zuckmayer refused the job and ended his time in the US working a farm in New England where he could retain his integrity.

Unlike the lesser lights – character actors, writers and 'technical advisers' – who clustered in national communities, émigré stars sought their friends among fellow exiles of their own eminence and wealth. In these circles, status rested less in property or possessions – if one had no Renoirs, it was seldom because one could not afford them – than in a personal style to which one's associates could be drawn. Some stars specialized in unconventional after-dinner entertainment; Gloria Swanson offered dinner guests a post-prandial exhibition of judo, Noah Beery responding with an Indian tribal dance. Will Rogers's polo and the millionaires and aristocrats it attracted to his house and private field; the fashionable fortune tellers, psychiatrists and religious mystics about whom the impressionable gathered; the semi-amateur productions of the Pasadena Playhouse, where actors could slum for a few days in a scratch production of Ibsen or Shaw for the benefit of their friends – these were the centres of status to which the stars aspired. If Wajda's Sunday Nights were a lodestone for literary Europeans, the soirées of Paul Lukas and his wife attracted the more sporty members of the same set, though the cream of émigré literati, as well as its homosexuals, tended to meet at the homes of Edmund Goulding or the mansion of George Cukor, the latter playing host to the greatest literary lions, including Somerset Maugham, though it was Goulding who created the most memorable Maugham film in his *The Razor's Edge*, with Herbert Marshall as the novelist, reviewing a Hollywood party with a phlegm bordering on paralysis.

Descriptions of high life in these circles verge on the ridiculous, with wild enthusiasm applied to projects of juvenile inanity. Anita Loos described a late 1930s picnic when the guests included Greta Garbo, Charlie Chaplin, Paulette Goddard, Aldous and Maria Huxley, Christopher Isherwood, the mystic Krishnamurti with a retinue of Theosophists and, making his first visit to Hollywood, Bertrand Russell. It was a bizarre scene.

The Indian ladies were dressed in saris which were elegant enough but the rest of us wore the most casual old sports outfits. Aldous might have been the giant from some circus sideshow; Maria and I could have served as dwarfs, but with our tacky clothes the circus would have been pretty second-rate. Nobody would have ever recognized the glamour of Greta Garbo and Paulette Goddard in that tatterdemalion group. To protect themselves from fans who might crop up out of nowhere, Greta was disguised in a pair of men's trousers and a battered hat with a floppy brim that almost covered her face; Paulette wore a native Mexican outfit with coloured yarn braided in her hair. Bertrand Russell . . ., Charlie Chaplin and Christopher Isherwood all looked like naughty pixies out on a spree . . .[45]

Food was understandably unconventional on this far-from-prosaic outing.

Krishnamurti and his Indian friends, forbidden to eat or cook from vessels that had been contaminated by animal food, were weighed down with crockery and an assortment of clattering pots and pans. Greta, then strictly a vegetarian, was on a special diet of raw carrots which hung at her side in bunches. The others could and did eat ordinary picnic fare, but Paulette, to whom no occasion is festive without champagne and caviare, had augmented the equipment with a wine cooler and thermos cases.[46]

The picnic ended in chaos when the group tried to light a fire in the dry bed of the Los Angeles River and a sheriff ordered them away; so effective was their incognito that he failed to recognize them even after they introduced themselves.

Aviation finally pricked the bubble of Hollywood's exclusivity, admitting the chill of East Coast fashion and, more important, Wall Street financial methods. The stock issues arranged throughout the 1920s by studios wishing to buy into the theatre building boom handed to Eastern investment bankers the control hitherto held by the studios' immigrant founders, and the new business brains had little use for the illusion of exclusivity built up by Zukor, Fox and Laemmle. Speed became the essence of every film deal, a policy reflected in transport. By the late 1920s it was possible, if uncomfortable, to fly the three thousand miles from New York to Los Angeles along the Transcontinental Air Transport 'Lindbergh Route' pioneered by the early airmail fliers. The trip began with an overnight rail journey from New York to Columbus, Ohio, from which the plane took off at 6 a.m. Since passenger night flying was forbidden, there were night stop-overs at Albuquerque and Wichita, increasing the trip to a marathon two days and exhausting the six or eight passengers on each flight, all of whom received a commemorative fountain pen and desk set by way of compensation. By the mid-1930s the Douglas DC3 Dakota had reduced the trip to sixteen hours, with three stops for fuel, the aircraft darting from field to field guided by a chain of illuminated beacons that were the only navigation points in a still sparsely settled continent.

With the Los Angeles/New York axis firmly established, the glamour ebbed from Hollywood social life and from the society of the Super Chief. Trains, while faster and more comfortable than ever, fell in status, though many who remembered the leisurely life continued to use them. DeWitt Bodeen never lost his affection for the Super Chief. He and fellow scenarist Leonard Spiegelgass were on board when a 1940s blizzard stranded them in the flat MidWest for three days. 'I went up into the observation car,' Bodeen says. 'The wind was so strong that the snow just came straight in at eye level. Leonard went up, and came down with a white face. "DeWitt," he said, "we have never been nearer death!".' The staff continued to serve free food and drink as the snow piled up around the cars, the passengers settling down to a house party at railroad expense. 'Things like that happened on the Chief,' Bodeen said nostalgically. But like the Hollywood society of which it was emblematic, the Chief had been passed by.

8 COLONIES

Director Robert Florey remembers social life among the Hollywood French community of the 1920s with warmth and affection. 'Many French lived at hotels like the Garden of Allah and formed separate groups gathering together in the evenings for dinners or parties where no one spoke English and everyone complained about the life in California. They went on Sundays to Santa Barbara, Arrowhead or Big Bear, below the border at Tiajuana to see the bullfights or the JaiAlai games. While working at the studio – any studio – the French ladies would bring baskets of food and bottles of wine – hard to get during Prohibition – and

Robert Florey (left) *with Noah Beery, Arlette Marchal and her husband Marcel de Sano at Beery's mountain resort in the San Bernadino mountains, 1933*

organize picnic luncheons, drinking and laughing, speaking loudly in French at noon time to the amazement of the Americans not accustomed to this kind of behaviour.'

A golden image – but too much so to be anything but gilt, the careful recreation of an imaginary idyll from the collective Gallic unconscious, as idealized as any canvas by Poussin or Fragonard. Like every foreigner in Hollywood, the French paid for their pleasure by playing a part. Unaccustomed it may have been to voluble and wine-bibbing French picnics on the lawns, but Hollywood knew from movies how the French should act, and accepted the scene as confirmation of their view.

Nor were the French alone in creating and pursuing a life-style rooted in national stereotype. When Cedric Hardwicke hit Hollywood, one duty occupied his mind above all others. 'As a recruit to the English colony, whose members kept the flag flying and poured tea each afternoon at four, I paid my due respects to C. Aubrey Smith, the senior member of the colony, whose craggy manner suggested that he had just completed a ceremonial tour of all four corners of Queen Victoria's empire.'[47] Only in Hollywood could such a community have existed; with its rituals and observances, its kipper lunches and the famous Hollywood Cricket Club, an established and viable organization for which most British expatriates played, the English community, like most other national groups in California, acted out its role as seriously as if it had been scripted by an MGM scenarist.

National communities were a feature of Hollywood from the earliest days, when language barriers made it essential for Germans or Hungarians to consort with their own kind, especially since immigration requirements often involved finding an American resident prepared to guarantee a newcomer work, a rule which accentuated the clannish nature of exile groups. Lubitsch in particular established a tight clique, but the Scandinavians ran him a close second, drawn together by their professional association with MGM, by far the largest employer of Danish and Swedish talent. Danish actor Jean Hersholt became the dean of the community, which included Lars Hanson and his wife Karin Molander, the comedian Einar Hansen, directors Hugo Ballin, Victor Sjöstrom, and the towering Nils Asther, probably the most successful of the Swedish actors brought to Hollywood – though, like most of them, his greatest successes were in bizarrely in-

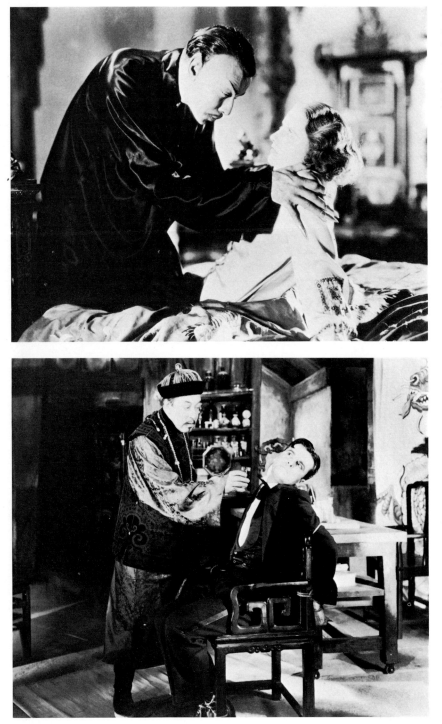

Nils Asther, his Swedish parentage well disguised, terrorizes Barbara Stanwyck in The Bitter Tea of General Yen

Warner Oland as the devilish Fu Manchu in The Mysterious Dr Fu Manchu

appropriate roles. Seeking acceptable Oriental character actors without the unacceptable accent or servant-class associations of Chinese or Nisei performers (who, except in the case of beauties like Anna May Wong, were relegated to the same menial type-casting as Negroes and Mexicans) the studios exploited the slightly Asiatic cast of some Swedish features by having its aristocratic Asians played by Swedes. Nils Asther earned high praise as the half-Chinese war-lord in Frank Capra's *The Bitter Tea of General Yen* and Warner Oland, born in Unea, Sweden, thrived as another half-caste in *Shanghai Express*, going on to become the best of many actors – all Occidental – to play Charlie Chan.

Greta Garbo, the most glamorous of the Scandinavian community, had little contact with her compatriots, preferring to hide behind an anonymity cultivated initially as a reaction against her first uncomfortable months in Hollywood. Tied to the concept of Swedish woman as a hard, Nordic sylph, MGM posed her for publicity shots in athletic gear crouching on a cinder track or having her stringy muscles fondled appreciatively by a bodybuilder. By the time her vividly erotic nature became apparent, Garbo had retreated into a secretive life-style which became her trade mark. Her widely quoted threat to MGM whenever she clashed with Mayer, 'I tank I go home', and the even more apocryphal 'I vant to be alone' set the style of her public image, and the actress quickly succumbed to it, cultivating a bleak disinterest and almost paranoid hatred of personal publicity. Hollywood society disliked both intensely, and particularly resented her habit of surrounding her homes with nine-foot high fences. David Niven recalled embarking on an alcoholic expedition with some other well-oiled stars to burrow under one such fence, but giving up when the foundations proved too sturdy. For herself, Garbo seems to have found Hollywood hypnotically frustrating. In the mid-1930s Cole Porter had a brief chat with her while waiting out his personal exile on The Coast. Asked by Garbo whether he was happy in Hollywood, Porter acknowledged that in general he was fairly content. She pondered this for some time, then commented dourly: 'That must be very strange.'

The 1917 Revolution threw Europe into the kind of confusion from which Hollywood always benefited, but the pattern of immigration to the movie colony reveals some of the subtle social

Garbo works out with a body-building coach in her early days in Hollywood

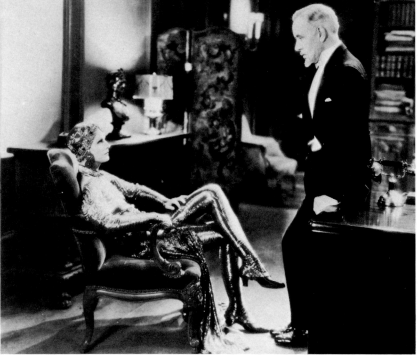

Mata Hari:*Greta Garbo and Lewis Stone*

distinctions between various types of émigrés which were to be accentuated in the 1930s. A new urge to politicize and nationalize the arts, including cinema, spread like a wave from Moscow, driving before it the artists who had depended on aristocratic patronage. Only a few months later, the flood to Vienna and Paris was swelled by another group, vastly different in political outlook: the leftist film-makers who had participated in the ill-fated nationalized cinema, the world's first, set up by the short-lived Hungarian Republic of Councils in April 1919 under an administrative board that included Sandor (Alexander) Korda, Mihaly Kertesz (Michael Curtiz), Laszlo Vajda and Bela Lugosi. After Horthy crushed the movement and restored authoritarian rule, the film-makers fled. Unlike the Russians, however, Curtiz, Korda and others remained in Europe, working mainly in the Vienna studios of Count Sascha Kolowratz, clinging to the Austro-Hungarian social life that was to them more important than the pursuit of wealth.

Exiled Russians, on the other hand, exploded out of Europe in a search for goals they seemed hardly to comprehend. Large

Bela Lugosi in his triumphant role as the blood-sucking count in Dracula

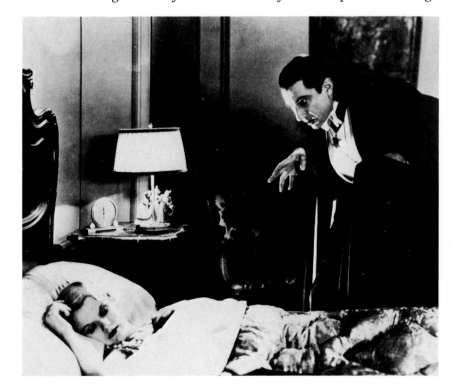

numbers found their way to Hollywood, where Revolution films became a fad. Many ex-Army men found themselves playing on screen a romanticized version of their own life stories, a phenomenon on which Josef von Sternberg commented wryly in his 1928 *The Last Command*, where a Tsarist general shattered by his experiences becomes a Hollywood extra and is cast as himself in a film being made by an actor he once tried to execute. With fantasy and reality totally confused in his mind, the general, played with typical extravagance by Emil Jannings, triumphs in the role and dies. Sternberg, who based the story on that of General Lodijenski, an officer of the Imperial Russian Army who had a brief movie career, had no trouble finding convincing extras for *The Last Command*:

I had fortified my image of the Russian Revolution by including in my cast of extra players an assortment of Russian ex-admirals and generals, a dozen Cossacks, and two former members of the Duma, all victims of the Bolsheviks, and, in particular, an expert on borscht by the name of Kolibianski. These men, especially one Cossack general who insisted on

In order to sustain the Russian atmosphere, director King Vidor (left) *hired a real Tsarist aristocrat to play the Grand Duke in his melodrama* His Hour. *Elinor Glyn, Aileen Pringle and John Gilbert stand by. For obvious reasons the Duke preferred to play under a pseudonym ('Mike Mitchell')*

keeping my car spotless, viewed Jannings' efforts to be Russian with such disdain that I had to order them to conceal it.[48]

Show business bristled with Russians in reduced circumstances. Appearing in *The Miracle* on Broadway in 1924 Lady Diana Manners found that one of the $16-a-week crowd extras was Volotskoy, a former diplomat who retained his impeccable manners and Academy French. When she asked him whether he had a better coat than the threadbare one he wore, the former courtier said delicately: 'Pas précisement'; Lady Diana obligingly cadged a replacement from among her friends.

The remarkable self-pity of Russian émigrés, their predilection for menial positions which accentuated their fall and the fanatical but romantic gloom that characterized their social life became a standing joke all over Europe. Jacques Deval's hit comedy *Tovarich* affectionately parodied a Russian Prince and Grand Duchess exiled in Paris with the entire Tsarist fortune, entrusted to them in the last throes of the Revolution, which they continue to guard even while living in total poverty. Offered jobs as butler and maid to a bourgeois French couple, they accept joyfully, enrich the life of their employers and finally hand the fortune back to the Bolsheviks, settling down happily to their servitude. 'Condemned to misery and hunger all the days . . .' the Prince reflects sadly before this dramatic change of fortune, and his wife agrees: 'Yes – misery and hunger – the greatest luxuries of our race! We were born to suffer and to love it. Life for us is so beautiful and so sad.' At one point the Prince essays an explanation of the bizarre Russian character for the family son:

We're congenitally savage . . . Sentimental barbarians! You can't emulate that. You have within you too great an accumulation of common sense. Your civilization goes back too far – all the way to Romulus and Remus, I suppose. We've had only two hundred years of the blessings of culture. And that isn't enough. We may wear the same clothes that you do, and read the same books, and know which fork to use at dinner – and be superficially presentable. But our souls are still roaming the steppes, wildly – baying with the wolves at the moon.[49]

The Broadway stage seized on the many Russian technicians and designers, once the envy of the theatre world, who arrived in New York dazed and broke during 1920. David Belasco snapped up Hartmann, the Kamerny Theatre's lighting expert, and

Richard Boleslavski demonstrates his hobby, brass-working, to actress Elizabeth Allan

Dmitri Buchowetzki (left), *with Marlene Dietrich and her husband Rudolf Sieber*

Moscow Art Theatre actor Leo Bulgakov and his wife Barbara later defected to set up a thriving New York Theatre School. Also a graduate of the Moscow Art Theatre, the towering Richard Boleslavski came to New York as an actor and acting coach after a wild flight during which he left the Tsarist forces to fight with Pilsudski's Polish army and then fled along the traditional route for Russian émigrés, to Berlin, then France and finally the USA, where he became a talented film director, his only real competition among the Russians being Dmitri Buchowetzki, a pre-Revolution arrival who had become famous in Berlin as the director of *Danton* and *Peter the Great*, historical sagas that earned him a Hollywood contract in advance of the Revolution. Other artists were less fortunate. In 1919 and 1920 Berlin became choked with fugitives and even the most distinguished found life difficult, partly because of the Association of German Artists, which made a protest to the government in 1922 about the over-abundance of Russian and Polish artists looking for theatre work. Some, like the actor/director Ivan Mosjoukine, moved on to Paris, where he had no lack of work, though a cautious visit to Hollywood in 1927 to play a young Cossack in yet another 'Russian' film called *Surrender* led only to poor reviews and his flight back to Europe.

Many, however, liked Hollywood and stayed. Alla Nazimova had already established herself at the centre of her epicene circle at the Garden of Alla, later – with a slightly amended name – a hotel and focus of Hollywood society. Olga Baclanova too had a cinema success, though by far the largest contingent was of ex-aristocrats too proud to work, a group who added spice, if little cash, to the town's society. Screenwriter Lenore Coffee remembered them with affection. Her husband, who could speak Russian, did his best to put jobs their way:

My husband had asked the DeMille casting director if he would like the list of Russians that Bucho [Dmitri Buchowetzki] always used and he was delighted to have it. Many of them had been in the Russian theatre but, whatever their background, all were extremely photogenic. Besides these, there were the two princes Mdivani, Serge and David, who acted as Cossacks. Serge was extraordinarily handsome, dark, tall and slender, with an almost Mediterranean cast to his features. He performed a marvellous sword dance, the *lesginka*, not unlike the Scottish Highland sword dance. David was blond, a bit plump and easy-going. There was a third son, Alexis . . . I understand there was a family con-

clave about who should restore the family fortunes and they all decided
that Alexis was the one. They were right, for he married first Louise
van Alen of a fine and moneyed family. This was not a success. His next
marriage was to Barbara Hutton, the first of her many marriages. This
lasted for a time and Alexis cut a dashing figure in the south of France.[50]

The Russians founded the Russian-American Art Club in an old
house on Harold Way in Los Angeles where members could eat
the traditional shashlik, served flaming on a sword, and listen to
Tina Zamina, a survivor of the anti-Bolshevik Woman's Army,
sing songs of the old days. But, like all Russians in exile, those in
Hollywood seemed set on self-destruction. Many died as bizarrely
as General Alexander in *The Last Command*; Alexis Mdivani in a
car accident in France, decapitated when he was thrown
through the windscreen, and his brother Serge, husband of both
Pola Negri and his own former sister-in-law, Louise Van Alen, in
a Florida polo match – unhurt after being thrown, he was helping
his horse to disentangle its legs from the harness when it kicked
him in the head. His sister Roussadana, married to the Spanish
painter Sert, became a leader of Riviera society and survived the
accident in which her brother Alexis was killed, only to die pre-
maturely a few years later. Like all the Mdivanis, 'Roussi'
attracted a remarkable and almost unhealthy personal devotion
from both male and female friends, including Sert's former wife
Misia Godebska, who made a vain pilgrimage to Lourdes in the
hope of averting her friend's death. Two men were needed to lift
the huge devotional candle she took to the shrine but her prayers
were in vain. 'In the grotto,' she later wrote, 'a drop of holy water
fell into my eye, and I have been blind ever since. At that very
instant – in Lausanne – Roussi died.'[51] In the context of the
Mdivanis's history, the story seems almost conventional.

To the Russians, Hollywood, like any place to which they were
exiled from their beloved homeland, was as much prison as
refuge, and in their manoeuvring for wealth one can see a shadow
of their desperation. Not only the Russians found Hollywood
sinister. Many observers of the 1920s recognized that the urge
for exiles to herd together in cliquey communities stemmed less
from companionability than from a horror of the alien landscape
and society of southern California. Eric Linklater's merciless *Juan
in America*, published in 1931, charting the reaction of a European

innocent to the horrors of Prohibition America, saw no symptom of cultural malaise more dangerous than the desperate refugees clustering like flies around the rich. A casual meeting puts Juan, a non-musician, into an orchestra supported on a caprice by millionaire Julius Pumpenstempel who has never asked it to play. When, unexpectedly, he demands a concert, the resulting cacophony reveals that the musical director, to line his own pockets, has filled the seats with tramps and loungers, pocketing most of their salaries. Later, at a film party, the German aristocrat husband of a status-seeking star reveals himself as a Berlin ex-waiter and, reverting to type, heads the guests in a boozy rendition of a comic song as he and his fellow hanger-on joyfully serve the movie millionaires foaming steins of beer. Reflecting on the German's invented duchy of Pretzel-Oppenheim, Linklater said: 'For its exiled aristocrats there were few places better than Hollywood, that was itself but half reality and seldom what it seemed.'[52]

Some expatriates regarded it as their duty to expose new-comers to the full hypocrisy of Hollywood before the studio fog descended on their senses. Robert Florey, a director who, throughout the 1930s and 1940s, was unofficial French ambassador to the movie colony, became more expert than most in de-mystification, as René Clair discovered on his arrival during the Second World War:

Florey, as soon as I arrived, insisted on showing me around in his own way – which is not most people's. He did not take me to the large modern studios, solid and white as New York banks, and organized on the scale of the motor factories of Detroit. He did not take me to see the mighty ones of the day or the fashionable stars, the private swimming pools or the night clubs where the clients are seated according to their weekly earnings . . . Florey drove me through nameless paths into the vacant lots where a few sheds were all that is left of the Hollywood of the past – which the Hollywood of today, like a wealthy courtesan un-willing to talk of her penniless, sensitive youth, doesn't care to re-member.[53]

Few expatriates had Florey's respect and philosophical regard for the past; such sights merely emphasized the ephemeral nature of everything for which they fought and intrigued. Hollywood for them was a game played in the eternal now, with companions

Ronald Colman relaxes with his crony Richard Barthelmess

Colman and Clive Brook (centre) – *professional Englishmen to the last hair – entertain friends to tennis*

chosen from among those who would have the sense, often in-culcated by the mutual favouritism on which Hollywood existed, not to destroy the illusion. No film community so respected the form of this tacit agreement as the British; nowhere was the pecking order more rigid, the rules more clearly defined, the rewards more lucrative.

Not that the British contingent was totally homogeneous. Faster members preferred to choose their friends at random. David Niven and Errol Flynn shared a beach house, soon nick-named Cirrhosis By the Sea, and such top stars as Ronald Colman maintained a disdainful detachment from Hollywood society of every kind. (Unlike most exiles, Colman refused to apply for US citizenship. 'A British passport is still the best in the world,' he assured his friends.) As one of the few actors under personal contract to Sam Goldwyn, Colman occupied a curious position, neither studio star nor free agent, which was emphasized by his unconventional private life. An early marriage to actress Thelma Raye broke up violently in Italy while on location for his first big American film *The White Sister*, and for years after Colman remained Hollywood's most eligible bachelor, heterosexual but preferring, in a long-standing British tradition, to share his life with a few male intimates. For some years he occupied a house with elderly British actor Charles Lane whom he met while mak-ing *Dark Angel* in 1932, and although protocol demanded that he retain the obligatory Filipino houseboy his only regular staff was an ex-Goldwyn prop boy named Tommy Turner who acted as secretary, valet and driver. The fan magazines struggled to find glamour in his staid existence. 'He lives quietly and unostenta-tiously,' *Motion Picture* commented in November 1935:

For years he had a little tucked-away house at the upper end of Vine Street. Recently he has moved to Beverly Hills . . . There his friends – Bill Powell, William Hawks, his business manager, Benita Hume, the Warner Baxters, the Dick Barthelmesses – come to dinner, usually on Friday evenings. Sometimes they run a picture, sometimes they play poker, though never for high stakes . . .

Only the British community saw Colman's life-style for the pose it was, a façade demanded by his standing and popularity in roles like Clive of India as the quintessence of British honour. David Niven recalled him 'aloof from it all, living the life of a hermit in his house at the end of March Street. . . . He had just overcome an unhappy marriage and was trying not to fall in love with Benita Hume.'[54] The liaison with Miss Hume became in time a sufficiently open secret for *Motion Picture* in 1938 to point out that for three years they had lived in adjoining Benedict Canyon houses and to add coyly 'in the community fence which runs along the border . . . there's a gate. The hinges are not rusty.' (Colman and Miss Hume married in September 1938.) Equally transparent was Colman's studied dislike of the movie business in which he had so sumptuously feathered his nest. ' "God, how I love the theatre," Ronnie was given to exclaim at least once a week,' his friend Cedric Hardwicke remarked. ' "Oh, for the good old days".'[55] But he later confessed to his agent, with rare candour for any star, 'Before God, I'm probably worth $35 a week. Before the motion picture industry I'm worth anything you can get.' Like many actors, Colman fell victim to the prevailing atmosphere

Ronald Colman in
A Tale of Two Cities

of fantasy that rotted the strongest personality, so that even so altruistic a gesture as a transatlantic and transcontinental dash to be with an ailing Ernest Torrence appears little more than a phoney Hollywood flourish, made more artificial by the fact that he arrived just two hours before Torrence died.

If Colman exercised a moral leadership over the British community, it was attenuated by the time it reached the lower echelons in which most of the British exiles earned their living. For them, Sir C. Aubrey Smith arbitrated in all things. An Old Carthusian and Cambridge graduate, Charles Aubrey Smith came from the richest British stock. His sister, Beryl Farber, had the reputation of being one of Edwardian London's most beautiful girls, and Smith's majestic and commanding personality made him a natural for aristocratic roles on stage and later in films. Going on the stage in 1892, he preceded almost every other British émigré to Hollywood, making his first film in 1915, and continued until his death in 1948, aged eighty-five, to play everything from a jungle trader in *Tarzan of the Apes* to various lords, bishops, admirals and generals, though he was at his most memorable as the bristling Colonel Zapt in David Selznick's all-star *The Prisoner of Zenda*. Douglas Fairbanks Jnr, who starred as the sinister Rupert of Hentzau, remembers Smith's unconcern for the pressures of film-making. Immersed in his airmail edition of the London *Times* and with his hearing aid switched off – for the bulk of his sound film career Smith was almost stone deaf – it took some time for Raymond Massey to attract his attention when he wished to ask his advice. Smith listened attentively as Massey explained his problems with understanding the character of Black Michael, the king's devious half-brother and instigator of the plot against him, then said: 'Ray, in my time I've played every part in *Zenda* except Princess Flavia' – Massey poised himself for the expected insight – 'and I've always had trouble with Black Michael,' he concluded, turning off his hearing aid and returning to *The Times*.

Smith's amiable acceptance of his role as a stage Englishman and that of the British community as comic cohorts seemed limitless. Few publicity schemes or crackpot casting ideas could not depend on British co-operation. In particular, David Selznick's publicist Russell Birdwell put them through the hoops more than once. On the news of George VI's coronation, Birdwell, seeing the rich publicity potential of the almost entirely British cast of *Prisoner of Zenda*, had the expatriates assemble for a well-reported ceremony of thanksgiving on the set and, shortly after, hearing that British author Robert Hichens, whose *The Garden of Allah* Selznick was about to film, had a similarly-named villa in Egypt, he persuaded the writer in a 45-minute phone conversation to offer it to the abdicated Edward VII and Mrs Simpson as a honeymoon retreat. Their acceptance boosted substantially the circulation of Richard Boleslavski's turgid adaptation. Aubrey Smith, along with Cedric Hardwicke, Roland Young, Nigel Bruce, Basil Rathbone and others, were once called by Darryl Zanuck to test for a collective role as the Japanese high command in a war film, the theory being that British actors, even in make-up, would have the same sinister authority playing Japanese as they showed playing Nazis in other films. After some hours of careful costuming the assembled actors made an impressive display, until Smith, as the chief of the Japanese war cabinet, rose and boomed: 'We are gathered heah to considah . . .' and the entire crew collapsed in laughter. The idea was quickly abandoned, but until the end of the war British actors enjoyed regular employment as Nazi beasts.

In time, the British colony declined into little more than a publicity gimmick. Its golden days were the late 1920s, when English actors, diffident, nervous, clubbed together for companionship in an alien land. 'My memories of Hollywood during that period?' actor Percy Marmont said.

The short answer to that is 'utterly delightful'. One had a lovely home life, and also one had a lovely home. It was particularly nice for us because we had our own little bunch of friends; some of whom were English, not all . . . Ernest Torrence, Ronald Colman, William Powell, Warner Baxter and another Warner, a wonderful man, Warner Oland, Jack Holt, Tim McCoy, and that was our little band of friends. We used to use each other's houses and get together at weekends, and we had a wonderful time. When I say at weekends, I mean it, because during the week one just could not be social. I mean, it was quite a usual thing if there was a party, and you were on a film, you unostentatiously left the party about nine o'clock – you wanted to go to bed. You had to be up at half past five in the morning.[56]

Some actors – usually those lower on the financial scale than featured players like Marmont – had livelier times, though the emphasis remained on a faintly phoney domesticity. During his Sennett days and later as a player for Fox, George Harris participated in all the social life open to him:

'We had a little clique of English actors – Lionel Belmore, Eric Snowden, Jameson Thomas, Lawford Davidson – who used to live near one another in an area we called "Little Tooting" – just off Sunset and Hollywood Boulevard. Every Sunday there would be a different sort of event: a kipper breakfast, for instance, with a box of kippers sent from England. Or Eric Snowden, who was a great cook, would get a piece of beef and we'd have roast beef and Yorkshire pudding. Or somebody would have a fish and chip evening. Our various girl-friends would come along, and since this was during Prohibition we had our own bootlegger who would get us the raw alcohol – God knows where it came from – which we would mix with orange juice and get fairly "kicked

Sir Charles Aubrey Smith – a former England cricket captain – presides over the Hollywood Cricket Club

up'' on. We had a great little gang.'

'Shortly after this, Aubrey Smith started the cricket team, with Ronnie Colman, Clive Brook and Herbert Marshall. I remember they sent round a little note to all of us to get together and discuss it. They wanted volunteers to play and others to keep records. I said: "Aubrey, I'm ready. What can I do?" He said: 'We may find it very difficult to play you, though we could make you one of the bails." We were even more interested in football – Association Football: soccer. There was a local team known as the Sons of St George. There were a couple of boys from Manchester United and other teams who had drifted to Los Angeles in business, and they used to play the Mexican teams that came up. We had almost a little football league with half-a-dozen teams, and a lot of us used to follow the games. I went along quite often with Victor McLaglen and his brother Arthur; Edgar Norton, Claude King, George K. Arthur and his sister-in-law Doris Lloyd. There would be picnics beforehand and we'd have a lot of fun. At these sort of events you met a lot of people you might not otherwise have known – just because they were British and liked to see other Britishers. Ronald Colman and Benita Hume were very select in their company but they would often come along to a British party and of course Victor McLaglen was just one of the boys. I'd been on the halls with him and his brother. We were on the same bill in 1913 at the Hippodrome, Richmond, when they were the Romano Brothers. They painted themselves white and posed nude, like Greek statues! So it was rather hard for me to think of Vic as a star.'

9 SHOUTS AND MURMURS

Film historians like to paint the coming of sound films in 1927 as a technical breakthrough commensurate with the invention of electric light, an advance, audacious and original, which revolutionized overnight the state of an art. As with all things to do with Hollywood, the reality is a good deal more prosaic. Sound film as a workable technique had existed almost as long as the cinema itself, and its pioneers, like those of colour film, widescreen, stereoscopy and most of the modern cinema's devices, hawked their ideas in vain from studio to studio for most of the 1920s. Notoriously nervous of change, the producers, notably William Fox, interested themselves in the inventions mainly to forestall their competitors, and when the high cost of adapting a cinema to the primitive sound-on-disc system became apparent – it could run from $10,000 to $30,000 per theatre – most companies decided the concept had little commercial potential. Respected film-makers from Thalberg to Chaplin saw sound film only as a gimmick, and declined to take seriously a future in which actors' accents would be a factor in their employment. Throughout 1927 and 1928, even after the first screening of Warner Brothers' sound films, European actors continued to arrive in Hollywood, and the colonies swelled with new arrivals. Renée Adorée, Sigrid Holmquist, Greta Nissen and a score of other European actresses made their debuts in the 1926–27 season. So did Vilma Banky, a beautiful Hungarian who spoke no English at all; for their love scenes in her first Hollywood film, *Dark Angel*, she spoke in her own language while co-star Ronald Colman chatted about cricket. Like the rest, Miss Banky was swept away when the sound craze flooded through Hollywood in the spring and summer of 1928.

Sound profoundly affected Hollywood in almost every department. Overnight, the emphasis in recruitment swung from stars, often European and well-versed in film technique, to directors and writers, generally from the theatre of Broadway or London, able, it was erroneously assumed, to handle the filmed stage plays into which Hollywood movies were destined, most people believed, to turn. Established stars like Blanche Sweet, Mae Murray and Alice White were pressed into clumsy imitations of Ziegfeld and Belasco shows which effectively ended their careers, a fate that also overtook poorly-voiced action stars like Allene Ray, Art Acord and Tom Mix. In 1928 *Photoplay* named the movies' top stars as John Gilbert, Emil Jannings, George Bancroft, Richard Barthelmess, Betty Compson, Gary Cooper, Joan Crawford, Marion Davies, Louise Dresser, Greta Garbo, Janet Gaynor, Jean Hersholt, Thomas Meighan, William Powell and Fay Wray. A year later, the popularity of Gilbert, Barthelmess, Compson, Dresser, Meighan and, at least in the US, Jannings, had declined almost to nothing, and Hersholt was confined for the rest of his career to avuncular mittel-European roles like the one he played opposite Shirley Temple in *Heidi*. Ironically sound was a greater disaster for English-speaking actors than for their European colleagues; while most continental performers had developed a polished stage delivery as part of their apprenticeship in the repertory theatre and could choose roles to accommodate their accent, American stars chosen for their face or physique and often lacking any formal acting experience found themselves at sea in the sound cinema, especially since primitive recording systems favoured a booming Broadway projection that few Hollywood-trained actors could boast.

As usual in the American cinema, the most crucial failure was one of nerve. Panicked by the problems of his accent, Jannings returned to Germany, where Erich Pommer, after a brief period supervising Paramount's European productions in Hollywood, was refurbishing UFA with Paramount money, building it into Europe's most modern production complex. With him, Jannings took Josef von Sternberg, another casualty of studio politics whose career was to change radically after his encounter with the young Marlene Dietrich. Although *The Blue Angel* revived Jannings's European career, American audiences, who did not see it until two years later, found it tepid by comparison with *Morocco*, the Hollywood film with which Paramount launched

(Above) *Josef von Sternberg on location before the coming of sound (Robert Florey is on the left) and* (below) *lording it over the set of* An American Tragedy

von Sternberg's protégée. Furious at the director's infatuation with his star and her instant American success, Jannings insisted on almost total control over casting, script and editing of his subsequent UFA films, a decision that reduced his sound output to a succession of studies in Rabelaisian barbarism laced with self-pity. Involvement with the Nazis – he became a top official in the wartime cinema – led to a trial for collaboration, and though the tribunal took pity on the ill and discredited old star, clearing him of guilt, he died still dreaming of the career he might have had, his ambitions to direct films unfulfilled.

Female stars fared better in Hollywood's sound purges, perhaps because a foreign accent often merely accentuated sexual attraction in a woman. A few, however, had no chance to try the new medium, the studios seizing on their doubt to dispose of stars whose popularity had been slipping for some time. Pola Negri found the balance of her contract sold to the British studio of Walter Mycroft, who thrived on exploiting Hollywood rejects and re-treads, and Greta Nissen was also sacked from Howard Hughes's employ when his decision to remake *Hell's Angels* in sound showed up the inappropriateness of her Nordic accent to the role of a sexy British society girl later played by Jean Harlow. Greta Garbo's success in sound, despite a similarly thick accent, suggests that, if a star failed to survive, studio ruthlessness rather than a lack of skill provided the reason. After delaying her sound debut for more than two years, MGM, reflecting that Garbo's greatest audience lay in Europe, elected to star her in Eugene O'Neill's *Anna Christie*, the part of an immigrant ex-prostitute perfectly suiting her Swedish murmur. Fluent in German, English and French, she played in all three foreign versions produced at the same time, though seldom with the same cast or director. For the German version, Clarence Brown was replaced as director by Jacques Feyder, a Frenchman who directed her in *The Kiss* (1929) and who later, because of his multi-lingual ability, became an expert in the re-making of Hollywood successes for the European market.

These new versions, shot on the same sets as the American films and often with the same supporting casts (though different stars), became a regular feature of Hollywood between 1929 and 1931, though other solutions to the foreign version problem were tried, including the use of the newly-developed travelling-

Jacques Feyder
rehearses Helen
Chandler and Ramon
Novarro for the MGM
film Daybreak

matte system to provide backgrounds into which other actors
could be incorporated overseas. For multi-lingual actors on both
sides of the Atlantic the system was a bonanza, and a lively
market developed, with German and American studios competing
for the best and most fluent performers. (British actor John
Stuart recalled that national loyalties ran high. Hired by G. W.
Pabst to appear in the English-language version of *L'Atlantide* in
1932, he and his French and German colleagues Pierre Blanchar
and Gustav Diessl consulted a roster each morning to decide who
went first onto the set, thus avoiding any national partisanship.)
For eighteen months Hollywood welcomed a stream of young
actors and actresses hired exclusively to appear in foreign copies
of films like *The Big House, The Trial of Mary Dugan, Olympia,
Anna Christie* and *The Sacred Flame*. Gustav Frohlich, Paul
Morgan, Hans Junkerman, Walter Hasenclever, Dita Parlo (star
of Vigo's *L'Atalante*), Lissy Arna, Theo Shall, Johannes Riemann:
all for the most part appeared in only one film before the fashion
petered out and they were sent home. A few hung on. Hans von
Twardowski, a veteran of *The Student of Prague* and *The Cabinet
of Dr Caligari*, sensed the risks of returning and resourcefully

accepted second-best to become a serviceable character actor. Others, unwilling either to return or take a back seat, learned that Hollywood could be cruel as well as kind.

One of the first French actors to be caught up in the craze was Charles Boyer, a promising Parisian juvenile hired initially by UFA to film French versions of its hits. Impressed by his showing, MGM, by then a UFA shareholder under the Par-Ufa-Met agreement, took him to Hollywood for the French remake of *The Trial of Mary Dugan* and George Hill's prison drama *The Big House*, the latter re-directed in French and German by Paul Fejos, a Hungarian bacteriologist who, by the curious alchemy of Hollywood, drifted into direction and is credited with, among other advances, the invention of the camera crane. For Boyer, the Hollywood experience, even with the help of a cultivated associate like Fejos, was painful. He called it 'a period of my life I would rather forget. I spoke painfully little English and could not seem to learn very quickly. Everyone knew me on the boulevards of Paris but here I was just another foreign actor.' His disenchantment was shared by Lily Damita, Lilian Harvey, Tala Birell and other actresses brought over in the first rash of enthusiasm for foreign versions and then left to hang around in unproductive idleness. True to type, MGM and other studios solved the problem with duplicity, goading the newcomers into breaking their contracts by offering them roles of a derisive smallness which also decreased their value to rival companies. Finding himself shoved into a tiny part as Jean Harlow's chauffeur in *Red Headed Woman*, Boyer, stung, exercised the clause in his contract allowing him to visit France for stage appearances and left America. 'My bitterness with Hollywood was so intense,' he said, 'that my ears rang with it,' and he did not return for another three years. He was luckier, however, than Morgan and Hasenclever, both of whom ended their careers and lives at the hands of the Nazis.

MGM and Paramount, the two main supporters of the foreign version policy, could afford to adopt a cavalier line with the multi-lingual stars because of a new development which appeared in France in 1930. Buying up the vast Joinville studios outside Paris, Paramount established a factory for foreign-language films, making as many as fourteen separate versions of a single film in various languages and combinations of languages under the control of Bob Kane, the Paramount producer who had

Charles Boyer – with Ingrid Bergman in Gaslight *and Garbo in* Conquest *(he played Napoleon, she Marie Walewska)*

laid down the law about re-editing the German epics and Expressionist classics of the 1920s. Babel would appear to have been a
tea-party compared with Joinville in 1931. Directors and writers
of every background and degree of talent flooded to Paris as the
American film business, one of the few to escape fundamental
damage in the Depression, poured cash into an industry still
rocking from the after-effects of successive political and economic
crises. One of the lesser arrivals was Michael Powell, who had
been working as assistant to the exiled American director Rex
Ingram at the ancient Nice studios to which he had fled when the
Hollywood star system made work in Hollywood increasingly
difficult for an artist of his wayward talent. 'Bob Kane was a
famous ruthless producer,' Powell said. 'He used to be with First
National, and later with RKO. I used to hang around his place
doing odd things, as I had hung around Rex Ingram' – first
mopping up the alkali dust footprints left on the black floor by
Alice Terry, his biggest star and wife; later acting – 'and Leonce
Perret, when he was making *Madame Sans Gene* in 1923 or '24. I
met Alex Korda there too, and Alberto Cavalcanti. European
directors from all over were flooding to Paris because they needed
people who knew every European language. For two years it was
bedlam. That's how Alex got his chance to make an English film.
He'd been to Hollywood and not done too well but he did such a
good job on the French version of *Marius* that Paramount took
him over to London to direct *Service For Ladies*. They just handed
him the script and he made it, and while he was making it he met
all these people who later worked with him or financed him.
Arthur Wimperis, who later scripted films for him, was on it;
George Grossmith, who became chairman of his company, played
the king, and Leslie Howard was a head waiter.'

Joinville carried the seeds of its own doom from the moment
Paramount set up the project. As producers discovered everywhere that foreign versions were made, regional variations in
language made the true international film an impossibility. As
Kevin Brownlow noted:

Some of John Barrymore's Warner Brothers successes were remade for
the South American market by Antonio Moreno, who was Spanish. And
Ramon Novarro, a Mexican, directed Spanish versions. The trouble was
that Hollywood soon discovered an irritating flaw to all this; there
were as many Spanish dialects as Spanish-speaking areas. French,

Ramon Novarro's Latin good looks made him one of Hollywood's most popular stars in the lucrative South American market. Films like The Call of the Flesh *enjoyed a brisk sale south of the border*

Carlos Villarias played the role of Count Dracula, originally done by Bela Lugosi, in the Spanish-language version of Dracula, *shot at the same time and on the same sets as the original*

German and Italian language versions ran into similar objections; audiences and renters frequently complained that the film, though in the right language, was still unintelligible.[57]

The situation was made all the more galling by the fact that Tobis, the German company which had cornered all the vital European patents in sound film, was making high-quality French- and German-language films at Epinay, just outside Paris, including Clair's *Sous Les Toits de Paris*, and the gradual improvement of recording techniques to the point where dubbing of films became practical spelt the end of Joinville. It quickly became a dubbing factory where sound men matched as far as possible the lip-movements of American actors to German, French or Italian glosses of the original script or, for inconvenient languages, superimposed sub-titles.

Back in the USA, the adaptation to sound bit deep into Hollywood's traditional isolationism. Except for William Fox, who as early as 1925 had installed a sound system in six of his cinemas, only to rip out the equipment when it became clear that silent films still satisfied the mass audience, no Hollywood studio owner saw the coming revolution or geared himself to it. After a confused period during which the majors watched with mingled astonishment and malicious expectation as Warner Brothers sank its meagre funds into producing sound films for the handful of cinemas able to show them, MGM, Paramount and Fox plunged headfirst into the currents and whirlpools of the sound maelstrom where the sharks of big business waited to snap them up. With Warners controlling the archaic but workable sound-on-disc Vitaphone system and Fox owning the more efficient sound-on-film Movietone, MGM and Paramount were forced to pay extortionate amounts to the radio interests, largely controlled by the Rockefeller family, for the vital patents that would allow them to produce sound films and, more important, convert their cinemas to screen them. Taking a lead from the Rockefeller-controlled Radio Corporation of America, which had cornered most of the radio patents in the early days of broadcasting (and exploited its advantage by buying the ailing Keith-Albee-Orpheum vaudeville theatres and converting them to the chain to be known as RKO), Western Electric consolidated all the sound film patents in Electrical Research Products Inc., from which studios were forced to purchase sound film licences. For the money to finance such purchases, studios appealed to New York finance houses, a move pioneered by Adolph Zukor in 1919 when he sold $10 million in Paramount stock to fund his attempt to monopolize the American cinema chains, but widely regarded by the immigrant moguls as dangerous, offering as it did a substantial degree of control to the native-born and generally gentile speculators of Wall Street.

Part of William Fox's control had slipped from his hands in 1925, when he re-capitalized the Fox Film Corporation by offering a million shares to the public, using the new funds to expand his impressive theatre chain. When the sound craze placed him in a commanding position, he tried to buy control of the less well-prepared Paramount and First National, being rebuffed on both occasions, and then to acquire control of Loew's Inc., the powerful parent company of MGM. In personal negotiations with Nick Schenck, the Loew's Inc. president who stood to gain millions from the deal, Fox and his backers won a tentative hold on Loew's stock, though only at the cost of vastly over-extending Fox's personal commitment, alienating the Loew's Inc. stockholders and alerting the government, then sensitive to the power of monopoly in American business, to the emergence of a new and dangerous power block in the film industry. Fox, a businessman of almost pathological cunning, might have resolved the situation in time, but he never had the chance. In July 1929, on his way to a golf game with Schenck during which they expected to discuss ways of neutralizing the growing anger of Adolph Zukor at their deals, Fox's car crashed. Laid up for three months in hospital he watched helplessly as his imperial schemes crumbled.

The Crash delivered the *coup de grâce*. Fox shares tumbled from $119 to $1 each, and in March 1930 he sold out his interest in the still-solid company for $18 million, a sum he quickly pyramided by selling short in the collapsing market, wrecking the company he helped to build. Still set on gaining control of the sound cinema, he bought the Tobis company's Klangfilm system, some of whose original features, though unpatented in America, were in wide use, and also acquired other patents owned by the German Tri-Ergon group. But Hollywood, now backed by its new Wall Street allies, could afford to defy a renegade like Fox. Long and costly legal battles eroded his patents, which the Supreme

Court ruled invalid in 1935, and in 1936 he declared himself bankrupt. A fortune of $100 million was reduced to nothing and in 1941, in the final humiliation, an attempt to bribe the judge in his bankruptcy trial earned him a $3000 fine and six months in jail.

Playwright Val Gielgud and Anna May Wong at Paramount's famous gate

Few of Fox's colleagues and competitors survived him. The last of those to retain control of his studio, 'Uncle' Carl Lemmle, sold Universal to East Coast interests in 1935 and died four years later. Most of the other moguls were not sorry to go. Their Hollywood had been superseded by something they had never expected, an industrial complex where ties of blood and birth counted for nothing. The new American cinema looked on Europe as a market to be exploited rather than as a source of spiritual power. If it imported European artists, it was to take advantage of the now totally Hollywood-oriented film audience of Germany, England and France rather than to improve the quality of its product. When European countries, particularly Britain, tried to stem the dollar imperialism by making it illegal for companies to siphon their enormous profits from cinema admissions back to America and forcing them to invest some funds in local production, Hollywood cold-bloodedly set up 'quickie' studios for the manufacture of inferior product intended merely to satisfy the law. British film-makers protested in vain that the 'quota quickie' system maintained the local cinema but kept it permanently undernourished; the new Hollywood, unlike the old, had no interest in what Europe thought, only what it paid to see.

The changes between 1929 and 1933 shocked and disconcerted Europeans who had relished the insouciance of Los Angeles movie society, its innocence and the generosity that could underlie its pursuit of status. Producer Bob Lord contrasted the mood at First National before sound with its re-birth as the hardest-driving of Depression film factories under the energetic Warner brothers. 'It was like a country club. The offices were beautiful, the café was beautiful. Everybody had lovely cars and used to stroll in around noon. But when Jack Warner arrived, it was like a bomb under the place.' Arriving on his second visit, British playwright Val Gielgud execrated the new Hollywood, 'its fake values, its meretricious pretentiousness, its vulgarity, its crazy paving of talent wasted or misused, of physical beauty exploited and degraded, of jewels and sweat-shirts, of fine intentions and com-

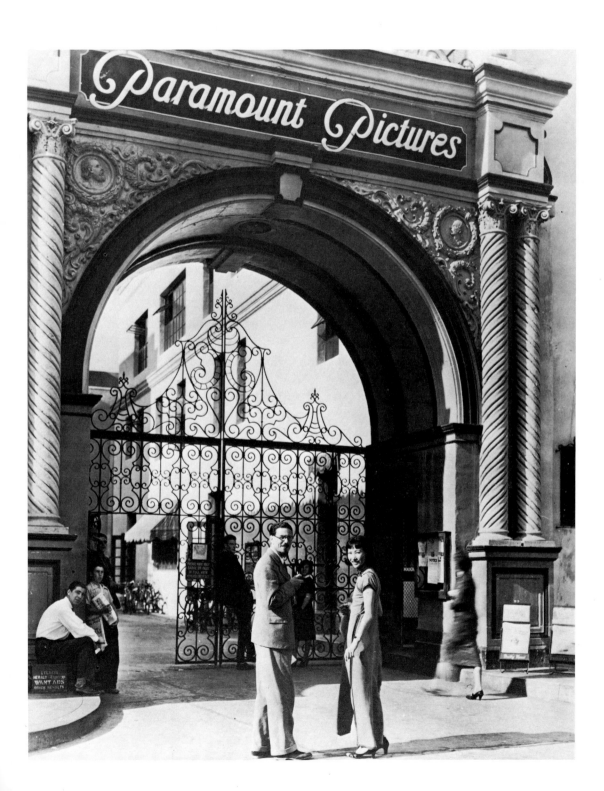

mercialism run mad. To leave Hollywood was for this traveller one of his most satisfying experiences.'[58] Hugh Walpole, a regular employee of MGM since his success in adapting *David Copperfield* for David Selznick, did not see the fundamental nature of the change until his return in the summer of 1935 after a long absence. As he explained in a letter, he found the writers' block at MGM 'like the grave. I have slipped back without a sound – no publicity this time whatever. It is all most pleasant, kindly, agreeable but, more than last year, completely unreal. There is more actual positive reality in one square inch of the beach at Scarborough than in the whole extent of Hollywood.'[59] Ever hopeful, Walpole saw a preview of *Broadway Melody of 1936*, then MGM's biggest musical, and quite liked it. 'In Hollywood itself, however,' he noted, 'nothing else is talked about, morning and night, but this and similar efforts. No wars, no politics, no death make any effect here. . . . We are all on a raft together in the middle of the cinema sea. . . .'[60] But the raft was soon to rock and almost capsize in the ripples of a problem which, though Hollywood had little part in it, confronted its people finally with the absurdity of all they said and did.

10 THE TASTE OF TRANSITORINESS

On 9 September 1933 Max Reinhardt celebrated his sixtieth birthday quietly with his wife. He had been in Oxford during the Berlin purges of the previous January, and had returned direct to Vienna, renouncing his Deutsches Theatre post in a letter commenting weakly: 'To have contributed to the national assets with the strength of my life softens the bitterness of my farewell.' By now, disparaging references to 'the Jew Goldmann' – his real name – appeared frequently in the Berlin press, and agents were already canvassing the possibility of an escape to Hollywood. But despite Hitler's growing influence on Austrian politics Vienna still retained its respect for The Master, and his Salzburg Festival productions of Mozart and Hoffmanstahl were as precise, and the midnight soirées in Leopoldskron as glittering as ever. Always, however, there was the shadow of an inevitable fall. As the horse-drawn carriages pulled up at two or three in the morning to carry away his guests, Reinhardt would whisper to a few close friends 'Stay for an hour'. 'That hour often stretched on to five or six in the morning,' Karl Zuckmayer said:

We sat in the small, dusty room above the baroque gallery . . . The mood was one of contemplative serenity, of wholly personal gaiety arising out of a common medium; art, literature and the theatre. In this world of doomed enchantment politics were underplayed, perhaps because everyone knew that in the long run he would not be able to escape their iron grip. It was somewhat like Versailles in the days of the Bastille, only more alert, more aware, intellectually more lucid. Once, at a late hour, I heard Reinhardt say almost with satisfaction, 'The nicest part of these festival summers is that each one may be the last'. After a pause, he added, 'You can feel the taste of transitoriness on your tongue'.[61]

161

The taste of transitoriness was an early symptom of the disease to which Reinhardt and many of his guests at Leopoldskron – Sokoloff, Basserman, Zuckmayer – were to succumb, the cultural ailment that forever barred Europe's intellectuals from any real entente with the pragmatists of Hollywood. Max Beerbohm isolated the virus in *Zuleika Dobson* – the assumption that only ideas are at all worth while – but its effects are apparent in every failure of the American film industry to nurture and learn from the great artists of its time and a corresponding inability of these artists to understand and exploit the resources and latent goodwill of the United States. The country stood to gain much from the Nazi horror; by saving the refugees, integrating them into its culture, the United States could have benefited as much as from the famines and wars of nineteenth-century Europe that drove so many Irish, Italians and Germans to the New World. And thousands of Europeans would have been saved from the ovens of Auschwitz and Belsen. The American failure to achieve this, and Hollywood's tawdry role in the débâcle, is one of the great tragedies of this century, but as dawn broke over Leopoldskron in 1933, the future was remote enough to be more melancholy than terrifying. The elegant langour that was a symptom of the European disease protected its sufferers from truth until the very end.

Marlene Dietrich scandalizes the première of The Sign of the Cross *by appearing in a man's tuxedo. Her companions are Maurice Chevalier and Gary Cooper*

In the years following the Depression, Hollywood drifted erratically, controlled by the gales of finance and the confused gusts of popular taste. For Paramount and MGM, the consistent popularity of cinema in Europe meant vast profits from the UFA complex, where Erich Pommer supervised a production team unexcelled in Europe. MGM even considered German actor Fritz Rasp as a replacement for Lon Chaney when the latter died in 1930, and only his nervousness about an irradicable accent prevented him from accepting Thalberg's offer; throughout the Nazi days he remained at the Berliner Volksbuhne, taken over from the exiled Piscator by Eugen Klopfer. Garbo's European popularity, though already showing the decline that eclipsed her as a star, continued with sufficient strength for Paramount to import Marlene Dietrich and Universal Tala Birell as competitors. The continental woman, sexually mature, explicitly erotic, had always been the most potent of imports into American art, and Paramount's

Marlene Dietrich, her daughter Maria, her husband Rudolf Sieber, and Josef von Sternberg

Mauritz Stiller (left) *presides over the introduction of beauty and the beast; Greta Garbo meets MGM's other top star, Lon Chaney, still in his make-up for* The Road to Mandalay

decision, urged by her director and lover Josef von Sternberg, to exploit Dietrich in a series of sensual melodramas, was endorsed by her immediate popularity. An uncomplicated young woman, she led a life of unexampled routine, more devoted to her young daughter Maria than to either Sternberg or her stage director husband Rudolf Sieber, who spent most of his time in Germany, conveniently remote from the rumours and eventual lawsuits brought by Sternberg's wife in which she charged libel and alienation of affections. Obsessed, the brilliant Sternberg put his star through every sexual hoop the Hays Office would allow, though it rejected his original script for *Blonde Venus* in 1932 with the terse comment in an internal memo that Paramount now led the way in exploiting sex in the cinema. Unalarmed, Paramount lavished its advertising budget on campaigns that underlined the film's sexual eccentricity, just as the slogan 'Marlene Dietrich, The Woman All Women Want To See' had sold the lesbian scenes of her first American film *Morocco*. A fashion for her mannish slacks swept America, Dietrich fanning the flames by appearing in top hat, long cigarette holder, tails and a monocle at such inappropriate events as the première of Cecil B. DeMille's *The Sign of the Cross*.

In what may have been unconscious imitation of De Maurier's *Trilby*, European glamour stars conformed to a pattern of which their ugly but brilliant director/protectors were a vital component. Garbo's Mauritz Stiller set the style; hulking, dour, with huge hands, his nickname 'Moje' disguised his Russian Jewish origin and real name of Mowscha. Sternberg too affected a European style – he was born Jonas Sternberg in Vienna but lived in the US most of his life: the 'von' was added by an obliging producer, allegedly to even up the lines on a credit panel – and made no attempt to reduce the contrast between his stooped, enigmatic physical presence and the mysterious elegance of his star. Jesse Lasky Jnr noted the impact of an early Dietrich arrival in the US, with Sternberg and Sieber in attendance. 'The golden, blonde, blue-eyed young Teutonic athlete, who might have stepped out of a Wagnerian opera, brimming with virility and bronzed from some Alpine ski-slope was her husband – the caved-in, dishevelled, unkempt, gnome-like von Sternberg her admirer and discoverer. A Hollywood cliché was shattered.'[62] Perhaps no film would have shown such a relationship, but in

Hollywood itself beauty and the brilliant beast went hand in hand.

After Dietrich's success, Hollywood was flooded with *femmes fatales* imported by hopeful producers, but no amount of publicity could sell those who lacked the sexual ingredient so superbly concocted by Sternberg. In 1933 Sam Goldwyn cold-bloodedly set out to build Russian actress Anjuschka Stenski into a star comparable to Dietrich. Changing her name to Anna Sten, he embarked on a campaign which announced that she had spent a year learning English, mainly by seeing three films a week, in preparation for her American debut. Though she had acted in Pudovkin's *Storm Over Asia* and played opposite Jannings in *Tempest*, Miss Sten proved too frail for Hollywood, and the copies of European films in which Goldwyn cast her – as the wronged girl in *We Live Again*, a version of Tolstoy's *Resurrection*; a middle-European immigrant in *The Wedding Night*; an unlikely Parisian courtesan in *Nana* – all flopped, and her Hollywood career petered out, its most eloquent epitaph an unpublished verse in Cole Porter's wry *Anything Goes*:

> If Sam Goldwyn can with great conviction
> Instruct Anna Sten in diction
> Then Anna shows
> Anything Goes'.[63]

Sten's failure was typical. Having hired an attractive European, studios seemed baffled by what to do with her. Tala Birell's career never took fire in America. Elissa Landi, an Italian, had routine roles in Fox films after 1930, but despite a success in DeMille's *The Sign of the Cross* drifted into obscurity; Hungarian Zita Johann, whose international education made her a promising Broadway ingenue in the late 1920s, went to MGM in February 1929 at the invitation of Irving Thalberg; by August, having been offered only two tiny parts, neither acceptable, she returned to New York, richer to the extent of a huge salary, a Russian wolfhound and a Croatian cook. It was not until three years later that she enriched Universal with fine performances in *The Mummy* and *Tiger Shark*.

In this circus atmosphere an actress sometimes succeeded despite her employers. After having a hit in the 1934 *Extase*, in which she had a much-publicized nude scene, Viennese actress Hedy Kiesler was signed by MGM, though Louis B. Mayer made

(Above) *The Goldwyn publicity machine worked manfully to promote Anna Sten, but to little effect.* (Below) *She makes her ill-starred bid for Hollywood fame in the disastrous* Nana

AMERICA'S GREAT NEW STAR

Anna Sten

The world awaits, with expectant thrill her debut in American pictures as the voluptuous lady of the boulevards in the Samuel Goldwyn Production of

NANA

with Lionel Atwill · Richard Bennett · Mae Clarke
Phillips Holmes · Muriel Kirkland
Directed by Dorothy Arzner   Released thru United Artists

Pretty Italian actress Elissa Landi owed her Hollywood contract to the claim by her mother, Countess Zenardi Landi, to be the illegitimate child of Empress Elizabeth of Austria. Valuable as she was to the Fox and Paramount publicity departments when she gave tea on the set to visiting royal relatives, her career declined along with the fashion for nobility in the movies

it clear in the terms – she received only a six-month contract at $125 a week and had to find her own way to America – that he did not approve of 'dirty pictures'; his advisers had merely urged him to sign up a potential hot property before his competitors. Also given a contract by MGM, the Czech director of *Extase*, Gustav Machaty, who had worked with von Stroheim in Hollywood during the 1920s, was dumped, like many other promising but inconvenient foreigners, in the short subjects department, where he turned out two-reel *Crime Does Not Pay* films in company with fellow émigrés like Fred Zinnemann, while Hedy Kiesler, renamed Hedy Lamarr – Kiesler was too like 'Kiester', then popular slang for 'buttocks' – filled a series of supporting roles. It wasn't until 1937, when independent producer Walter Wanger borrowed her from MGM to appear opposite another unsuccessful émigré in *Algiers*, a remake of Jean Gabin's success *Pepe Le Moko*, that her career and that of Charles Boyer took off in America.

Actors and actresses were far from the only victims of Hollywood's rudderless progress of the early 1930s. Desperate for words to fill the vacuum, studios bought up any writer who

Hedy Kiesler (later Hedy Lamarr) in her famous nude sequence in Extase

looked remotely able to produce scenarios. Playwrights and novelists flooded into Hollywood between 1930 and 1935, many of them condemned to unproductive idleness on full salary while the ex-newsmen and magazine writers who had trained in the silent days continued to crank out the scripts that were actually filmed. George Kelly, author of the Broadway hit *Craig's Wife*, spent two months at MGM without even seeing Irving Thalberg, who had hired him. Angered at last by his inactivity, Kelly returned without notice to New York. A few weeks later, in Los Angeles on business, he dropped by his old office to see if any mail had accumulated. On his desk he found a pile of weekly salary cheques, and, as he turned to leave, Thalberg breezed by in the corridor, shook him warmly by the hand and said: 'I'm so sorry not to have had time to see you. Let's get together next week for sure.' The diffident English playwright Frederick Lonsdale, signed for movies on the basis of such successes as *The Last of Mrs Cheyney*, arrived in New York almost on the eve of *The Jazz Singer*'s opening, commented tersely to reporters, 'This will destroy the silent screen', and returned gratefully to London. J. B. Priestley spent two 1930s winters in the California desert with a nine-strong household that demanded that he prostitute himself to the movies. 'I could motor in a day to Hollywood and there pick up some odds and ends of script work,' he reported. 'An inspection of credit titles in the middle and late thirties will not reveal my name, for I surprised and gratified my script-writing colleagues by demanding to be left out of the credits.'[64]

Priestley found Hollywood 'daft but not boring'. At parties, he said, 'I held on to my drink and listened to talk about films, agents, Louis B. Mayer, diet, astrology, Louis B. Mayer, agents, films, always hoping I would think of something witty and memorable to say and be given a chance of saying it.'[65] Almost alone among the imported writers, Hugh Walpole found Hollywood congenial and the contract writing system unobjectionable. In 1933 MGM bought his novel *Vanessa* for $12,500; the following year a phone call from David Selznick in the early hours of the morning summoned him to spend 'a few weeks' in America writing the script for *David Copperfield*. He remained there, on and off, for the rest of his life. Producers anxious not to be beaten to any promising talent would offer a seven-year contract to people about whom they knew no more than could be discovered from a telephone book. During the early 1930s MGM had one hundred and eight writers under contract. It was enough for an agent to mention a wonderful novelist in Shanghai for him to be hired. C. S. Forester, in the 1930s a minor novelist with no particular reputation, had a brief spell in Hollywood as the result of just such a recommendation.

Hugh Walpole, whom I had never seen, nor spoken to, nor corresponded with, was at work in Hollywood . . . [He] was asked, inevitably, who among the young writers in England showed promise and might be useful in handling the new medium; it happened that he gave my name. So a letter arrived for me asking if, were I to be invited to come to work in Hollywood, would I accept the invitation? I wrote back saying that I would accept the invitation if it came, but I was quite sure that the invitation would never come. Yet it came, charged with all the desperate urgency of Hollywood, so that after forty-eight hours of active visa-seeking and desperate packing I found myself sailing for New York in the old *Aquitania*.[66]

Forester found Hollywood's skin-deep emotionalism stimulating, but his lack of interest in or facility for screenwriting soon became apparent.

After going along from one job to another I found myself engaged by Irving Thalberg . . . to write a screenplay about Charles Stewart Parnell. No two people on earth, perhaps, were less suited to work together than Thalberg and me; and perhaps the spirit of Parnell did nothing to soften any personal difficulties. Then, idly, I noticed the announcement of a sailing next day from San Pedro of the Swedish ship *Margaret Johnson* . . . with freight and passengers for Central American ports, the Panama Canal and England . . . There was the instant realization that I wanted no more of Hollywood . . . Within the hour I was a free man.[67]

Forester's first Hollywood visit – he was to have one other, equally unproductive – resulted in nothing filmable. *Parnell*, with Clark Gable in the title role as the Irish patriot, finally saw release in 1937 scripted by a bizarre but distinguished committee including John van Druten, Lenore Coffee and S. N. Behrman. But the long voyage back to England gave Forester the peace he needed to develop the first of his novels about the popular character of Captain Horatio Hornblower.

Any foreign artist, not only a writer, could expect a Hollywood offer if their work had any application to sound film, even when the slightest pause for reflection would have revealed some absurd drawback. Diminutive tenors and haggard sopranos trickled into Los Angeles off every train, and in one case the wayward impulse of Fox's production head Winfield Sheehan prompted him to offer a two-film contract to English night-club star Florence Desmond, an accomplished mimic who in 1933 enjoyed some popularity with a record called 'The Hollywood Party' on which she imitated Garbo, Dietrich, and Janet Gaynor. Apparently tickled by the accuracy of her mimicry, Miss Gaynor mentioned the record to Sheehan, who cabled his London office to arrange a screen test. When her manager, Archie Selwyn, told Sheehan that MGM's Edmund Goulding, then visiting London, had told Miss Desmond he was planning to make a film called *The Hollywood Party* in which she might have a part, Sheehan, afire at the prospect of losing someone to another studio, cabled: 'To hell with the test. We'll take a chance and sign her up.'

Miss Desmond signed a Fox two-picture contract at $1000 a week – just as well, since the film of *The Hollywood Party*, when it appeared, was a clumsy fantasy starring Jimmy Durante in which both Goulding and Miss Desmond would have been ashamed to take part. Clearly baffled as to how an impersonator could fit into sound films, Fox sent her around its theatres to do her night-club act as a warm-up to the night's movie, matched her with Will Rogers in an inconsequential comedy, *Mr Skitch*, then used up the balance of her contract by having her imitate Garbo, Dietrich and Zasu Pitts for a puppet sequence in one of the last American films of another unsuccessful import, Lilian Harvey. Eight months after her arrival, a slightly shopworn Miss Desmond, wasted by her employers and skinned by her manager, was on her way back to London.

Those who remained in Hollywood and succeeded often found problems the nature of which they had never remotely expected in England. Walpole in particular found the society initially delightful, especially its casual hedonism and the company of stars like Norma Shearer and Anne Harding. (H. G. Wells too thought Hollywood's greatest delight its beautiful women.) 'It is lovely to sit under the moon at midnight,' Walpole wrote, 'and watch these beautiful creatures with practically nothing on play tennis under artificial light. But I think why I am really happy is that I am free for the first time from all the English jealousy that I've suffered from for years. No one here cares a hang about the relative merits of English writers;'[68] Walpole was still smarting from the vicious parody inserted by Somerset Maugham in his *Cakes and Ale*. After the difficult apprenticeship of *David Copperfield*, complicated by the casting of an intransigent Charles Laughton as Mr Micawber, a role later played by W. C. Fields, Walpole steamed through *Little Lord Fauntleroy* in a month, was delighted with the film version of *Vanessa* and even acted as a garrulous vicar in one of Selznick's films. The director ordered take after take, hoping that the writer's improvised sermon would dry up, but his invention never flagged.

When Walpole finally succumbed to a variation of the Hollywood malaise, it was, as in many other cases, a result of the community's self-satisfaction and indolence emphasizing a defect in his personality. He wrote to a friend:

This place is making me lazier and lazier. It isn't a good sort of laziness in which you recuperate but a bad sort in which your character becomes weaker and weaker, and you care less and less whether you do anything properly or not. I've just been telling John Collier [the

English short-story writer] that he'll be completely and utterly damned, body and soul, if he stays here much longer, but he tells me that he wants to be damned, is longing to know what it's like.[69]

The bulk of new arrivals in Hollywood during 1933 and 1934 could not afford the luxury of Collier's search for self-illumination in the movie crucible, involved as they were in the more mundane task of merely staying alive.

In February 1933 the Reichstag burned down, Hitler assumed power and, among other policies, brought his plans to purge Germany of Jews and Communists into the open. The events came as no surprise to most Jews and Germans of the Left; the pattern of Nazi expansion was traditional enough to be transparent, and the wisest had already made their plans. When, on the day after the Reichstag fire, storm troopers moved to arrest known left-wing intellectuals, most, including playwright Bertholt Brecht and other socialist ideologues, had gone to ground. From then on, the pattern of escape from Germany became, as it would later do with the Jews, almost ritualistic. From Berlin, Brecht, his wife and son fled to ostensibly neutral Austria. In April, friends also smuggled out his daughter Barbara, whom it was feared the Nazis would use to blackmail him back to Germany.

From Vienna the escape route divided. The leftists often went to Czechoslovakia. After Hitler outlawed all political parties save his own, Prague became the headquarters of what had been the country's biggest party, the German Social Democrats, and Karls-bad, on the German border, a convenient distribution point for anti-Nazi literature. For the Jews and Communists, Czechoslovakia seemed too close to Germany for comfort, and the refugees of 1933, who included Thomas and Heinrich Mann, Lion Feucht-wanger, Arnold Zweig and, among the film-makers, Erich Pommer and Fritz Lang, preferred the remoteness and comfort of France. The richer émigrés settled down on the Riviera, where they had been joined by 1935 by such luminaries as Toscanini, Sholem Asch, Maurois, Jules Romains and Stravinsky. Less elevated names, including Emeric Pressburger, made for Paris, where there was work, even if it was not always as regular as they liked:

'The French were always very generous with visas, so I went to Paris. I arrived on the first of May, 1933, speaking not a word of French. In the next two years I learned some French and got a little name in the film industry, but I couldn't stand it for any longer. The French film industry took gladly all those people who had worked in Germany, because they had made some very successful films, but France was entirely different to Germany: haphazard. A contract didn't mean anything. I worked first for a small film producer who also ran a racing stable. Friends of mine said: "You know, he will never pay you." But they told me to learn the names of some horses he owned and look in the paper to see when they were running. If they were running I would go to the racing and when his horse won I, with one or two other people, would go up to him and say: "Look, I need the money very badly and it is sixteen months I am waiting for it", and he would put his large hand – he was a large man – into his pocket, which was full of banknotes, take out a handful and say "Count that".

'One day I had a visitor from America, another ex-Hungarian, who was in a rather important position with a finance house. He was coming to France looking for businesses in which he could invest. I was the first person he telephoned in Paris and we dined at Fouquets. I told him, "I can't stand this situation any longer," and told him about my troubles. "What was that name again?" he asked. It turns out that this very chap has requested some money to put into his business. My friend said: "From what you tell me I don't think I can do business with him, but I will make sure you get your money." He had written my friend saying that he had never signed his name to a contract he hadn't kept. "Give me your contract," my friend said, "and I will make sure you are paid." So I was very glad, but when I met two days later my friend he said: "I am afraid I didn't get your money." When the producer was shown my contract he said: "It is true I have always honoured any contracts I have signed – but I did not sign this one." It turned out he had someone in his office who signed small contracts like mine, but since the signature was not readable I had thought it was his. So I never got my money. It was then I decided French films were not for me.'

In September 1935 Pressburger sailed for London and a long and successful career as writer/director in association with Michael Powell.

British/Hungarian producer Alexander Korda (rear left, in glasses) exhibits some of his international team – including Marlene Dietrich, Conrad Veidt, Elsa Lanchester, Edward G. Robinson, Googie Withers and Douglas Fairbanks Jnr

Although Pommer and Lang managed to set up *Liliom* in Paris, with Charles Boyer, a production which gave them an entrée to Hollywood, most expatriates soon found England a more promising base, and for the next five years an émigré community grew in London, particularly at the Denham studios owned by Alexander Korda. Robert Mayer and Carl Wiene settled in the precarious safety of Britain; Conrad Veidt, driven from Hollywood by sound, preferred London to the dubious delights of Berlin and signed with Korda, though Hungarians predominated in Korda's casual regime. His brothers Zoltan and Vincent, director and décor expert respectively, and ex-Hollywood scenarist Lajos Biro controlled an eccentric but productive studio which profited

from the growing resentment of America's domination of the British film industry, an irritation that culminated in the largely ineffective legislation which forced Hollywood to plough part of its British profits back into local production. A businessman of sporadic genius, Korda backed his hunches with reckless courage – as when he placed his two biggest stars, Charles Laughton and Conrad Veidt, under generous long-term contract – only to let his advantage slip away; though the US success of *Rembrandt* and *The Private Life of Henry VIII* made Laughton an international star, Korda's personal arguments with the actor prevented him from using him in a film for almost the entire term of his agreement.

By contrast, some of the films made by his London Films teetered on the lip of absurdity. Deciding to make Anthony Gibbs's *Young Apollo*, a somewhat tiptoe sketch of university life at Oxford, Korda imported the German director Leontine Sagan, whose greatest success had been *Maedchen in Uniform*, a famous study of sexual repression in a girls' school. 'Leontine Sagan,' Gibbs said diplomatically, 'was a bit mannish. . . . "Take me," she said, "to a very high place. I must go where I can see all Oxford. . . ." So I took her to the roof of the Bodleian. . . . She sat on the parapet for a long time, smoking a Turkish cigarette, with her chiselled face half turned to look over Oxford and be revered. . . .'[70] She outlined to Gibbs some additions she required to the script, a leitmotif of *A Midsummer Night's Dream* plus some new scenes.

'I want a kaffeehaus scene. Perhaps a brothel? There is a well known house in Oxford?' 'Well,' I said, 'there's Fullers, and the Kardomah, and of course . . .' 'A scene, you know, where the boys are sitting with their women, and the camera passes from one table to the other, and you hear snatches of conversation, the sort of thing boys talk about, you know, when they are with their women.' I said I thought that was a very good idea. 'Tell me,' she said, 'is there much homosexuality among the boys?'[71]

Korda had his competitors. Ex-Berlin journalist Max Schach set up Trafalgar Films, which specialized as energetically in Austrian émigrés as Korda did in Hungarians. For Schach, Elizabeth Bergner and her husband Paul Czinner made *Dreaming Lips*, and Richard Tauber appeared in an abortive version of *I Pagliacci* directed by Karl Grune and with a script allegedly contributed to by Bert Brecht. Schach also, without much success, imported Americans like Anne Harding, Jimmy Durante and director Rowland V. Lee to make films in London. The incomparable Fritz Kortner, star of *Danton* and *Warning Shadows*, who had fled to Britain in 1933 after hearing of the fellow supporters of Brecht who had been arrested in their dressing-rooms shortly after Hitler took power, struggled to perfect his English, a task which took two years. Writer John Kahan would often see him in the lobby of the Dorchester, where Kortner would shout proudly, after consulting a little book he carried: 'I am now knowing so-many-thousand words of English.' Schach finally backed Grune in an ambitious production of *Abdul the Damned* in which Kortner, with typical Viennese relish, played the dissolute last Sultan of Turkey. Lavish oriental sets, sound support from Nils Asther and John Stuart and a score by Hanns Eisler, another refugee, unfortunately failed to save the film from disaster, but it remains a fascinating fossil from the disordered days during which Hitler's armies ate into the capitals of Europe and pressed on towards England.

Like Korda, Schach financed his activities by fiscal presti-

Fritz Kortner (left) *with John Hodiak and Madeleine Lebeau in* Somewhere in the Night

digitation and personal drive. With insufficient money existing for a true film industry, producers could only exploit a devalued cultural currency and hope the attractions of Hollywood did not wake one's actors to their exploitation. When the bubble burst, it did so explosively, and from 1938, when the new Films Act forced Americans to leave a large percentage of their profits in the UK, a rule which accelerated the production of 'quota quickies' with wholly British casts and crews, émigré production almost ceased. Only Korda, inconveniently at large in Britain and the USA, survived, surprisingly unresented by the finance companies whose millions he had lost. In the 1940s Emeric Pressburger was surprised to hear that Korda had taken an apartment in the same luxury block as an ex-London Films shareholder of whose fortune the producer had lost millions. Did the two old partners, Pressburger asked, ever meet on the stairs? And, if so, what happened? 'Oh, they often run into one another,' he was told. And? 'The financier is always hoping that Alex will invite him to dinner.'

By 1938 most émigrés had lost faith in England as a refuge. The government, once generous in the matter of entry permits, was clamping down, and new arrivals often had to undergo humiliating searches and interrogations. Jewish refugees, and some British film artists also, prudently made plans to retreat to America when the inevitable invasion came. For some, however, the running had to stop. Stefan Zweig, among the most distinguished of the refugee writers, escaped from Austria with most of his fortune and library intact, and was thus able to turn down the offers made by Hollywood in 1933. He did lecture tours of the USA, collaborated desultorily on a few film scripts, all with little real interest. 'You know,' he told Karl Zuckmayer, 'we've about had what life has to offer. From now on it's a downhill course. However the war turns out, there's a world coming into which we won't fit any longer.' After a visit to Brazil in 1936 for a PEN conference, Zweig conceived a passion for the country and when he left Europe decided in common with many other refugees – Mexico in particular played host to a large group of German radicals and Communists – to settle in South America. But even there life offered little. In February 1942 he and his mistress took overdoses of veronal and lay down together to die. André Maurois delivered a eulogy on their deaths which seems appropriate to all the artist refugees who did not have the guts to claw their way to the barred shelter of the USA. 'Many men of feeling,' he wrote, 'must have meditated, the day when they learned of this double suicide, on a responsibility which is that of all of us, and on the shame of a civilization that can create a world in which Stefan Zweig cannot live.'

11 THE GOLDEN DOOR

'Give me your tired, your poor,' reads the conclusion of Emma Lazarus's 'The New Colossus' engraved inside the base of the Statue of Liberty, 'Your huddled masses yearning to breathe free/The wretched refuse of your teeming shore./Send these, the homeless, tempest-tost, to me/I lift my lamp beside the golden door.' A moving promise but one which, to students of contemporary history, ironically encapsulates the United States' talent for rhetoric at the expense of action. Although a wave of middle-European and Irish immigration fuelled the industrial dynamism of the 1880s, America remained deeply suspicious of any attempt by foreigners to establish themselves on her soil, an attitude reflected and often magnified to a phobia in the foreign communities where refugees tended to cluster. Many centres of immigrant life had as their nucleus a political or religious minority which fled from Europe to escape nineteenth-century persecution, and while their original beliefs had often faded away, a suspicion of the European past, combined with a pride in and intention to protect their American success, discouraged any sympathy for later arrivals.

The first refugees from Hitler in 1933 encountered a German-American community divided on social, political and geographic grounds which, far from welcoming them with open arms, viewed their compatriots with suspicion. Hitler, it was pointed out, had done nothing to them, except perhaps threaten a little investigation, from which they had nothing to fear – if they were innocent. The rest had been mere discriminatory noises, hardly enough to cause one to flee from a legally constituted government. 'The relationship of the German anti-Nazi exiles to the *Auslanddeutschtum* in the US,' one historian said, 'can be described as singularly unharmonious. The latter did not provide the kind of support which, for example, émigrés from Italy, Poland, France and Czechoslovakia found, and were on the whole opposed or indifferent to the efforts of the anti-Nazis.'[72] A minority of established German-Americans opposed Hitler's policies, the majority declared themselves uninterested, while about 5 per cent were active Fascist supporters.

If the first refugees found the attitude of their own people lukewarm, that of the US government was glacial. Following the anti-German hysteria of the First World War and the growth of isolationism, the American tradition of free entry to immigrants had rapidly deteriorated. With the lame justification of wishing to maintain the racial balance that existed pre-1914, Congress in successive Acts had set national quotas for immigrants, ignoring the fact that European conditions had changed utterly during the war. Political unrest drove thousands of Poles and Czechs to America in the 1920s just as famine had starved the Irish from their homes in the 1880s. Now, in the late 1920s and 1930s, the victimized Jews, Catholics and Socialists of Germany and Austria looked to the US for a new home, only to discover that most places in the US allocation of immigrants (slashed from 900,000 in 1900 to 153,774 in 1929) were reserved for the Polish and Irish who no longer needed a haven. As the Immigration Department increased the financial, social, legal and political obstacles for prospective immigrants it became clear that regulation had become a pretext to impose a discriminatory barrier against middle-Europeans, and against Jews in particular.

The story of America's discrimination against the refugees from Hitler's Germany has been told in greater detail elsewhere, and one cannot read it without a horror and despair made even more painful by the fantasy which the media, and particularly Hollywood, erected to cover the truth. Films like *Casablanca* and *Above Suspicion* showed the USA as alert to the Nazi menace, sympathetic to Hitler's enemies but hampered by the necessities of diplomacy from aiding them. When their entry into the war made it possible, the tale goes on, mountains were moved to rescue those who could be saved. Yet, because of a tacitly discriminatory policy, only a fraction of even the heartlessly small quota of immigrant places was ever filled. Between 1 July 1933 and 30 June 1943, 476,930 aliens were taken into the USA – only 165,756 of them Jews. The total US quota from Nazi-controlled countries for that decade was 1,500,000 – 400,000 *more* than were admitted. One observer is scathing in his summation of the Immigration Department's policies. 'In the years between 1933 and 1943, the American tradition of sanctuary for the oppressed was uprooted and despoiled. It was replaced by a combination of political expediency, diplomatic evasion, isolationism, indifference and raw bigotry.'[73]

For the Jewish or leftist émigrés with literary or film experience who waited in Zurich, Vienna or Paris for Hitler's next move, Hollywood became the focus of all their hopes. The necessity for some guaranteed employment in America before a visa could be issued, the possibility that colleagues already admitted to the USA could steer a course through the maze of bureaucratic barriers, and the promise of massive material success for those who reached California made an American movie contract the most sought-after of prizes.

Those still in Europe looked with envy at shrewder compatriots who, from the moment that US investment in Europe began to shrink during the Crash and the traditional isolationism reasserted itself, had seen that one had to be in Hollywood to succeed in the international film business. In the late silent and early sound period, a number of ambitious middle-European directors seized the opportunity of a Hollywood contract. Jack L. Warner, on one of his European buying expeditions of the mid-1920s, saw the work of both Mihaly Kertesz and Wilhelm Dieterle, inviting them to Hollywood where they became pillars of the Warner Brothers newsy low-budget drama style. After the disasters of the first sound days, studios hesitated to import actors purely for their value in foreign areas, though Fox did recall the exiled Charles Boyer in 1934 for the first step of a rich Hollywood career culminating in *Algiers*, and Universal, hoping for a performer comparable in menace to the late Lon Chaney, found Peter Lorre loitering nervously in Paris along with many fellow colleagues of Brecht, and offered him the contract that was to make him one of the cinema's most memorable character players. But directors remained the most valued quarry. Though its industrial skill and technical polish had given the American cinema total ascendancy over European rivals, a sense of artistic inferiority remained. It was a weakness on which the clever resourcefully played, as producer Robert Lord discovered at

Peter Lorre in one of his most famous roles, as the soldier-of-fortune Ugarte opposite Humphrey Bogart in Michael Curtiz's Casablanca

Warner Brothers in 1937.

'One day I was going about my business when I was told Mr Warner wanted to see me. All producers are in or out of favour – you are either a hero or a bum, depending on the last picture and the boss's mood – and at this time I was in favour. He said: "Since you have done so well, I am going to do you a big favour. I'm going to let you work with the best director in the world. Have you ever heard of Anatole Litvak?" I said "No". He said: "I am surprised. You have not heard of Litvak, the best director in Europe?" "I'm sorry, Jack. I haven't." "Well, I'm sorry for you. He is under contract here and he is going to make a picture *Tovarich* from a French play of Jacques Deval. This is a great privilege, because you will learn from this man; we will all learn from him. Go to New York and see the play." I went to New York – living in a suite at the Plaza – saw the play and was thrilled to peanuts. I said: "I can write this. It doesn't really take much writing." Warner said: "No, no, no, no! We don't want you to write this. We don't think you have the finesse to write this kind of thing. Casey Robinson is going to write it." I knew Casey and why he had more finesse than me I didn't understand.

But Warner was so high on this thing that I didn't want to start making waves. I said: "Do you want us to start on the script or do you want us to wait for Mr Litvak?" "You will have to start the script because Mr Litvak is now in this country. He is at RKO finishing an English version of a French picture he made; one of the greatest pictures ever made." He showed me the name – he had it written on a piece of paper: *L'Equipe* – The Team. "Have you ever heard of this picture?" he said, and I had to say: "Jack, I never heard of it." He said: "I'm beginning to wonder about you," and I said: "I'm beginning to wonder about *myself*." I always thought I was a fairly hip guy and I knew pretty much what was going on.

'At any rate I asked: "Do you want me to go over to RKO and meet Mr Litvak?" He said: "Oh, my God, no! Don't disturb him. Don't bother him. He's very, very busy. He's quite sensitive. Don't call him. He has accepted you." I said: "He did?" So Casey got to work on the script. Weeks passed and weeks and weeks. I said to Hal Wallis: "Hal, should I call this gentleman?" He said: "Don't bother him. When he gets through over there, he'll come over here." They really had the red carpet treat-

Anatole Litvak and Anthony Perkins clown on the set of Goodbye Again

ment for him. I found out later that the whole thing was the work of the master bullshitter of all time, Charlie Feldman, the agent. Charlie did the whole thing. He was good at that.'

The relationship between Lord and Litvak did not improve when they finally met. After delaying shooting through his romance with Miriam Hopkins, whom he later married, Litvak insisted on using three cameras for a trivial rooftop sequence inserted into the play, consulting on the casting with Feldman and writing into his contract an agreement that the film should be cut by his personal editor, the Dutchman Henri Rust. Litvak's reputation soon evaporated. *Tovarich*, despite good performances from Charles Boyer and Claudette Colbert, emerged as a routine filmed stage play to the cost of which Litvak's delays had added $400,000, and when the US version of *L'Equipe* also flopped the director became more accessible.

In Vienna and Berlin, film-makers who had rejected Hollywood overtures in the early 1930s reassessed their decision in the light of events. Otto Preminger, the meteoric young Jewish producer

Otto Preminger, one of the most successful of the Viennese refugees to Hollywood

who had succeeded Reinhardt at the elegant Josefstadt theatre, changed his mind about Gilbert Miller's offer to direct a Broadway play and also seized the opportunity of a 1935 Vienna buying visit by Fox's Joe Schenck to sign a Hollywood deal. Joe Pasternak, a Hungarian who, after experience at Universal in the 1920s as an assistant director, returned to Berlin as the company's German manager, prudently moved in 1933 to Budapest, where he made two pictures with Fransiska Gaal (an actress being groomed for possible Hollywood stardom but who had what little US success she achieved on the Broadway stage), and thence to Vienna. In 1935 he appealed to Universal for a safe post and came to Hollywood accompanied, as Lubitsch had been, by an équipe, which comprised director Henry Kosterlitz and writer Felix Joachimson. The Pasternak coterie exemplified everything that had ever been said about Hungarians in Hollywood. Pasternak glimpsed a pudgy soprano named Deanna Durbin in a short and built her, against studio inclinations, into a major star, a coup Joachimson – renamed Jackson – clinched by marrying her, after which he wrote a number of Durbin vehicles which Pasternak produced and Kosterlitz – renamed Koster – directed. With the Universal studios as an anchor, Pasternak threw a lifeline to a number of stranded relatives, among them composer Nicholas Brodszky and Pasternak's brother-in-law S. Z. 'Szöke' Szakall, the cherubic comedian, then stuck in London playing comic counts in shoe-string operettas, who later, as 'Cuddles' Sakall, built his broken English and quivering jowls into a successful Hollywood career.

For many Viennese, the decision to abandon Europe was hastened by Max Reinhardt's defection to Hollywood. With The Master gone, most felt, little of worth remained. In retrospect, those who knew Reinhardt must have seen the decision as inevitable. The European unease about his work which had been growing in the wake of Brecht and his iconoclastic new drama had not reached the USA, where, mainly on the strength of his success in the 1924 tour of *The Miracle*, both public and theatre regarded him as the stage spectacle's supreme master. Hollywood's efforts to lure him into making a film had seldom flagged, despite his poor record in the field. After Zukor's failure to import him at the same time as Lubitsch, Reinhardt signed a four-film contract with a German company but produced only three works,

Viennese comedian S. Z. 'Cuddles' Sakall, with his wife. The caption claimed: 'Although Cuddles may play schmaltzy Viennese musicians on the screen, he prefers boogie woogie in private life'

The Island of the Holy, Venetian Nights and a static record of *The Miracle*'s Berlin production. Put off by the grasping Berlin film people, he founded his own company, but it never made a film. Finally Joe Schenck, known for his hectoring persuasiveness, managed to coax Reinhardt into contemplating a production for United Artists, and between 1925 and 1928 even Reinhardt and Hugo von Hoffmansthal, who was to write the script, began to believe a film might actually reach the screen.

To star, they chose Lillian Gish, whose icy purity he and Hoffmansthal found fascinating. 'She is the descendant of twenty generations of puritans,' Hoffmansthal explained. 'A religious ecstatic. Goodness and pain are what she inimitably brings to expression.'[74] After considering a picture on Joan of Arc – Miss Gish declined on the grounds that she could never make such a role convincing to French audiences – they elected to film the true story of Theresia von Konnersreuth, the Austrian peasant woman in whose hands the stigmata – bleeding wounds in imitation of Christ's – had appeared. Miss Gish visited Reinhardt at Leopoldskron, made a pilgrimage to Konnersreuth, and Reinhardt prepared to sail for Hollywood to begin work on the nearly completed Hoffmansthal script; but in 1929, partly because of the sound revolution, the project collapsed and Reinhardt's career entered a final decline.

In December 1928, Hoffmansthal, never the easiest man with whom to work, had announced abruptly that he found Reinhardt's vision of Theresia 'passive' and pulled out of the film. Political in-fighting among the Reinhardt circle was unceasing, and Hoffmansthal appears to have taken offence at some real or imagined slight connected with the Salzburg festival. Before the rift could be patched up, he suddenly died, depriving Reinhardt of his most glittering collaborator and of the support his prestige drew from sections of the establishment. A few weeks later, in an even greater loss, Reinhardt's brother died in a plane crash. For years, Edmund Reinhardt, a skilled businessman, managed the teetering Reinhardt empire, keeping it miraculously intact despite his brother's wild expenditure and vaulting ideas. Reinhardt had relied on him totally for business advice as he had depended on his *dramaturgs* like Arthur Kahane and Stefan Hoch – combination play-readers, dramatists, associate producer/directors – to realize the generalized conceptions of a work he was so skilled in creating. The double loss of Edmund and Hoffmansthal disturbed him deeply. In a rare personal letter to an actress who had written consoling him, he said: 'I often travel again the long wonderful road which I travelled with Hoffmansthal, and on which I many times met you. It is dark. Around us the lights are going out. We are lost always in time. My heart is heavy from all that remains unsaid and undone.'[75]

In 1927 Reinhardt had revived his American reputation – if revival was needed – with a three-play season in New York. Brooks Atkinson called his colossal productions in German of *A Midsummer Night's Dream*, *Danton's Death* and *Everyman* at the Century Theatre 'superb; organized and played with an easy versatility beyond anything comparable in America at the time. . . .'[76] Reinhardt received with little enthusiasm an invitation to stage the same three plays elsewhere in the USA as he had *The Miracle* in 1924–25, notably in California, where he was offered the 25,000-seat Hollywood Bowl, the largest audience

Jack Warner (left) *with Max Reinhardt* (centre), *imported to direct* A Midsummer Night's Dream, *and William Randolph Hearst*

with which he had ever worked. In common with many other artists, Reinhardt found the offer more seductive in 1932 than he had in 1928, when the Konnersreuth film had occupied his attention. In America the lights had not gone out. With little heart-searching he packed his possessions and sailed for New York.

For the Hollywood Bowl, Reinhardt decided to stage his most lavish version yet of *A Midsummer Night's Dream*, a play he had produced several times since 1905, seldom with any major alteration in costume, playing or setting. Drawings of Berlin presentations in the early 1920s are almost identical with those from the Hollywood production of 1934. From the start Reinhardt took a high hand with his hosts. After one look at the Bowl, a vast saucer sliced out of the hillside, he ordered the large music shell dismantled so as not to interfere with his staging, and sent his son Gottfried to the casting director with his schedule of preferred stars. These included Charlie Chaplin as Bottom, Greta Garbo as Titania, Clark Gable as Demetrius, Gary Cooper as Lysander, John Barrymore as Oberon, W. C. Fields as Quince, Wallace Beery as Snug, Walter Huston as Theseus, Joan Crawford as Hermia, Myrna Loy as Helena and Fred Astaire as Puck. How seriously he

(Above) *The Holly-wood Bowl, scene of Max Reinhardt's* Midsummer Night's Dream, *which Warner Brothers later filmed* (below)

meant this list is debatable. Reinhardt accepted without fuss the non-availability of his preferred stars and decided quixotically to cast the production mainly with minor character players and even unknowns. Gloria Stuart, the female lead in John Ford's *Air Mail*, became Hermia, with Jean Rouverol as second choice. As Rouverol's understudy he gave a chance to a young theatre student, Olivia de Havilland, who, when the other ladies dropped out to take up film offers, became Hermia and, overnight, a star.

Miss De Havilland was in Chicago with the road-tour company of the *Dream* a year later when Reinhardt cabled her to return to Hollywood. He had at last been invited, after some politicking among the studios by Ernst Lubitsch, to prepare for Warner Brothers a definitive film version of the play with no expense spared. 'For the first time in my life,' he told the press, 'I have realized my own dream of doing this play with no restriction on my imagination. . . . This is only the beginning of Shakespeare's alliance with the motion pictures.' Since Reinhardt had only a general notion of film production, technical control was handed to William Dieterle who, before becoming one of Warner's top directors, had acted in the Deutsches Theatre under Reinhardt, including a role in an early production of *A Midsummer Night's Dream*. The husky Dieterle, with his booming voice and white gloves, had his work cut out to realize Reinhardt's grandiose vision. As hordes of kindergarten 'fairies' milled amid a confusion of interlopers and hangers-on his voice roared desperately at the hordes of fussing parents: 'All mudders off der set; all mudders off der set!'

Confident of his ability to extract good performances from anyone, Reinhardt accepted a cast made up almost entirely of Warner Brothers contract players, including Dick Powell, James Cagney and Joe E. Brown. But in his staging he felt the lack of his skilled technical assistants, now scattered all over the world after being snapped up by eager producers the moment they left Vienna. Both Hock and Ernst Stern, the Deutsches Theatre designer, were in London, though even they might not have been able to solve the unique problems of making a film in Hollywood at a time when the studio machine worked with a speed even old hands found disconcerting. Shortly after shooting started, cameraman Hal Mohr had a call to hurry to the studio. Head of production Hal Wallis intended to close the film down as being impossible to shoot. In Mohr's words:

Part of Warner's advertising campaign for A Midsummer Night's Dream

They got so filled with what Reinhardt was going to do with Shakespeare the perspective in their thinking got beyond the realm of motion pictures . . . When the art director built the sets, they were going to make the damnedest forest you'd ever seen. He built a forest set that covered two full stages. It was so realistic you couldn't photograph it . . . The trees were so natural and so dense and so huge that there was no place to get any light through the damn things.[77]

Mohr took over the film, sprayed every dark area of the sets with aluminium paint and, with Reinhardt's approval, scattered glittering flakes through the rest to reflect the light – efforts for which he received an Academy Award.

Reinhardt's dream of an unfettered film of Shakespeare had little hope of achievement. His own languid approach to the production, which merely repeated the effects and action of his Hollywood Bowl staging, guaranteed this. But the film shimmers with reflections of his brilliance, coups that anyone who loves the play cannot fail to find affecting. Victor Jory's saturnine Oberon, erupting into the clearing at the head of his demonic guards with a chilling 'Ill met by moonlight, proud Titania', Olivia de Havilland's melting Hermia, and brilliant comic playing from James Cagney as Bottom, all augmented by Mendelssohn's music – adapted by another Viennese, Erich Wolfgang Korngold, an ex-child prodigy whom Reinhardt whisked to Hollywood specially for the film – do much to compensate for the lack of any real imaginative leap. Faced with what was plainly a box-office disaster, Warner Brothers gambled on a lavish advertising campaign to 'put the film over', even hiring hot-shot Broadway publicist Nathan Zatkin to cook up stunts to push the production. Zatkin spent several days in Washington with Senator Carter Glass, President of the American Bacon Society, coaxing him to seek an injunction against the film on the grounds that it misrepresented Shakespeare as the author when in fact it could be proved that Francis Bacon had written the play. Happily, the Senator thought better of the idea and declined at the last moment to co-operate. Warners compromised with a 'transatlantic première', with simultaneous showings of the film in both America and Britain, but with $1,300,000 sunk in it they had little hope of a profit. *A Midsummer Night's Dream* flopped and with it

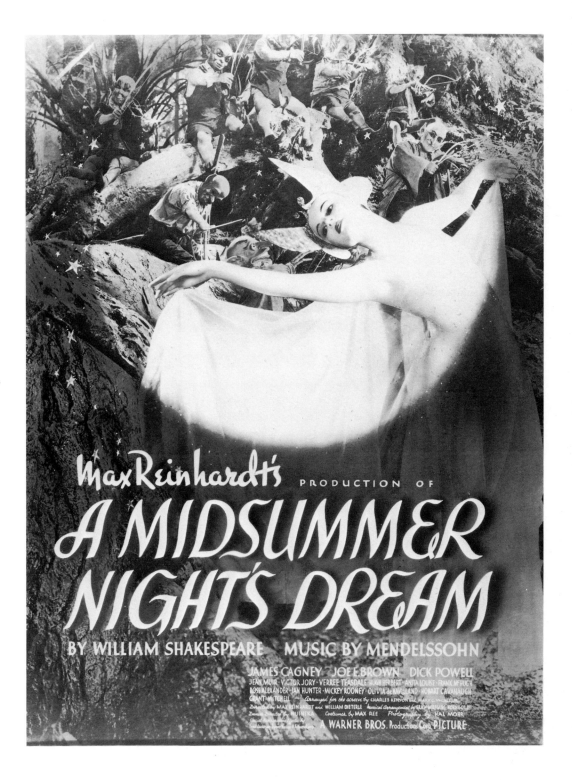

Reinhardt's hopes of a Hollywood career. Of the seven pictures provided for under his long-term contract, only one more was made, a travesty of *The Miracle* directed by his assistant on the *Dream*, Irving Rapper, and designed to cash in on the craze for religious films that followed *The Song of Bernadette*.

If Reinhardt had any cause to congratulate himself, it was for his foresight in leaving Vienna when he did. For those who remained in the hope that Nazi domination would be averted, 1935 ended their dreams. Hitler announced an Anschluss with Austria and the Nazis marched in. (Ironically, Reinhardt's Leopoldskron was immediately annexed by the Party as a conference centre.) Austrians, predominantly Catholic and middle-class, accepted the move with equanimity, though, as musicologist Hans Keller noted dryly, 'their enthusiasm tends to be underplayed these days.' In March 1935 he estimates that 70,000 people were arrested and subjected to indignities ranging from seizure – 'Aryanization' – of their property, through humiliating interrogation – standard questions all Jews were required to answer included 'How long have you been a homosexual?' and, paradoxically, 'How many Aryan girls have you seduced?' – to arrest, torture and murder. No respecters of persons, the Nazis inflicted the same indignities on even the most gifted Austro-Hungarian artists, but the actions of foreign embassies in Vienna, besieged for visas, were no less callous. Despite pleas that Jews who queued outside the British consulate all night for visas would certainly be brutally beaten by Nazis, the staff firmly refused to let them shelter inside, and the US consulate stolidly declined, despite pleas that delay could mean torture and death, to speed up the cumbersome immigration procedure which demanded such impossible submissions as an official copy of one's police record (obtainable only from the Nazi authorities). Other countries declined to make any move at all; the Australian consulate merely let thousands of visa applications pile up unopened on its desks.

In this climate of desperation and despair even the oldest friendships broke down. Jewish artists who approached colleagues with a real or fancied influence in Nazi circles seldom received much sympathy. Composer Emmerich Kalman, a Jew, hoped that his old friend Franz Lehar, whose wife Sophie was also

Jewish, could intercede on his behalf, since the Lehars had considerable contact with the German government. Lehar counselled co-operation until the situation was clearer, but when Nazi officers arrived to seize the Kalmans' house and belongings, phone calls to the Lehar residence remained unanswered. As the soldiers reluctantly left with promises to return later, Sophie Lehar finally answered Vera Kalman's call, telling her angrily: 'Don't you know we have our own troubles? Don't ask Franz to come.' Hitler later declared Mrs Lehar an 'honorary Aryan' in appreciation of her husband's gesture in writing a new overture to *The Merry Widow* in his honour. Not all artists could wield Lehar's influence, even if they wished to. In March 1938 Karl Zuckmayer rang his old friend Emil Jannings, then undergoing a rest cure in the Vienna Cottage Sanatorium, in the hope that he could influence the Nazis to allow him and his wife to escape to America. Jannings, Zuckmayer felt, sincerely wished to be of assistance. In his presence, he rang the German Embassy in Vienna and obtained an assurance from attaché Clemens von Ketteler that Catholics like Zuckmayer had nothing to fear. Two hours later, Nazis took Ketteler to a park in the middle of the city and murdered him. Zuckmayer left as soon as he could pack his bags, arriving in America with nothing – unlike the fortunate Kalmans, who gained protection from the Hungarian government and got their possessions safely out of Vienna. Few had such luck. In November 1938 the last vestige of safety for Jews in Austria was swept away in the orgy of 'Kristallnacht,' the Night of Broken Glass, when Hitler used the shooting of a minor officer in the Paris embassy by a desperate Jewish boy as the pretext for a fury of destruction throughout 'Greater Germany'. One hundred and ninety-five synagogues were burned, 800 shops destroyed and 7,500 looted, 20,000 Jews arrested and sent to prison camps.

One would like to record that, as these horrors became generally known, the world's publishers, recording companies and film producers declined absolutely to trade with the murderers of German art and artists, but in fact the market for German material remained strong until the outbreak of war. When publishers and writers set up in exile, Goebbels dumped confiscated books, both 'acceptable' and 'unacceptable' in Nazi eyes, on the world market at a 25 per cent discount, thus undercutting foreign émigré editions, bringing in valuable hard currency – and compounding the offence by seizing the royalties of refugee writers, all of whom were 'stateless' under Nazi law. German films continued to show in both the US and Britain, particularly since Goebbels, to encourage the illusion of normality, approved the production of frothy fantasies like *Amphytrion* which had wide international appeal. Film exhibitors and distributors, particularly in Britain, took the bait. Gaumont-British, the mainly Jewish producers of Robert Flaherty's *Man of Aran*, documenting the harsh life of the Aran islanders and their struggle for survival, agreed as a condition of its sale to Germany that the names of writer John Goldman and musical director Louis Levy be removed from the credits and a laudatory foreword by Goebbels be added praising the film as one which 'exemplified all the virtues of simplicity, courage and endurance that Hitler wished to become characteristic of the German people'.[78]

Faced with this moral vacuum, minor Jewish entrepreneurs frequently set the only standards. When Basil Dean wanted a Tyrolean-type interlude for a 1930s Broadway production of *Autumn Crocus*, a horrified Shubert stage manager protested: 'You should ask for me to find someone to play *German* music?' Elsie Cohen, owner of London's prestigious Academy Cinema, recalled:

We showed German films up to 1937. From 1937 we more or less stopped. I saw the way things were going and didn't like it . . . In 1938 two Germans came to see me, and said: 'We'd like to buy the Academy.' I thought they were crazy. But they were serious. I said 'Not for sale' and they said 'And if we offer you a million pounds?' And I said 'Still not for sale. Who are you?' They belonged to some German state department, and they came back every day for a week. And I saw why. The Academy would have been the most wonderful propaganda for Hitler if he got hold of it.[79]

Far from protesting about the situation in Europe, Hollywood studios reflected the USA's prevailing isolationism, confirmed in this policy by the government, anxious not to offend powers still technically friendly. Paramount's tepid Spanish Civil War drama *The Last Train From Madrid* required special censorship permission before going into production; Fox halted *Alcazar* because of political fears; Walter Wanger shelved a film with a similar background; and MGM abandoned its adaptation of Sinclair

Lewis's *It Can't Happen Here* in the face of murmurs from
America's thriving Fascist groups, whose 'Brown Houses' all
over the country offered centres for protest and demonstration.
The studio initially tried to deny that the Lewis film had been
censored, claiming that Sidney Howard's script would cost too
much to film. Howard responded that he had seen a letter from
the Production Code Administration's Joseph I. Breen referring
to the story's 'dangerous material'. But, as Lewis's biographer
notes: 'Whether or not MGM had acted on the advice or orders of
the Hays office, the motive for stopping the film was probably
less political than economic. Not only would this film have been
banned in Germany and Italy and other foreign markets, but
probably all Metro films would henceforth have been kept out of
Germany and Italy.'[80] Rather than risk such reprisals, Hollywood
studios often shot alternative endings to films which might
offend, and were abject in their apologies if criticism slipped
through. In 1935 Adolph Zukor publicly repudiated Josef von
Sternberg's *The Devil Is a Woman* when Spain protested its
cavalier attitude to the Guardia Civil, and even burned a 'master
print' of the film on the front lawn of the Spanish Embassy in
Washington. Justifying the move Zukor commented without con-
scious irony: 'We do not make pictures with any idea of depicting
real life.'

Reality, particularly of the political kind, troubled Hollywood
to its core, and the few films made about Fascism followed the
prevailing cautious view. Even the trenchant *March of Time* documentary series used its 'Nazi Germany, 1938' to show an indus-
trious, apparently happy and well-cared for people united in a
common cause, a mildly critical commentary doing little to strip
the gloss from these pleasant visuals. Despite this placating policy,
Germany continued to ban American films – Fox's *My Weakness*
in 1934 because 'the lace panties on the girls would contaminate
the morals of the New Germany', *Country Doctor* (1936) on the
grounds of Jean Hersholt's alleged Jewish birth. Too greedy to
protest, the studios acquiesced, even entering into correspondence with the German censors to prove that Hersholt had no
Jewish relatives for three generations, but the ban naturally
stood. Only Warner Brothers took an anti-Nazi stand, and their
motives were less ideological than personal. Brownshirts had
beaten and killed Joe Kaufmann, their distribution man in

Berlin, encouraging Jack Warner in an uncharacteristic gesture to close the company's offices there. Partly for this reason, but also out of traditional interest in 'spot news', almost every 1930s film which stigmatized the Nazi regime came from Warner Brothers, notably *Confessions of a Nazi Spy* (1939) and the biographies of Zola, Juarez and Dreyfus whose sentiments were rephrased to bear on current events.

Their efforts made Warner Brothers a target for America's many Fascist groups, and both Hal Wallis and Jack Warner had calls threatening to burn their homes. Robert Lord, who produced *Confessions of a Nazi Spy*, and other members of the crew received threats. 'One of the assistants on the picture, Jesse, was a powerful guy, a bar-room brawler and very, very anti-Nazi. He had just learned that there was a Brown House in Los Angeles. It was on Georgia Street, near the Georgia Street police station. There was a museum of Nazi documents, with the Horst Wessel song. They met three times a week and drilled. Jesse said: "I'm going down there. You can take care of yourself – will you come with me?" I was scared to death. But the night we went there it was like a German restaurant. German waitresses with dirndls. We had some kind of pot roast, and beer – the best beer I ever drank. Everyone was immensely polite. We walked around the museum and they had pictures of everybody – Goebbels, Goering, Speer. There was a kind of librarian, a motherly-looking lady with grey hair. She said: "Good evening, gentlemen. Thank you for coming," Jesse was disappointed. He had brass knuckles. He was going to rip the place apart.'

Nazi influence in Hollywood could be more sinister. Immigration authorities frequently arrested German sailors who jumped ship in Los Angeles and were assumed to be potential Nazi infiltrators. Two servants in the house of Cedric Hardwicke, who led the émigré actors' committee, were found to be not Dutch, as he believed, but German, and some émigré performers did little to hide their Hitlerian sympathies. Dita Parlo, who had been imported to appear with Charles Boyer in the German version of *The Big House* in 1929, was later deported from France as a suspected German spy.

The abuse heaped on *Confessions of a Nazi Spy* and threats of blanket banning in Germany hardly encouraged anti-Fascist gestures. Hollywood's political conscience was non-existent. *Variety*'s

Dita Parlo with Paul Reno, production manager of Paramount's Joinville Studios

response to the events of March 1939 was an unbelievably bland: 'Hitler's reshuffling of central Europe in the past ten days is an additional blow to the American companies' foreign film income. . . . For the major companies, the German sweep through central Europe this month represents a loss of $2\frac{1}{2}$ to 3 per cent of the total foreign business.' Predictably, the USA showed little inclination to succour refugees whose names often stood high on Nazi 'wanted' lists. Countless Jews and Socialists, the latter particularly suspect to the Immigration authorities, were abandoned to the Gestapo and certain death. Nowhere in the world could refugees rely on consistent help. Half in sympathy with Hitler's stigmatizing of the Jews as the scourge of Europe, most countries refused to interfere in case the gesture should limit their own diplomatic manoeuvres. Even traditionally welcoming Switzerland tightened its restrictions, particularly on writers, many of whom could not publish under their own names while living in the country; a brisk market grew up in established Swiss writers 'renting' their names to the émigrés. Physical search and unfeeling interrogation faced many visitors to Britain, and when war broke out France interned all German nationals, Nazi and anti-Nazi alike, then, by refusing to release legitimate refugees as the Germans advanced, condemned most of them to eventual death in prison camps. But at least France had offered no 'golden door'. America's callous promise of sanctuary which it withdrew when an attempt was made to redeem it makes the USA's offences harder to forgive.

12 A JOURNEY OF NO RETURN

By 1940 Hollywood could no longer ignore the fact that thousands of men and women were dying when a word from the more influential members of the film community could save them, but this realization was not always easily translated into action. Even when a studio contract was ready and waiting for some stranded artist, a jungle of red tape had to be penetrated. Refugee intake was stemmed to a trickle by Immigration Department rules which demanded two personal guarantees from American citizens for each prospective visitor as well as absurdly detailed proof of their ability to support themselves. Some émigrés, having been admitted as visitors, had to leave and return via Cuba or Mexico to have their visas renewed, putting them through the same humiliations all over again. To the groups of desperate hopefuls in Paris, London and Zurich were added colonies in Havana and on the Mexican border; in *Hold Back the Dawn* (1941), directed by Billy Wilder, himself an ex-Viennese, Charles Boyer played an international charmer who marries a visiting American old-maid school teacher to secure his escape from Mexico, a far-from-rare solution for resourceful visa applicants.

On the East Coast small rescue committees had been fighting for years to force a realization of the situation on the government, but their generally leftist or Jewish sympathies had made it difficult to obtain the official ear. In 1940 Roosevelt belatedly set up the Advisory Committee on Political Refugees, a figurehead organization which did at least authorize the admission of a trickle of émigrés whose intellectual achievements made them special cases. But in October 1940 the Committee pointed out that of 567 distinguished European artists recommended for visas, only forty actually received them, the State Department delaying issue of the rest for fear of 'enemy agents' among those admitted. (Some émigrés were actually interned as suspected security risks, including Karl Völlmoller, whose confinement in various Californian prisons – without, his associates claim, any justification – broke him in health and spirit.) Fewer than half the 3,000 visas endorsed by the Committee were ever granted. Jewish, Communist and non-ideological agencies did their best to save those still free. American journalist Varian Fry ran an 'underground railway' from Marseilles for the most wanted refugees. Those he rescued included sculptor Jacques Lipschitz, painters Max Ernst and Marc Chagall, harpsichordist Wanda Landowska, and the authors Franz Werfel and Lion Feuchtwanger, the latter smuggled out of a French internment camp in women's clothes. Hundreds owed their lives to his thirteen months of intensive work, cut short when the Vichy government expelled him.

A disproportionately large percentage of the émigrés admitted to America headed for California. More than 5,000 Jews alone settled in Los Angeles between 1933 and 1945, and entrenched movie cliques regarded the influx with suspicion. The *New York Times* in March 1941 hinted uneasily: 'Not yet at the alarming stage, Hollywood's refugee problem is nevertheless giving some concern to certain people here.' It estimated that

forty or fifty well-known film workers from middle Europe have been more or less recently employed by the studios – at whose expense doesn't seem quite clear just now – and there are twice or three times that number waiting around on the off-chance that a job will be found for them. Technical jobs are pretty well protected by guilds and unions, and for the moment no concern need be felt over them. A scattering of secretaries, research workers, readers, messengers and the like have been brought in; but probably no more than are being absorbed by other Southern California business and industry from the 6,000 to 25,000 refugees believed to have sought home and work here in the past year and a half.

These careful generalizations disguised a scheme whereby a vaguely-titled European Film Fund, chaired by Ernst Lubitsch, slipped distinguished émigrés into minor jobs at the studios so as to justify their continued presence in Hollywood. A noted historian could find himself 'researching' some costume drama, a musical academic like the Vienna Conservatory's Dr Eugen Zador 'apprenticed' to Herbert Stothart at MGM. 'How on earth can I tell Dr Zador what he does for a picture isn't right?' a technician told the *Times*. 'He has forgotten more about music than I will ever learn.' Minor actors who had prudently come to Hollywood in the 1930s now guaranteed the visas of their late superiors. Adolf Licho, once General Manager of the Volksbuhne and Deutsches Theatres, came to America in 1941 with the help of Fritz Feld, who had once performed for him as a character actor and now thrived playing mercurial head waiters in movie comedies. Feld found bit parts for the penniless Licho, but the aged and dispirited old man died in 1944, one of many who arrived in Hollywood only to succumb, it seemed, to hopelessness.

Among the established communities, particularly the British, war in Europe posed problems as embarrassing in 1940 as they had been in 1914, when foreigners established in the movies had usually found excuses to explain their inability to enlist in the armies of their homelands. According to Robert Florey, 'Erich von Stroheim – Lieutenant Erich Oswald Carl von Stroheim von Nordenwald of the Imperial Mariahilfe Military Academy, as he introduced himself – told his intimate friends that his Uncle Emil – or was it August? – having paid a debt of a few thousand kronen that he had contracted, he, von Nordenwald, had been obliged to leave the service of his Imperial Majesty Franz Josef, a condition imposed by his uncle (?). The same uncle had then obliged him to emigrate to America in 1909. . . . When Austria and the other European powers mobilized, Stroheim said that not being rich enough to purchase a ticket for Vienna he was obliged to remain in Los Angeles and was heart-broken not to be able to go and serve his Emperor and Vaterland on the battlefield . . . not mentioning that the Austrian Consulate-General (and also the German, French, British, etc.) had advised the men under the jurisdiction of the Consulate that the Austrians living in southern California should present themselves at the Consulate to receive a free ticket allowing them to rejoin their country for military duty (and money for expenses during the train/boat trip). Many of the foreign men didn't go and after the war couldn't return to the country of their birth having been declared defaulters to the Army during war-time.'

Many Britons made no secret of the fact that they were unwilling to return home in 1940 and face the draft, and the accusation of the British press that they had 'Gone With the Wind Up' had some foundation. On the other hand, those who did return often found their gesture unappreciated. Novelist Michael Arlen was rejected by the British army on the grounds that his Armenian parentage made him politically suspect, and the RAF implied to David Niven that his move to enlist was a mere publicity stunt. An actors' deputation finally approached the British Ambassador in Washington, then Lord Lothian, for guidance. He told them to stay put. 'It is quite unfair to condemn older actors who are simply obeying this ruling as "deserters",' he explained later to H.M. Government. 'Moreover, the maintenance of a powerful British nucleus of older actors in Hollywood is of great importance to our own interests, partly because they are continually championing the British cause in a very volatile community which would otherwise be left to the mercies of German propagandists, and because the production of films with a strong British tone is one of the best and subtlest forms of British propaganda.' This directive hardly covers the handful of British producers, directors and stars who suddenly found American opportunities too pressing to ignore as Hitler's armies massed across the Channel in 1940–41. In particular, Elizabeth Bergner, who accepted a part in Michael Powell's *49th Parallel*, which was to be shot in Canada, only to defect shortly afterwards and flee to the United States, leaving her role to be completed by Glynis Johns, earned considerable criticism.

Singer Gracie Fields also fled to Canada, her husband, Italian-born comedian and director Monty Banks, having been threatened with internment if he remained in Britain. They reached Canada a few days before Italy entered the war, and Banks went on to the USA while Miss Fields stayed in Canada to appear at concerts for the Navy League. She recalled that 'At the end of that week the storm broke. Every British newspaper screamed that I had deserted my own country and taken all my money and £100,000-worth of jewellery out of England with me. I was a traitor. I had run away. I'd smuggled heaven knows what fortune out of Britain. I was stunned. . . . Questions were asked in Parliament about me, and the Financial Secretary of the Treasury, Captain Crookshank, issued an official statement that I had not taken any unauthorized sum of money out of Britain. But this was not published till long after all the mud had been slung.' Despite her considerable efforts entertaining troops all over the world, Gracie

Elizabeth Bergner was originally cast as the Hutterite girl in Michael Powell's 49th Parallel. *She still appears in the longshots, but when she fled to the United States Glynis Johns (seen here) replaced her in close-ups*

Monty Banks in his days as a slapstick comic: his Italian ancestry was to make him liable for internment during the Second World War

Fields's career never recovered from the perhaps unjustified attacks following her flight to America.

Never as powerful as the British community, Hollywood's French enclave was inundated after the invasion, and Robert Florey found his services in considerable demand. 'The wave of French motion picture people started in 1939 when Jean Renoir arrived at the end of the year,' he explained. 'Other directors followed: René Clair, Leonide Moguy, Henry Diamant-Berger, Julien Duvivier, with his production manager Levy-Strauss, the writers Maurice Dekobra and Kessel; later Saint-Exupéry, who wrote *Le Petit Prince* while in Hollywood, two production managers, Charles David, who became Deanna Durbin's husband, and Roger Woog. Producer André Daven was hired by Darryl Zanuck at Fox. Among the actors arriving from Paris, Jenine Crispin, Madeleine Lebeau, Micheline Cheirel, Michele Morgan, Vera Korena, Fernando Albany, Jean Gabin, Victor Francen, Jean-Pierre Aumont, Marcel Dalio, Jaque Catelain, Bernard Deschamps, Georges Rigaud (back from Buenos Aires) and at the end of the war Louis Jourdan, Micheline Presle, Claude Dauphin and Barbara Laage. . . . Some just passed through Hollywood,

(Right) *René Clair directs Marlene Dietrich in his first Hollywood film,* Flame of New Orleans. *(Below)* The French community in 1942: *(left to right) Micheline Cheirel, producer Robert Hakim, Christiane Tourneur, Lulu Hakim, John Loder, Olga Duvivier, René Clair, Christian Duvivier, Robert Florey (at back), Levy-Strauss, Bronja Clair, Julien Duvivier*

staying but a few weeks. They came from South America and
went to French Canada or New York. I always did everything
possible to help and assist these artists – help them to find their
way about – to find a home – to know the region. I introduced
some of my colleagues to the Directors' Guild where they were
immediately admitted. Most of them came to my home for dinner,
to listen to French recordings or to borrow French books. No
government regulations ever tied my hands. Hollywood helped
not only the French but all the foreign refugees. They never
starved and all got good jobs in the studios for which they did not
always express their gratitude when returning to France after
the war.'

Charitably, M. Florey glosses over the problems many French
film people faced restarting their careers in America. The big
names – Gabin, Morgan, Simone Simon – found some work, but
lesser stars encountered a brick wall. As John Houseman observed, Hollywood in 1939 'was still a closed society whose social,
financial and professional structure, though subject to constant
shifts, remained basically rigid and unchanged.'[81] An unwillingness to admit the newcomers was, as usual, disguised by lavish
hospitality. Marcel Dalio wandered disconsolately from party to
party until Dorothy Parker started a whispering campaign,
nudging likely employers with a confidential: 'Who is that
fascinating-looking man? He looks a bit like Marcel Dalio, who
was in all those wonderful French films.' Roles like the charmingly
bent croupier in *Casablanca* soon made him a familiar Hollywood
face. Directors found equal difficulty getting their ideas across at
the endless round of celebratory dinners. Asked if he had the
chance to see many of his French colleagues during his sojourn
in Hollywood, René Clair remarked: 'If you weren't working at
the same studios, it was like being on two different islands. When
you came home after shooting, you wanted only to eat and sleep –
except on Sunday, at the famous "Sunday Parties", where people
were classified by the amount of the weekly cheque they got.
You never met a cameraman, for example, at these parties: big
stars, directors or producers only. My idea of a Hollywood party –
to which I didn't go very often – is one where I finish seated on a
staircase eating cold spaghetti with Ernst Lubitsch.'

On arrival in America in 1940 Clair had many ideas for films,
notably comedies starring Henry Fonda, then a promising young

juvenile, and a period comedy with Chaplinesque overtones starring W. C. Fields and Deanna Durbin as father and daughter. 'They had an eerie quality,' Clair said. 'They were both of another world. But when I approached Universal, to whom both were under contract, they thought I was nuts.' As an alternative, they offered him a frothy period sex comedy with the uncommercial Marlene Dietrich, clearly their idea of an appropriate film and star for a French director. After *The Flame of New Orleans*, to which Clair lent all his refinement and wit – and which, with its costumes by René Hubert and photography by Rudolph Maté, both old friends from Paris, is a perfect expression of the French spirit in American cinema – he reluctantly retreated into a series of fantasies as an alternative to the war films offered him. He regrets the type-casting which robbed him of a chance to work with the light comedians of Hollywood he so much admired – 'I would have loved to do more with Veronica Lake, but she had nothing to do with the Philippines' – and his return to France as soon as hostilities ended is hardly surprising.

Hollywood engulfed the contemplative elegance of Renoir and Duvivier as it had that of Max Ophuls, the Viennese who

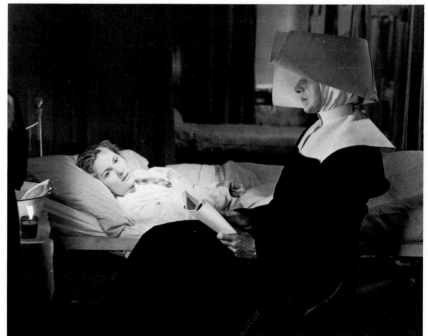

The elegant Viennese romanticism of refugee Max Ophuls, exhibited superbly in his adaptation of Zweig's Letter from an Unknown Woman *in 1948 for Joan Fontaine, puzzled Hollywood. Nicknamed 'The Oaf', he found the film colony an impossible milieu and soon fled*

changed the spelling of his name to "Opuls" when the usual mis-pronunciation 'Offals' and related nickname of 'The Oaf' with which he was saddled by Howard Hughes (briefly his employer) grated on his ear; and though all three men, the cream of pre-war Parisian cinema, produced some notable work, their careers there left them unsatisfied. 'I tried to get Renoir involved in making films with me in Hollywood,' said James Mason, 'but at that time people had decided that Jean Renoir was not the kind of director that they wanted to work with. He'd done two or three films in Hollywood which were unsuccessful and they did not like his manner. His method of working was very unHollywood. He didn't like to plan things; he liked to improvise a little.'[82] Studios remained as uncomprehending as ever towards the artistic temperament of these exiled artists. Deciding to leave MGM in 1939 to return to Britain, Luise Rainer told Louis B. Mayer: 'My sources have dried up.' 'Why do you need sources?' he snapped. 'You've got a director, haven't you?' There is also a story, perhaps apocryphal, that Alfred Hitchcock, asked on his arrival in 1940 what kind of films he liked, astonished the questioner by telling

Luise Rainer and Paul Muni in MGM's block-buster The Good Earth

Carmen Miranda, the 'Brazilian Bombshell', whose popularity in South America did much to bolster the sales of American films when European markets shrank at the outbreak of war

him he never saw any. 'But if you don't see any movies,' the man said, 'where do you get your ideas?'

The panic-stricken financial situation afflicting Hollywood in late 1939 and early 1940 did nothing to help the Europeans adjust to their new homes in California. As Hitler and Mussolini seized American-owned cinemas and banned the circulation of foreign films, losses in revenue as high as 60 per cent were glumly forecast. Before it became apparent that vastly increased audiences at home and in Britain would more than compensate for the loss, the studios turned to the South American market. Spanish versions of Hollywood successes persisted long after sub-titles took over in Germany and France, and now Hollywood invested in stars whose films would sell in Argentina and Brazil. Fox snapped up the most commercial of these performers, the Broadway dancer Carmen Miranda, the 'Brazilian Bombshell', and starred her in such pan-American successes as *Down Argentina Way*, *That Night in Rio* and *Weekend in Havana*, all placing coyly-disguised emphasis on the 'Good Neighbour Policy' then being pursued by the American government. For *The Gang's All Here*, director Busby Berkeley spent the first ten minutes drumming into geographically-hazy audiences the fact that Brazil was 'where the coffee comes from', after which Carmen and the girls mingled with night-clubbers to teach them 'The Uncle Samba' as a gesture of intercontinental amity. Miranda's performances gained spice from the fact that she never wore underwear when she danced, and Fox had to compensate with tight skirts and attention-getting hats made up largely of fruit.

By 1941 European immigration had peaked, and assimilation was under way throughout the country. While many theatrical and artistic émigrés headed for California, others, particularly keen Christians or those with strong political views, stayed in New York, attracted by an entrenched German community into which they could comfortably sink. Academics in particular found New York congenial. Six hundred and thirteen displaced professors entered the US between 1933 and 1945 under a rule giving exemption from the quota to any who had taught during the previous two years and had a guaranteed American teaching position. The Emergency Committee In Aid Of Displaced Foreign Scholars found places for 459 of them; 167 staffed New York's University in Exile, set up by the New School For Social Research, a Rockefeller Foundation-funded college which since the 1920s had represented radical scholarship and education in the US. The School also took on Erwin Piscator as head of its Drama Department, offered Hanns Eisler the funds to leave Hollywood and do research into film music, while Karl Zuckmayer was one of many indigent artists pressed into teaching special courses. Legendary names from European intellectual circles wandered through New York, searching for reminders of the world they had lost. Bela Bartok, who arrived in 1940, eked out his last years alone in a skyscraper office, indexing Hungarian folk melodies and avoiding the sad groups who, with memories of coffee afternoons at Vienna's Schonbrun or in Berlin, met at New York's zoo to chat.

Only a handful lived in the style they had enjoyed in Europe. Kurt Weill's skill in eluding Hollywood to write consistently for Broadway suggested to his old colleagues that he earned as much from his shows as he had in Berlin and Paris, leading producer Gabriel Pascal, on arriving at Weill's rural haunt in Nyack, New Jersey, to glance around and ask 'Are there horses?' One of the few exiles to maintain his old life-style was playwright Ferenc Molnar, who moved into the Plaza Hotel; like many Budapest-born Hungarians, he had lived in hotels and worked in cafés all his life. His ex-wife Lily Darvas and friends already living in New York urged him to come earlier, but he eventually fled from Budapest late in 1939, only a few hours in front of the Nazis – too quickly to bring with him more than twenty of the fifty volumes in his Collected Works. In a market starved of good film material Molnar's accumulated plays and stories supported him in ease, helped by his legendary unwillingness to part with money. When a studio approached him for the film rights to his comedy *The Swan* the executive sent to negotiate with him at the Plaza assured Molnar that, as far as money was concerned, the sky was the limit. In fact, he proposed to let the amount be settled by later negotiation, filling the space on their contract with a dash. Molnar contemplated the stroke and shook his head: 'Not long enough.'

Ferenc Molnar's genius for sly comedy made his work among the most sought-after by Hollywood. Alfred Lunt and Lynn Fontanne (seen here with Roland Young) made their only film appearance together in an adaptation of his comedy The Guardsman *in 1931*

Characteristically, Hollywood pursued those like Molnar who disdained their offers but behaved coolly towards the many who clamoured for movie work. As part of the belated rescue effort MGM and Warner Brothers offered more than seventy 'blank' contracts to the Emergency Committee as proof that the prospective immigrant could work. It was a laudable gesture which, in Thomas Mann's words in a letter to Louis B. Mayer, 'not only enabled these men to emigrate to the United States but also gave them at least a certain breathing spell in which to secure the foundations of their existence.' A miscellaneous collection of Expressionist poets, art historians, historical novelists and political satirists thus found themselves in Hollywood in 1940, drawing token salaries of $100 a week and contemplating without enthusiasm a movie career. Among those chosen, largely at random, for this help were Alfred Döblin, Wilhelm Speyer, Walter Mehring, Alfred Neumann, Alfred Polgar, Bertholt Brecht, Bruno and Leonhard Frank, Friedrich Torberg, Heinrich Mann, Ludwig Marcuse and Ernst Lothar. Franz Werfel and Lion Feuchtwanger, both moderately well off from accumulated American royalties, declined.

Of this group, only Brecht made a determined, if cynical, attempt to succeed. In his poem *Hollywood* he commented tartly:

> *Every morning to earn my bread*
> *I go to the market, where they buy lies.*

In the words of historian Martin Esslin:

He moved largely in the narrow world of German and Austrian refugee intellectuals and was frequently at loggerheads with those American circles one would have thought most likely to appeal to him: the many left-wing, fellow-travelling and Communist Americans of Hollywood. But these writers, actors and producers were largely under the spell of the Russian theatre and enthusiastic followers of the Stanislavsky method, which was a red rag to Brecht ... Ironically enough, Brecht, whose writing in his youth had centred around a mythical conception of the Anglo-Saxon and largely American world, found very little contact with the real America. After he had set foot in America, the American scene ... disappeared from his writing. And while he admired the productive achievements of the United States, he ... distrusted its politics, wrongly believing that after the war the USA would eventually lapse into isolationism, and disliked the cooking ... As to

the beauties of the Californian landscape . . . a friend once took him on a drive along the coast road through the most breathtaking scenery. Brecht remained silent and morose. But when the car turned into the disreputable quarters of the Los Angeles waterfront his face lit up. 'What beautiful scenery!' he said. And he meant it.[83]

Brecht's only Hollywood credit, for Lang's story of the Heydrich assassination, *Hangmen Also Die*, was removed from the film, allegedly because Brecht, as an émigré, would not derive the same benefit from it as his native collaborator, but he seems to have cared little. Hollywood eminence was not a goal any of the exiles cared to compete for.

Marcuse summed up the general disenchantment of Brecht's compatriots in the studio writing departments: 'without a knowledge of English or of film-making, full of scorn for the industry – and also without even being asked to undertake anything serious. Physician and novelist Döblin was shown the story of *Mrs Miniver* and asked for recommendations . . . and they received the grotesque answer that the material suggested a Chaplinesque treatment.'[84] 'One does nothing, absolutely nothing,' Döblin com-

Bertholt Brecht received a brief mention in the advertising for his only American film, but the Hollywood hokum is totally in command

plained to a friend. 'Supposedly we are collaborating on something, but up to now that is only a rumour.' Like generations of
movie writers before them, the Germans learned to stay out of the
corridor and thus avoid awkward questions. 'We take care of our
correspondence, telephone, read newspapers, write on our own –
whatever one can do in a sitting position.'[85] Alfred Neumann
wrote of '$100 a week charity' and his 'senseless existence' at
MGM. (Not only foreigners experienced this frustration. While
Döblin and Zuckmayer cooled their heels, in a nearby office the
young Tennessee Williams, having been hired as part of a 'pack-
age' with a ballet dancer to create a new film, used his time to
write *The Glass Menagerie*.)

Perhaps the most pathetic figure in Hollywood was the aged
Heinrich Mann. He and his wife lived in virtual retirement,
refusing financial help from his younger brother Thomas who,
through a combination of diplomacy, literary eminence and the
possession of a Czech passport exempting him from suspicion of
hostile attitudes to the USA, became the colony's moral leader.
The 70-year-old author of *The Blue Angel* spent hours in ante-
rooms, hoping to catch the ear of a story department head. Many
lesser figures existed on charity doled out by a committee headed
by the wife of Bruno Frank; in January 1942 Döblin said his income consisted of $18 a week unemployment benefit and $50
from Frau Frank. But still the proprieties were observed. 'When
we recently celebrated the 70th birthday of Heinrich Mann at the
house of Salka Viertel,' he wrote, 'everything was as in former
times. Thomas Mann pulled out a manuscript from which he read
his formal congratulations. Then his brother pulled out his paper
and thanked him with equal formality. We sat at dessert, some
twenty men and women, and listened to German literature.'[86]
Other gatherings, though no less distinguished, have an air of
absurdity. S. N. Behrman described a dinner party at the home of
Franz Werfel, then married to the widow of Gustav Mahler.
Alma Mahler Werfel, as she called herself – following Werfel's
death it became Alma Werfel Mahler – regaled the guests, who
included Arnold Schoenberg, with tales of her conquests: the
painter Oscar Kokoschka had been so in love with her that he took
a life-sized model of her on his travels; Alban Berg had dedicated
Wozzeck to her; the architect Walter Gropius was a devoted
slave. Coming to the end of the list, she looked straight at Werfel

and said: 'But the most interesting personality I have known –
was Mahler!' Her current husband nodded in fervent agreement,
and the party ended with Mme Werfel producing the lock of
Beethoven's hair which the Vienna Symphony had presented to
Mahler on his departure to America. Hollywood would have been
hard put to achieve this level of subtle eccentricity, though it
came close on the occasion of a dinner party thrown by Frau
Bruno Frank for Thomas Mann on his arrival in Hollywood.
Among the guests was Carl Laemmle, then still influential at
Universal. As the guests were departing, Laemmle offered his
warm congratulations on the evening, and told Frau Frank that
his secretary would ring the next morning for Mann's address
and a complete list of guests. 'I want to have exactly the same
party at *my* house next week.'

The studios did buy works by Werfel, Feuchtwanger (who
later settled in California), Bruno Frank, Martin Gumpert, Hans
Habe, Stefan Heym, Gina Kaus, Ferenc Molnar, Neumann, Re-
marque and Toller; and two lesser writers, Hans Lustig and
Georg Froschel, had successful careers as screen writers, but
most chose to mark time until the end of the war freed them from
a servitude that to some, deprived of their beloved German
language, was almost as galling as life under the Nazis. 'If I had
the dollars,' the 80-year-old Heinrich Mann said in 1949, 'I
would have tried to emigrate' – but, lacking even the money to
return to Germany, he died an exile.

Though European writers found Hollywood difficult to encom-
pass, most did at least know enough of popular fiction and the
cinema to recognize what was required, even if they chose not to
supply it. For musicians, however, the movie music scene bore
no relationship to anything they knew in Germany or Austria. In
European cinema, music played a minor role. Few producers cared
to engulf a drama in the sort of all-enveloping score beloved of
Hollywood, and when music was needed a good composer could
generally be found to do the job discreetly and with taste. Fleeing
musicians arriving in Los Angeles during the 1930s faced an
entirely different situation, one which derived from film music's
curious position in the days of silent film.

It is a truism that 'silent pictures were never silent', but few émigrés realized the extent to which music was an integral part of the silent movie programme. Only the tiniest of country cinemas offered a solo piano accompaniment. Any respectable theatre provided at least a trio, and in larger towns twenty-piece orchestras were far from uncommon, while cinemas in New York or Los Angeles dazzled audiences with symphony-sized orchestras, organs and dancing girls. A corps of composers, arrangers, orchestrators, conductors and song-writers existed solely to fill the need for movie music. With every film the studio issued a music cue sheet listing in detail the suggested selections to be played with each scene, cued for the conductor's benefit with specific references to individual titles or shots. For longer films, they offered specially commissioned scores, and song-writers vied for the chance to write tunes which would benefit from the wide publicity. Both Irving Berlin and Victor Schertzinger offered new ballads as title songs for Lubitsch's *Rosita*. When Mary Pickford chose Berlin's lesser and now-forgotten tune Schertzinger retitled his 'Marquita' and watched with satisfaction as it became a hit.

When the companies needed musicians to handle their music departments after the coming of sound, it was to these silent movie composers that they turned. William Axt, who had scored *Madame Dubarry*, *The Big Parade* and *Ben Hur*, was chosen to write, with David Mendoza, the score for Warner Brothers' first 'synchronized music and effects' film *Don Juan* in 1926. Largely indistinguishable from a silent movie score, with its plethora of motifs and broadly descriptive romantic or swashbuckling themes, the *Don Juan* score nevertheless struck Hollywood as ideal, and most studios recruited their heads of music from men hitherto employed as conductors of the major cinema orchestras. Leo Forbstein, who managed Warners' music section, had conducted at Grauman's Los Angeles Metropolitan; Herbert Stothart, who occupied a similar position with MGM, had been a minor song-writer and collaborator with Rudolf Friml on *Rose Marie*, hardly an adequate basis for such an onerous job.

Men like Forbstein and Stothart imprinted on their departments a view of film music derived directly from silent film, one which aimed at an easy manipulation of the audience by the use of familiar tunes and 'mood' themes; for effect they relied heavily on leitmotifs, broadly descriptive programme music and cliché national colour. From a composer they required the simplest thread of a tune which their arrangers could, as the department heads had done while running their own theatres, expand into a score appropriate to the instrumentalists available and the overall 'house style'. Stravinsky railed against 'Hollywood composers who farm out their orchestrations and whose scores should be marked "colour added" like the labels on food cans.'[87] The most articulate critic of movie music was Hanns Eisler, who came to Hollywood in 1937. In addition to the widespread practice of farming out orchestration, he castigated the rigid structure of film orchestras, confined by union agreement to a strict number of strings, woodwinds and brass, the habit of handing conducting jobs to 'conventional performers from night clubs or musical shows, or to orchestra players who have worked their way up through diligence or connections'. He had considerable sympathy for the musicians, excellent players driven by the studio schedules to work long hours to complete a scene, then dropped back into weeks of unproductive idleness; but in particular the programmatic structure of the music they were asked to play and he to write made Eisler furious.

There is a favourite Hollywood gibe – 'Birdie sings, music sings'. Music must follow visual incidents and illustrate them either by directly imitating them or by using clichés that are associated with the mood and content of the picture ... Mountain peaks invariably invoke string tremeloes punctuated by a signal-like horn motif. The ranch to which the virile hero has eloped with the sophisticated heroine is accompanied by forest murmurs and a flute melody. A slow waltz goes along with a moonlit scene in which a boat drifts down a river lined with weeping willows ... When a scene is laid in a Dutch town, the composer is supposed to send over to the studio library for a Dutch folk song in order to use the theme as a working basis.[88]

As in the silent days, a knowledge of the popular classics provided the basis of any Hollywood composer's career. Max Winkler, inventor of the silent film cue sheet, confessed: 'We murdered the works of Mozart, Grieg, J. S. Bach, Verdi, Bizet, Tchaikovsky and Wagner – everything that wasn't protected by copyright from our pilfering.' The policy persisted into sound and was adopted enthusiastically by the musically literate émigrés. The use of *Swan Lake* for *The Mummy* and other early horror films, Friedrich

Hollander's plunder of Siegfried's funeral march for Don Siegel's *The Verdict* and Herbert Stothart's medley of Tchaikovsky favourites for *Romeo and Juliet* are just a few examples of the disreputable technique Eisler so despised.

Success or failure for an émigré composer generally depended on the amount of money with which he had escaped from Europe. Where Eisler's limited funds obliged him to submit to the studio regime, Erich Wolfgang Korngold, whose possessions and family, including a distinguished musicologist father, had been successfully smuggled from under the noses of the Nazis, could be choosy about the projects on which he worked. He alone among Hollywood composers declined to accept Max Steiner's pompous Warner Brothers fanfare at the head of his scores, agreed only grudgingly to write the music for Errol Flynn's swashbuckling adventures, and only after long experience in Hollywood settled down as a regular composer for Warners. Some major musicians, whose past work earned them enough to live comfortably in exile, had no need to work on films. Nadia Boulanger, Mario Castelnuovo-Tedesco and Igor Stravinsky all spent their Los Angeles exiles in comfort, relieving the tedium with teaching and the occasional Hollywood chore.

Stravinsky in particular lived like a prince – as W. H. Auden once remarked sardonically, 'With the old boy, obviously, the mother figure is money' – surrounding himself with such congenial fellow émigrés as Aldous Huxley, painter Eugene Berman, Franz Werfel, author of *The Song of Bernadette* and one of the few foreign writers who prospered in America, Nadia Boulanger and ex-Reinhardt actor Vladimir Sokoloff, with whose wife Mme Stravinsky opened a successful art gallery. 'Before age and America changed Stravinsky's character,' Vera Stravinsky said, 'he opened his heart only to Diaghilev.' Now, as part of a stylish international set, comfortably wealthy and free of worry, both his personality and his music flowered anew. The discovery of some Mozart masses in a Los Angeles bookshop encouraged him to write his own ascetic Mass as a response to these 'sensuous suites of sin', and he agreed with surprising willingness to let his work be adapted for films, though the results were often disastrous. In 1938, before he had arrived in America, Walt Disney asked his permission to feature *The Rite of Spring* in the film *Fantasia*, remarking with typical Hollywood candour that, since the work was not copyrighted in America, they would use it whether he agreed or not. Under the circumstances Stravinsky felt 'obliged to accept' the $5000 fee. At Christmas 1939 he saw the film in Hollywood with George Balanchine. 'I remember someone offering me a score and, when I said I had my own, the someone saying "But it is all changed". It was indeed. . . .'[89]

But despite the violence it did to *The Rite of Spring*, *Fantasia* gave Stravinsky an entrée to the movies. In 1942 Columbia hired him to score *Commandos Strike at Dawn*. 'At the initial discussion of the film,' critic Tony Thomas says, 'the plot was outlined to Stravinsky: Norway during the war, the underground resistance of the Norwegian patriots, the raids of British commandos etc. Stravinsky said he found all this fascinating. Some weeks later he called the producer and said the score was ready, which surprised the producer because the film wasn't.'[90] Nor did Columbia like the music, which Stravinsky – not forgetting to collect his fee – later adapted as a concert work, *Four Norwegian Moods*. In a similar way, the Apparition of the Virgin music he wrote for the film of his friend Franz Werfel's *The Song of Bernadette*, but which was never used, became part of the *Symphony in Three Movements*. No commission deterred Stravinsky, no matter how bizarre. In 1942 he wrote *Circus Polka* for the dancing elephants of Barnum and Bailey's circus, and a few years later flirted with jazz to write *Ebony Concerto* for clarinettist Woody Herman. In retrospect his 1945 decision to become an American citizen merely solemnized a natural affection for and understanding of the United States and its way of life.

Arnold Schoenberg too found Hollywood congenial, even though his eminence in Berlin and subsequent fall had been more dramatic than most. At a meeting of the Senate of the Berlin Academy of Arts on 1 March 1933, the Academy President, minor composer Max von Schillings, made known the government's wishes that the Jewish influence in the Academy should be eliminated. Responding angrily that he never stayed where he was not wanted, a recently-elected Schoenberg walked out. Robbed of his contracted two years' salary he fled penniless to Paris, then to New York and, when the damp East Coast climate endangered his health, to California. From his writings, Schoenberg emerges as a man of great warmth and an innocent enthusiasm which disconcerted hard-bitten Hollywood. He wrote to a friend:

We have a very charming little house, not too large, furnished, with
many amenities customary here but hardly known at all in Europe . . .
Hollywood is a sort of Floridsdorf or Modling [Viennese industrial
suburbs] of Los Angeles, only with the difference that here they produce
those splendid films whose highly unusual plots and wonderful sound
give me so much pleasure, as you know. Los Angeles is a complete
blank page so far as *my* music is concerned.[91]

Actually well respected by fellow musicians in California,
Schoenberg gratefully accepted the teaching jobs offered to him,
giving courses at both USC and UCLA. Movie composers also
approached him for private, even secret tuition, hoping that his
lustre would rub off on their indifferent talents. Baffled by the
insistence on programmatic writing, he tried without success to
start them with exercises in counterpoint and harmony, about
which most were entirely ignorant. When one desperate composer badgered him for a theme he might use to accompany the
sound of roaring aero engines, Schoenberg solemnly suggested:
'Use the same music as for bees, but much larger, of course.'
Thereafter he always referred to movie scores as 'big bee music'.

Interested by his growing underground reputation as the
resident genius of European music, Irving Thalberg offered
Schoenberg a contract to score MGM's mammoth version of Pearl
Buck's *The Good Earth*. According to legend, Herbert Stothart
clinched the deal by playing to Thalberg a record of Schoenberg's
most accessible work, *Verklärte Nacht,* and wordlessly indicating
the large entry under his name in the *Encyclopaedia Britannica*. A
minion who called on Schoenberg to discuss the project described
the film's climax. 'Think of it! A terrific storm is going on; the
wheat field is swaying in the wind, and suddenly the earth begins
to tremble. In the midst of an earthquake, O-Lan gives birth to a
baby! What an opportunity for music!' Schoenberg looked
puzzled. 'With so much going on, why do you need music?'
Deciding that Thalberg's legendary talents of persuasion were
needed, Stothart fixed an appointment between the two men. In
his 61 years Schoenberg had never waited for anyone, but it is an
index to his forebearance and Thalberg's respect – he had been
known to leave major writers in his outer office for weeks – that
Schoenberg endured the relatively brief twenty-minute wait
Thalberg inflicted on him. Their meeting lasted no longer. Asked
for his terms to score the film Schoenberg said briskly: 'I want

$50,000 and an absolute guarantee that not a single note of my score will be altered.' The fee presented no problem to MGM, but that a composer should have control over his work was clearly impossible. Stothart personally scored *The Good Earth*.

Undeterred, Schoenberg settled down to his life of teaching and society. He often played tennis and swam with George Gershwin, who painted an evocative portrait of his friend. Schoenberg responded with one of Gershwin's sincerest epitaphs: 'There is no doubt he was a great composer.' Among American popular musicians not only Gershwin responded to Schoenberg's charm. Some time after his arrival he was nominated for the American Society of Composers and Performers, membership of which allowed him to collect American royalties on his work. Duly proposed and accepted, he attended a celebratory dinner for new members at which he was seated between two writers from Tin Pan Alley. As the party warmed up, one of his companions turned to Schoenberg and confided: 'You know, Arnold, I don't understand your stuff, but you must be okay or you wouldn't be here.'

The ease with which Schoenberg penetrated Hollywood's tight professional ranks contrasts with the problems faced by most performing musicians, who found work difficult without an almost unobtainable union card. Bootleg work flourished. European virtuosi could be had cheap – it was not unknown for Americans to take foreign names to get work – and absurdities proliferated. German exile Ignaz Hilsberg recorded the Tchaikovsky Piano Concerto heard on the sound track of *Song of Russia*, but the pianist appearing on screen was Albert Coates, actually the conductor of the orchestra seen being led in the film by a musically illiterate Robert Taylor. To have a movie career, the imported singer or performer needed to act, a fact which elevated some moderately talented opera singers like Lily Pons, Melitza Korjus, Gladys Swarthout, Jan Kiepura and the great *heldentenor* Lauritz Melchior to character star status. Melchior amiably trundled his bulk through various Esther Williams musicals and Paramount's 1951 *The Stars are Singing*, briefly convincing in the latter as an aged alcoholic Polish opera star. Melchior and other émigrés must have found the plot wryly amusing, concerning as it does an illegal immigrant girl pursued by evil Iron Curtain authorities and finally succoured by a compassionate Immigration Department,

Tenor Lauritz Melchior in a publicity shot for the musical Luxury Liner

but it did not do to be flippant about one's livelihood, a fact which makes even more surprising the dialogue of *My Favourite Brunette*, a 1947 Bob Hope comedy in which Peter Lorre plays a soft-voiced mobster. 'You're a pretty good guy, for a foreigner,' cop Ray Teal observes patronizingly after Lorre has fended off their enquiries. 'Thanks. But I'm studying to become a citizen,' he purrs. 'Perhaps you gentlemen could tell me who was the eighth president of the United States?' The police retire in confusion while Lorre returns to memorizing the Constitution while practising his knife-throwing on a ham.

Melchior's clown status was rivalled by other important performers. Concert pianist Jose Iturbi swapped quips with Frank Sinatra and acted as mentor to Kathryn Grayson in *Anchors Aweigh*. In a scene typical of Hollywood's attitude to serious

*Pianist Jose Iturbi
goes through the
hoops for Hollywood
in* Anchors Aweigh.
(Left to right)
*Kathryn Grayson,
Carlos Ramirez, Jose
Iturbi, Bill Forrest
and Ray Teal*

*Famous conductor
Bruno Walter shared
the star honours with
Artur Rubinstein,
Jascha Heifetz,
Leopold Stokowski,
Lily Pons, Gregor
Piatigorsky, Harry
James and other
musical luminaries in*
Carnegie Hall

music, Grayson, a budding soprano reduced to extra work in an opera film, says meltingly: 'Iturbi gets so much out of a singer. I'd give anything to work with him,' as he conducts Figaro's aria from *The Barber of Seville*, sung by a reedy tenor dressed as a Mexican spiv standing in the plaza of a fishing village watched by peasantry and grenadiers. At the end of the shot Iturbi asks brightly: 'When do we do the boogie-woogie?' (and does later lead an orchestra in a hotted-up performance of *Donkey Serenade* arranged for him by a teenaged immigrant prodigy named André Previn). Leopold Stokowski appeared as an imposing silhouette in *Fantasia* and the cream of European music, including Arthur Rubinstein, Bruno Walter and impresario Walter Damrosch, were roped into *Carnegie Hall*, where a budding young musician, despite advice from Rubinstein to 'play nothing but Bach, Bach, Bach, Bach', elects to break his mother's heart and take to jazz. The great names dragooned into this farce rated at least a decent fee. For the Viennese orchestral player or Berlin bass there was little but blackleg labour and a perhaps welcome anonymity.

As war threatened to engulf London, where many of them had fled after 1933, some of Reinhardt's old colleagues moved to join him in California, but found there none of the old cameraderie and collaborative fervour they had enjoyed in Salzburg and Berlin. After the débâcle of *A Midsummer Night's Dream* only Broadway offered any opportunities for ambitious work. In 1936 Reinhardt staged Werfel's huge encapsulation of Jewish history, *The Eternal Road*, in New York, luring Kurt Weill from Paris to do the music and reducing the Manhattan Opera House to total con- fusion in order to accommodate Norman Bel Geddes' sets. When the orchestra pit proved too shallow for part of the spectacle, they drilled into the bedrock and struck an underground stream; water spurted twenty feet into the pit. After ten postponements the play, with a cast of forty-three principals and countless lesser actors, opened to packed houses; the opening night audience re- mained rapt even though its four acts did not end until 3 a.m. From the second night two acts were discarded, but despite capacity crowds every night *The Eternal Road* lost $5000 a week, a figure not atypical of Reinhardt's experiences with Broadway. In Hollywood he opened a drama school, attended mainly by stage-struck children and relatives of his many friends – including Aldous Huxley's ward and the daughter of Marlene Dietrich – and supported, without Reinhardt's knowledge, by Gert von Gontard, a local patron of the arts. Karl Zuckmayer noted that 'he occasionally gave performances with the more talented of his students. But these performances were attended only by connoisseurs, professionals and Europeans.'[92]

The old colleagues who joined Reinhardt in Hollywood often fitted resourcefully into the movie machine. Turning his chancy English to advantage, the impish, bearded Vladimir Sokoloff specialized in foreigner roles, ranging from an Italian physicist in Fritz Lang's *Cloak and Dagger* (in which Reinhardt's wife Helene Thimig had a small but effective part as a refugee scientist) to a blind Chinaman in von Sternberg's *Macao*. Later in his career Sokoloff, who was born in Moscow, estimated he had in his time played thirty-five nationalities. Tall, distinguished Albert Basserman arrived in 1938, his stooping bulk and punctilious good manners elevating those films in which he had small parts. His almost total lack of English was remedied by his wife, who coached him phonetically in all his dialogue. Indefatigable even in his eighties, he died in 1952 while flying back from playing the ballet designer in Michael Powell's *The Red Shoes*. One of Reinhardt's most striking protégées, dancer Tilly Losch,

Reinhardt star Vladimir Sokoloff adds another nationality to his collection – here he plays a blind Chinese beggar in Macao, *with Jane Russell*

also cut a niche in Hollywood. With a face so *chien* as to border on ugliness and a body capable of contortion into poses of absolute lasciviousness she had dominated the productions of *The Miracle* and the Weill/Brecht/Balanchine ballet *The Seven Deadly Sins* in Paris and London, then exploded on Hollywood to take dancing roles in *The Garden of Allah*, *The Good Earth* – 'She is like a dream person,' one watcher breathes as she creeps on stage in heavy white brocade, jewelled head-dress and gem-encrusted fingers – and *Duel in the Sun*, before marrying into the aristocracy and retiring from a career unlikely ever to be equalled.

Ernst Matray, the choreographer and movement expert Reinhardt trained to handle crowd scenes for his productions, did better than most in America, a rare example of the exile who forgot 'former times' and determined to succeed. Under the wry heading 'From Reinhardt to Sinatra' he detailed his experience in a February 1944 issue of the New York émigré newspaper *Aufbau*:

When I left Europe I realized that I would probably have to abandon all artistic ambitions, which dated from my early youth in Budapest and which I had kept up through my first struggling 'leaner' years at the Deutsches Theatre in Berlin to the 'fatter' years later on . . . There is only one way to success – an open, positive attitude towards the new country. To be liked, you have to like first . . . I made up my mind to settle down and learn. When I came to the United States as an immigrant – I had been in New York twice before, with the 'Reinhardt-Gastspeile' – I was with the Folies Bergere shows, for whom I did the staging. We played sometimes four shows a day. It was hard work, but it was also a priceless experience.

Then I went to Hollywood and studio work. I staged dances and musical sequences for Jeanette Macdonald-Nelson Eddy pictures such as *Bittersweet* and *I Married an Angel* and coached dramatic actresses with little or no dancing experience, as for instance Vivien Leigh in the Swan Lake ballet in *Waterloo Bridge*, Joan Crawford in the Swedish folk dances in *A Woman's Face* and Greer Garson in her vaudeville act in *Random Harvest*. More musicals followed . . . twenty-three altogether. Then, it seems, I was ripe for Frank Sinatra. First came *Higher and Higher* . . . and right now I am working on his second, more pretentious RKO picture *Manhattan Serenade*. What is he like? I would call him an American institution like Coca Cola, chewing gum or Yellowstone Park. Why did they promote just him to this extraordinary position? Even his friends don't insist that he is outstanding in any way, as a singer, a performer or as a personality. In my humble opinion the reason for his tremendous success is the fact that he is the perfect embodiment of all the qualities you would describe as 'average'.

Even the success of old friends and associates like Matray failed to revive Reinhardt's hope for his future. It may have destroyed the little resilience not eroded by the 'European disease' from which he and the disdainful German writers of Hollywood suffered. His few Broadway productions of the 1940s failed, Hollywood showed no interest in his film plans and even the school petered out for lack of support. In 1943 he celebrated his seventieth birthday in New York with a few friends. Karl Zuckmayer came down from his Vermont farm and found Reinhardt, fresh back from a seaside holiday, 'healthy and vital . . . his face taut and bronzed, his hair like a cap of silver. A few weeks later I had to go to New York again for his funeral.'[93]

Even with hindsight, it is difficult to analyse the fundamental change experienced by Hollywood during the last three years of the war. One sees it clearly in the films, the elegance of wisecracking thrillers like *The Thin Man* replaced by *film noir*, where rich gang bosses, high in penthouse apartments, rule over empires of dark, wet streets and desperate men, the marzipan of Jeanette MacDonald and Nelson Eddy superseded by a tart Judy Garland and an agile Gene Kelly, the 1930s softly feminine women eclipsed by square-shouldered Lauren Bacall and the overtly erotic Rita Hayworth. Americanism had found its most potent expression in war-time Hollywood as the studios, pressed by an audience anxious to be confirmed in its vision of the way of life for which it was fighting, distilled the quintessence of American man, American woman, the American way of life.

The exiles who contributed so much in technique, content and style to these new ideals were paradoxically forced out by their acceptance. European comedy, classical drama and the stars of both had no place in this world, and when the war ended many of them quietly fell away. Marlene Dietrich remained, adapting to whatever the public seemed to want, but Garbo retired as most of her imitators had done already. Emigrés who had settled in New York and survived the struggle for the legal right to work

*In 1937 Marlene
Dietrich swore the
oath of allegiance to
the United States as
part of her admission
as a US citizen*

stayed on and thrived, but most of the Californian exiles – Bruno
Frank, Franz Werfel, Thomas Mann were among those who did
not – returned to Europe, even though, as Karl Zuckmayer
remarked: 'Going into exile is "the journey of no return". Anyone who sets out on it dreaming of coming home is lost.'[94] With
NeuBabelsberg in Russian hands, later to become headquarters of
DEFA, the East German film industry, UFA's old staff had nowhere to go. Yet like an addictive drug, movie-making could sap
the energy as it increased the craving. One of the most revealing
portraits in the literature of film exile is a *Motion Picture Herald*
interview of June 1945 with Emil Jannings. Hoping to return to
the movies as a director, he whined to the reporter, between gulps
of sparkling red wine on the terrace of his house in the Salzkam-
mergut Valley in Austria, that he had disliked the Nazis, broke
with Goebbels over the question of casting, refused the directorship of the German film industry in 1939 when he was told he
could not have total control. 'He did not refer to nor explain his
long term, apparently with the approval of the Nazis, as a top
executive of UFA,' the report concluded coldly, and though the

War Crimes Commission cleared him he never worked again.

The war, which did so much to unify most American industries, left the cinema deeply split, its native members embittered by a conflict out of which they seemed to have gained nothing. 'In wartime no group is quicker to volunteer its services than actors,' Groucho Marx said in a rare moment of seriousness. 'The automobile factories, the aircraft manufacturers and all the other industries grow pretty fat on their wartime profits. The actor gets his expenses, ten or eleven miserly dollars a day, and when the war is over they hand him a plaque.'[95] Directors and producers who had spent their war service in training work returned with a determination to produce films which explored the world as they saw it, socially unequal and morally bankrupt. Their disenchantment and the conservative establishment's resistance to such exposure led inexorably to the House UnAmerican Activities Committee hearings which finally drove out of the film business many of those émigrés who had settled in Hollywood after the war.

With an absurdity that must have delighted him, Bert Brecht, still marking time in Hollywood while deciding which European offer to accept, emerged from the HUAC trials with a cleaner bill of health than almost any other witness. Deliberately misleading and lying to the court, he earned their approval and praise. They even recommended him to other witnesses as an example of the ideal.

'With the influx of the refugees in the thirties,' said S. N. Behrman, 'Hollywood became a kind of Athens. It was as crowded with artists as Renaissance Florence. It was a Golden Era. It has never happened before. It will never happen again.'[96] Behrman paints the picture of an idyll, yet none who lived through those days thought them perfect. Art flourishes in isolation, society and scandal in a crowd, and it was society and scandal that the émigré community of the 1930s and 1940s mainly produced. Towards the end, Hollywood became a community obsessed, as its fans always had been, with celebrity. A 1930s tennis match such as that described by musician Larry Adler, with he and champion Bill Tilden against Charlie Chaplin and Salvador Dali, reduces the cult of personality to its true absurdity. Typical, therefore, that the last great survivor of the exiles, Ernst Lubitsch, should have had his final fatal heart attack at a party given for an official of the Nuremberg war crimes trials. As the guest recounted his stories

of Nazi humiliation to an absorbed table, only Lubitsch's collaborator Walter Reisch noticed the director's distress. Not even
the servants saw Reisch help Lubitsch to his car. Though he survived to begin another film, within a few weeks Lubitsch was
dead, and with him something unique in the world's most durable
popular art.

SOURCE NOTES

1. *A Victorian in Orbit,* Sir Cedric Hardwicke, Methuen, 1961.
2. *Weimar Culture,* Peter Gay, Secker and Warburg, 1968.
3. Ibid.
4. *In My Time,* Anthony Gibbs, Peter Davies, 1969.
5. *The Sociology of Film Art,* George A. Huaco, Basic Books, 1965.
6. *Fun In a Chinese Laundry,* Josef von Sternberg, Secker and Warburg, 1965.
7. *Popular Scenario Writer,* December 1924.
8. *Fun In a Chinese Laundry.*
9. *A Part of Myself,* Karl Zuckmayer, Harcourt Bracc, 1970
10. Ibid.
11. *New York Times Book Review and Magazine,* 26 March 1922.
12. *Fun In a Chinese Laundry.*
13. *Benjamin Christensen,* John Ernst, Det Danske Filmmuseum, 1967.
14. *Film Culture,* 20, 1959.
15. *Bright Day,* J. B. Priestley, Heinemann, 1950
16. *Memoirs of a Star,* Pola Negri, Doubleday, 1970.
17. *Tales of a Wayward Inn,* Frank Case, Frederick A. Stokes Company, 1938.
18. *Tribulations and Laughter,* S. N. Behrman, Hamish Hamilton, 1972.
19. *Letters of Aldous Huxley,* Chatto and Windus, 1969.
20. *Look Back Look Forward,* Edward Beddington-Behrens, Macmillan, 1963.
21. Ibid.
22. *Seven Ages,* Basil Dean, Hutchinson, 1970.
23. *The Show Must Go On,* Elmer Rice, Viking, 1951.
24. *Broadway,* Brooks Atkinson, Macmillan, 1974.
25. *Fun in a Chinese Laundry.*
26. *The Refugee Intellectual,* D. P. Kent, Columbia Univ. Press, 1953.
27. *Mrs Patrick Campbell,* Alan Dent, Museum Press, 1961.
28. Ibid.
29. *Fun In a Chinese Laundry.*
30. Ibid.
31. *An Unfinished Woman,* Lillian Hellman, Little, Brown, 1969.
32. *The Letters of Bernard Shaw and Mrs Patrick Campbell,* ed. Alan Dent, Knopf, 1952.
33. *Movie Merry-Go-Round,* John Paddy Carstairs, Newnes, 1937.
34. *Letters of Aldous Huxley.*
35. *Films In Review,* April 1965.
36. *Picture Show Annual,* 1927.
37. *In My Time.*
38. *Hugh Walpole: A Biography,* Rupert Hart-Davis, Harcourt Brace, 1962.
39. *Run-Through,* John Houseman, Simon and Schuster, 1972.
40. *Memoirs of a Star.*

41. *The Light of Common Day,* Lady Diana Cooper, Hart-Davis, 1959.
42. *Picture Show Annual,* 1927.
43. *Films In Review,* April 1965.
44. *A Part of Myself.*
45. *Aldous Huxley: A Memorial Volume,* ed. Julian Huxley, Harper and Row, 1963.
46. Ibid.
47. *A Victorian In Orbit.*
48. *Fun In a Chinese Laundry.*
49. *Tovarich,* Jacques Deval, adapted by Robert E. Sherwood, Random House, 1937.
50. *Storyline,* Lenore Coffee, Cassell, 1973.
51. *Salute to the Thirties,* Horst. (Notes by Valentine Lawford.) The Bodley Head, 1971.
52. *Juan In America,* Eric Linklater, Cape, 1953.
53. *Reflections On the Cinema,* René Clair, William Kimber, 1953.
54. *The Moon's A Balloon,* David Niven, Hamish Hamilton, 1971.
55. *A Victorian In Orbit.*
56. *The Silent Picture,* Summer 1970.
57. *The Parade's Gone By,* Kevin Brownlow, Alfred Knopf, 1968.
58. *Years In a Mirror,* Val Gielgud, Bodley Head, 1965.
59. *Hugh Walpole.*
60. Ibid.
61. *A Part of Myself.*
62. *Whatever Happened to Hollywood?,* Jesse Lasky Jr., W. H. Allen, 1973.
63. *Cole,* Brendan Gill, Michael Joseph, 1973.
64. *Margin Released,* J. B. Priestley, William Heinemann, 1963.
65. Ibid.
66. *Long Before Forty,* C. S. Forester, Michael Joseph, 1967.
67. Ibid.
68. *Hugh Walpole.*
69. Ibid.
70. *In My Time.*
71. Ibid.
72. *German Exile Literature in America 1933–1950,* Robert E. Cazden, American Library Association, Chicago, 1970.
73. *While Six Million Died.*
74. *Neue Zurcher Zeitung,* 18 November, 1973.
75. Ibid.
76. *Broadway.*
77. *Behind the Camera,* Leonard Maltin, Signet, 1971.
78. *Movie Merry-Go-Round.*
79. *The Silent Picture,* Summer/Autumn 1971.
80. *Sinclair Lewis,* Mark Schorer, McGraw-Hill, 1961.
81. *Run-Through.*
82. *Focus On Film.*
83. *Brecht: A Choice of Evils,* Martin Esslin, Norton, 1974.
84. *German Exile Literature in America 1933–1950.*
85. Ibid.
86. Ibid.
87. *Retrospectives and Conclusions,* Igor Stravinsky and Robert Craft, Knopf, 1969.
88. *Composing For the Films,* Hanns Eisler, Dobson, 1951.
89. Ibid.
90. *Music For the Movies,* Tony Thomas, A. S. Barnes, 1973.
91. *Schönberg: A Critical Biography,* Willi Reich, Praeger, 1971.
92. *A Part of Myself.*
93. Ibid.
94. Ibid.
95. *Memoirs of a Mangy Lover,* Groucho Marx, Manor Books, 1964.
96. *Tribulations and Laughter.*

Index of Names

Figures in *italics* refer to illustrations

Index of Film Titles

Figures in *italics* refer to illustrations